Praise for *Sun Signs i*

"Easy to read and can help you build extraordina[...]
ner." —**Pamela Chen, author of** *Enchanted Crystal Magic*

"Informative, intriguing, and so refreshing." —**Valerie Mesa, celebrity astrologer**

"An essential must-have for anyone interested in deepening their relationships or compression of themselves." —**Lisa Stardust, celebrity astrologer and bestselling author**

"Desiree's style is clear, accessible, and informative." —**Skye Alexander, author of** *Magickal Astrology*

"When [sun sign] interactions get dicey, these pages help you navigate what's going on." —**Steven Forrest, author of** *The Inner Sky*

"An insightful astrological companion for falling in love and staying in love." —**Catherine Urban, author of** *Your Astrological Cookbook*

"Written in a refreshingly easy to read and understand style … both pointed and poignant." —**David Pond, author of** *Astrology and Relationships*

"A must-read for those looking to the stars to help guide their path in all relationships. "—**Jen CK Jacobs, founder of** *Age of Sail*

"A helpful guide to understanding your relationships on a deeper level." —**Rebecca Campbell, bestselling author and mystic**

"An incredibly in-depth overview of why each zodiac sign is the way they are." —**Natalie Walstein, founder of Soulshine Astrology**

"Students of astrology to the professional astrologer can benefit from *Sun Signs in Love*." —**Wayne Gonzalez, Astrologer To The Stars**

"A beautifully written book to help us understand our many relationships through the lens of the sun." —**Kay Taylor, author of** *Soul Path Way*

"*Sun Signs in Love* will become your tried and true heart-centered guide." —**Liz Simmons, Astrology.com**

"Desiree combines her years of experience and observations with her poetic writing style." —**Cannelle Farnault, astrologer**

"The absolute best book on astrological compatibility out there!" —**Narayana Montúfar, author of *Moon Signs***

"An amazing journey into the heart and soul of each astrological sign and how they can find connection and love." —**Kira Sutherland, medical astrologer**

"Desiree offers the magic of astrology to help you find the love you long for and to understand, deepen, and strengthen the love you have." —**Phyllis Curott, author of *Book of Shadows***

"Desiree is an incredibly gifted and insightful astrologer, and it shows on every page." —**Kasandra Martinez, founder of Style by the Signs**

"This book is like alchemy for relationships, blending elements, aspects, signs, and modalities." —**Tara Aal, author of *Astrology by Moonlight***

"Desiree masterfully details the signs, their personalities, and their relationship qualities." —**Raven Brinson, radio and podcast host**

"A bible for many who are seeking love and wanting to understand themselves and their partners." —**Amber Harkin, professional astrologer**

"An immersive and poignant entry into the nuance of dating and relating by sun sign." —**Clarissa Dolphin, astrologer and writer at SiderealSoul.com**

"Beautiful work… Desiree blends her wisdom and spellbound spirit to bring true magic to the reader." —**Dr. Alyse Snyder, cofounder of Cosmic AF**

"Rich, appealing, and descriptive, and you will really understand the energy of each Sun sign." —**Louise Edington, astrologer and bestselling author**

"When an astrology book makes you gasp and cover your mouth with the shock of astonishing accuracy, then you know the book is one you have to have." —**Colin Bedell, author of** *Queer Cosmos* **and horoscope writer for Cosmopolitan.com**

"*Sun Signs in Love* brilliantly answers our most probing questions of how each sign navigates romance." —**Nadine Jane, author of** *Magic Days*

About the Author

Desiree Roby Antila specializes in sun signs and astrological relationships. She has been studying astrology for several decades and has written numerous articles on matchmaking, cosmic timing, forecasts, and more. Desiree also teaches astrology classes in her local community and has conducted hundreds of natal chart and synastry readings.

Visit her online at SimplySunSigns.com / @simplysunsigns.

SUN
SIGNS

in Love

SUN SIGNS

in Love

Relationship Compatibility by the Stars

DESIREE ROBY ANTILA

LLEWELLYN PUBLICATIONS
WOODBURY, MINNESOTA

FIRST EDITION
First Printing, 2022

Book design by Christine Ha
Cover design by Cassie Willett
Constellations and astrological glyphs by the Llewellyn Art Department

Llewellyn Publications is a registered trademark of Llewellyn Worldwide Ltd.

Library of Congress Cataloging-in-Publication Data (Pending)
ISBN: 978-0-7387-7165-6

Llewellyn Worldwide Ltd. does not participate in, endorse, or have any authority or responsibility concerning private business transactions between our authors and the public.
   All mail addressed to the author is forwarded but the publisher cannot, unless specifically instructed by the author, give out an address or phone number.
   Any internet references contained in this work are current at publication time, but the publisher cannot guarantee that a specific location will continue to be maintained. Please refer to the publisher's website for links to authors' websites and other sources.

Llewellyn Publications
A Division of Llewellyn Worldwide Ltd.
2143 Wooddale Drive
Woodbury, MN 55125-2989
www.llewellyn.com

Printed in the United States of America

In the limitlessness of the universe, through the trillions of stars, and in the vastness of time, it is all my joy to spend my days with my Pauls: through infinite lifetimes, through endless galaxies, and in every form of existence.

Acknowledgments

First and foremost, thank you to one of the most alchemic writers and astrologers ever known: Aries author Linda Goodman. You were my first teacher and instructed me on how to understand the synastry of the stars. The first time I picked up *Love Signs*, I knew I had come across something special. Out of the several books on the shelf, your book seemed to jump out at me as though it was choosing me. Even though your earthly life has come to an end, you have taught me from the heavens, and I consider you to be my guru and guide. Your books are where I go when I need inspiration, when I get stuck, or when I feel like learning more. Even though I have read your works hundreds of times, I still find bits of magic hidden in the pages. It has always been as though you were speaking to me directly from your manuscripts, and I thank you for your incredible works, which have inspired my own writings. I pray you have now reconnected with your Sally.

To my Scorpio husband, Paul, thank you for being such an unwavering constant. Even though astrology is not your cup of tea, you have always supported my passion, which I appreciate more than you know. To my Virgo son, Paul Trey, you have given my soul wings and healed holes in my heart that I never thought could be mended. Being your mother is the greatest gift I will ever receive. I love you more than all the stars in the universe. To my family, thank you for always adding extra joy and laughter to life. You have all been a blessing on my journey.

Thank you to the astrological community, especially my dear friends Leo Queen Cannelle and Aries stellium Liz. Your ongoing support and the safe space you create to talk shop has made me a better astrologer and has inspired me in more ways than I can count. C, if you would not have pushed me to submit my manuscript to Llewellyn, we may not be reading this book right now. Thank you to all the astrological authors, especially those on my recommended reading list, who have shared their life's work and blessed us all with their knowledge through the written medium. I deeply credit the brilliant astrology community for encouraging my own continued learnings and journey with their endless amount of expertise and insight, which amazes and inspires me on a daily basis.

Thank you to all of the amazing and talented people I have worked with through my publisher Llewellyn Worldwide. You have all been an absolute delight to partner with, and I am incredibly grateful that you saw potential and had faith in my writing abilities. Your support has allowed this dream to come true, and there are days I still have to pinch myself to believe that this is really happening. Thank you for making this experience so special and one I will never forget.

Lastly, thank you to my loyal friends and acquaintances, along with everyone and anyone my life has allowed me to cross paths with. It is you and your relationships that I have had the honor of observing and studying, which is how this book came to fruition. If I knew you at some point in my life, there is a very good chance that you are secretly sprinkled across the pages of this book. It is your love stories that inspired the breadth of this manuscript. To my past relationships and lost love, thank you for teaching me the lessons I needed to obtain so that I could end up where I am right now. It was in those seasons of life that I learned even more about the archetypes of how sun signs love and lose love. My Chiron in the seventh was meant for this because, through the wounds of love, I am now able to help other relationships heal. It is the collection of my life's experiences, both good and bad, and my personal journey through love that gave me the insight to create this piece of literature, and I am eternally grateful.

Contents

Introduction

In my multiple decades of astrological study and the honor of performing hundreds of chart readings, the most frequently asked questions I receive are in regard to love. And why wouldn't they be? From the day we are born, love is one of our deepest and most profound needs. No matter our religion, race, gender, sexual orientation, biases, wealth, or health, we, as humans, want to love and be loved in return. We were not created to be alone but to have a companion, and therefore, we will use whatever tools we have in our box to find, gain, and keep love. The notion of love is incredibly illusive and abstract, and it is experienced differently by everyone. These traits make it difficult to acquire and even more difficult to retain. It is our longing for love and tireless search for our missing half that is the secret of life itself. Astrology gives us answers about love that we can then use to find and obtain it. Astrology also allows us to understand our partner on a deeper level and even sympathize with parts of them we may not have understood without this esoteric knowledge. It is my understanding that we must master the positive traits of our own sun sign to be the partner we desire to be and to open our hearts to the love we all deserve.

Before you start reading this book with a preconceived notion of which zodiac pairings are favorable and which ones are unfavorable, I invite you to wash away any stereotypes that you may have heard in the past. There is no such thing as a bad match in astrology, and to base that belief on simply looking at sun signs is like judging a book by its cover. You are not destined to fail because you have some more "difficult" aspects in your synastry. *All* relationships are difficult, and *all* relationships have beauty and lessons to be learned. Astrology is meant to be used as a device to assist bringing you and your partner clarity in areas of opportunity and to show the splendor between your unique compatibility. I believe that when you meet your soul mate, there will be karmic tests that you are both put through, but not even death can separate the bond between soul mates, so certainly synastry in astrology could not break it either. There is a saying that goes, "Astrology is not meant to predict a storm, it is meant to tell you to bring an umbrella." This concept applies to how to use astrology in your relationship.

While it's important to understand that there is more to you than just your sun sign, it is my wholehearted belief that the location of the sun at the moment of the first breath is the key to the true essence of who you are. The characteristics imprinted upon your personality when you drew your first breath were caused by the sun and planets in our solar system exercising their powerful influences through the zones of the zodiac. This magical process is what creates your personal sun sign and natal chart. The alchemy of the stars at the time of your birth was electromagnetic and magically cosmic. Therefore, when the sun is vibrating its force through a certain sun sign at the exquisitely timed cosmic moment of your birth, it is exercising its powerful pulsations through the characteristics of that archetype wholly.

The sun makes up for roughly 99 percent of the mass in our solar system, which is why it is believed that an individual's sun sign composes at least 80 to 90 percent of their characteristics. The other 10 or 20 percent are the intricacies and details of their chart that influence their sun sign. The other planets, orbs, and asteroids in our solar system simply refine the details of your complex personality. Where you were at the exact time and place you took your first breath will never be there again in our lifetime. This fact helps make you and your personality 100 percent original.

This book is organized by using the karmic wheel's order of astrological signs, which means we start with Aries. In the Aries chapter, you will find that it includes all twelve love matches for Aries. Second is the Taurus chapter, which will not include Aries, and then Gemini, which will not include Aries and Taurus, and so on and so forth. Although this book was written with the intention of comparing compatibility between sun signs, this manuscript does not contain gendered pronouns, and it is written from a viewpoint of how that zodiac sign's energy is experienced. Therefore, you can apply these chapters to all of your planetary aspects. For example, if you have a Sagittarius rising and your partner has a Capricorn rising, it is highly likely that the Sagittarius and Capricorn section will resonate with your relationship. This applies to your moon, Venus, and other planetary placements as well. The intent and takeaways of this book are to finds seeds of wisdom to make your love stronger, to understand yourself and your partner on a deeper level, and to have fun reading through the magical mysteries of the karmic wheel.

Astrology's Secrets of Synastry:
Aspects, Elements, and Modalities

There is more to sun signs when it comes to understanding love astrologically. Synastry between all of the planets is crucial to understanding the overall vibration between individuals. Synastry is defined as a way to determine a couple's likely compatibility and dynamics through comparing their natal charts by overlaying them on one another. The three factors used when determining a match's harmony are their aspects, elements, and modalities.

Aspects

Astrology's secret of compatibility is in the distance between your zodiac signs, and we call this distance an aspect. Some aspects do make for a smoother relationship, but here is something I have learned: easy does not necessarily mean better. Why are these frustrating relationships in your life, you wonder? It is because there is something for you to learn from them. In today's modern world, we are looking for a partner that challenges us, makes us a better version of ourselves, and pushes us to our full potential. The following are the seven major aspects that are used in astrology to understand the synastry between a pair.

Conjunct: 0 degrees

The conjunct aspect is when you are the same sign as your partner, and it gives an energy of self-recognition. Couples in conjunct relationships may find it easy to disappear into their own worlds, which seems effortless at first but can backfire in the future. Couples with this aspect must create independence in their unions for the relationships to work.

Semisextile: 30 degrees

The semisextile aspect is when you and your partner are one sign apart, and it can initially be met with resistance and variance. These couples may feel jealous or intimidated by each other's differences. Couples with this aspect must learn that it is not a competition. Instead, they must be supportive and complementary of one another.

3

Sextile: 60 degrees
The sextile aspect is when you are two signs apart from your partner, which gifts a vibe of friendship and communication. Vanquishing a sextile relationship is all about understanding that your partner's way of doing things is equally as important as your own, even if they are incredibly different. There will be a lot of enthusiasm when these couples discover the many things that they have in common. However, because of their many commonalities, things can seem a bit monotonous and predictable.

Square: 90 degrees
The square aspect is when you are three signs away from your significant other, and it creates a tricky, competitive, and vigorous atmosphere. The feel of this relationship usually leaves one or both partners requiring more from the other. They will both need to be very careful not to unload their negativity on each other because it will create friction. There is so much to learn from relationships with this aspect, but it must be done in a supportive and constructive manner.

Trine: 120 degrees
The trine aspect puts you and your lover four signs apart and brings synchronization and comfort to your union. These relationships are effortless and enjoyable. You truly enjoy being around each other and naturally vibe together. Throughout astrological teachings, you will learn that this is the most favored of the aspects when in a love relationship. However, because the energy is so easygoing, it can become lazy.

Quincunx: 150 degrees
The quincunx aspect is when you are five sun signs away, and it will bring correction, learning experiences, and conciliation to your relationship. The quincunx combination feels bizarre because the two signs have nothing in common astrologically regarding their elements or modalities. To make the relationship work, both partners need to be a karmically developed version of themselves, which is why these combinations usually work better when they are in the later years of their lives, or if both have gained philosophical knowledge early on in their journey.

Opposite: 180 degrees
The opposite aspect is when two signs are six places away on the karmic wheel, giving them a new viewpoint, differences, and stability. The tendency of opposites is to push each other's boundaries. If they want this relationship to work, they'll both need to find compromise in their divergences. These two will have a strong attraction and will gravitate to one another like magnets due to their polarizing personalities.

Elements

When considering compatibility between two sun signs, the nature of their elements is one of the most important—if not the most important—things to take into consideration. By breaking each sign down into a tangible organic matter, one is given the ability to paint a picture of what those two signs are like when they combine. The elements are as follows:

- *Fire:* Aries, Leo, and Sagittarius
- *Earth:* Taurus, Virgo, and Capricorn
- *Air:* Gemini, Libra, and Aquarius
- *Water:* Cancer, Scorpio, and Pisces

The element of fire radiates an active and enthusiastic energy. These sun signs possess an independent and groundbreaking spirit. They are known for their aggressive personalities.

The element of earth relates to tangible and carnal energy. These sun signs possess a practical and cautious spirit. They are known for their steady and persistent personalities.

The element of air relates to intellectual and communal energy. These sun signs possess a restless spirit. They are known for their logical, adaptable, and communicative personalities.

The element of water relates to emotional and intuitive energy. These sun signs possess a transitional and emotional spirit. They are known for their enigmatic personalities.

Blending the Elements
When fire meets fire, it results in higher heat and hotter flames. It may even cause an explosion that damages all in its path. It can consume everything and burn out

quickly, or it can light the darkness with its positive glow. The control lies in the decisions of the torch holders.

When air meets air, there are no barriers and things flow with ease. The blending of two mental signs can add up to a beautiful, uplifting, and intellectual experience. However, if one air sign is hot and the other cool, things can be whipped into a frantic tornado.

When earth meets earth, the two can build themselves into a tall mountain that symbolizes faith and steadfastness, or the relationship can be a dry desert containing no life. When two earth signs rub each other the wrong way, it can cause a damaging earthquake.

When water meets water, there is no resistance, causing things to flow into a stream of enlightenment. However, too much water can create a flood that drowns all life around.

Air feeds fire and causes it to burn even brighter, but too much air can push fire into a frenzy or blow it out completely. If the fire is overbearing, it can use all the oxygen in the air, making it impossible to breathe.

When earth meets fire, they will often be able to figure out who is the stronger of the two elements. Earth remains where it is unless moved by an outside force, whereas fire creates its own course. Fire can scorch earth but can never destroy it. Earth can support fire by giving it a foundation to burn upon, but remember, even the brightest flame can be put out if covered by dirt.

When fire meets water, couples must be careful. With enough heat, fire can evaporate a small amount of water or turn it to steam. On the other hand, with enough liquid, water can put out flames. Instinctively, fire respects and fears water and vice versa. Both understand the danger of one another and know that they could destroy each other. Balance is the key with this elemental blend.

Earth contains air and needs it. However, air does not contain earth and does not need it. Earth is obligated to remain where it is and only moves in the event of an earthquake, whereas air moves freely above it, choosing wherever it wants to go. Wind can destroy things with its tornado forces, but it is temporary. The earth protects the roots in its soil, and life will return to grow.

Water is always flowing to find its home, and it can find it within the earth by soaking into the soil, which is a blessing to the earth because it creates life. Without the enrichment of water, the earth would be a barren desert. These elements were designed to be symbiotic. However, too much water can create mud, which nothing can grow in, and too little water would get lost within the dry dirt.

When air meets water, air stirs, turns, and can cause waves in the water but then quickly moves away, giving the water no control. When water penetrates the air, it creates moisture and ignites the process of rain. Rain is needed for life and rebirth, which air has no control over. There is no choice of these things occurring in either of the elements, so it is better if these elements appreciate one another's differences and individual energy.

Modalities

The third thing to consider when looking at love, communication, and compatibility among sun signs is modality. Modality is defined as a way in which something occurs, is experienced, or is communicated. In astrology, there are three modalities, and each one includes a sign from each element.

- *Cardinal:* Aries, Cancer, Libra, and Capricorn
- *Fixed:* Taurus, Leo, Scorpio, and Aquarius
- *Mutable:* Gemini, Virgo, Sagittarius, and Pisces

Cardinal

Cardinal signs are the natural-born leaders and self-starters of the zodiac. In nature, these signs begin each of the seasons and are excellent at getting things moving. They are the ones who have a get-up-and-go attitude. They tend to give out a lot of energy by being assertive and influential. Cardinal signs promote change—sometimes for others—but mostly for their own sake. They like to be at the head of the pack and typically dominate most situations.

Fixed

Fixed signs are the organizers and steady souls of the zodiac. These signs prefer to keep their energy contained by leaving their environment as it is. They were born at a time when the seasons were in full swing. They are extremely consistent people in that they conserve their energy usage. Fixed signs are creatures of habit who tend to be very hard workers, but at times, they can be very resistant to change.

Mutable

Mutable signs are the communicators of the zodiac. These signs both give out and keep energy, making them unstoppable and most flexible in all environments. They were born at a time when the seasons were transitioning and changing. They have the gift to be able to be content with their environment, as well as having the need to control it. Their duality can be a blessing and a curse by causing indecisiveness.

Chapter 1

Aries

Aries's love archetype is the warrior of love. They are a brave and bold lover who enjoys taking the lead. They're inspirational, aggressive, and dynamic. Aries's lesson in love is to impart that love is virtue and absorb that love is faith.

Element	Fire
Modality	Cardinal
Polarity	Yang, positive, and masculine
Mantra	"I am."
Hue	Red
Deity	Ares, god of war
Glyph	♈
Flowers	Honeysuckle, poppies, and tulips
Tree	Hawthorn
Jewel	Diamond
Crystals	Bloodstone and pyrite
Fragrance	Geranium
Body Parts	The head, face (except the nose), and brain
Animals	Sheep and rams
Food & Herbs	Onions, leeks, shallots, cayenne pepper, capers, mustard, yarrow, wood betony, borage, and strong-tasting food, such as curries

Aries's Ruling Planet: Mars

Mars in love rules energy, physical stamina, and motivation. Mars reveals how we act out our sexual impulses, passions, challenges, and masculine sexual expression. Mars (Ares in Greek mythology) is the god of war. He was regarded as the father of the Romans. Many soldiers worshipped and prayed to Mars for a successful battle. Mars also represents bodily energy and how one acts and reacts in situations.

Aries Mythology

The ram had originally been bestowed to Nephele, the goddess of the clouds, by Mercury. Nephele's husband took a new wife, Ino, who despised Nephele's children, Phrixus and Helle, and plotted to kill them. To keep them safe, Nephele put Phrixus and Helle on the back of the golden ram, which flew them away. Helle fell off into the Aegean Sea, but Phrixus safely made it to Colchis. Phrixus gave the ram to Zeus and presented the Golden Fleece to the king of Colchis as a gesture of appreciation for his hospitality and protection.

Aries's Positive Qualities and Negative Forms

The positive qualities of Aries are a heart-tugging innocence and wonder, blind faith, and raw courage. If these qualities are expressed in their negative forms, Aries can become selfish, narcissistic, thoughtless, aggressive, and take impulsive action with no regard for the consequences.

How an Aries Loves

Aries falls in love the way they go about everything in their life: forcefully and all at once. Aries is a warrior when it comes to romance, and they never step into a partnership halfheartedly. Most of the joy for a ram in love is the pursuit. Their wild vigor, impulsive energy, and intense enthusiasm is what they use to entice the one they want into their arms. They love to sweep the one they want off their feet with physical and mental expressions. Aries does not believe in boundaries when it comes to the pursuit. So, if they have found the apple of their eye, infinity is where they will stop to win their affection.

The ram's energy vibrates to the number one since they are the first sun sign of the zodiac. Because of their innate mentality of being primary, they like to be put first when they are in a partnership. They are known to be called selfish, but if you give them some time, you will learn that they are incredibly generous with the ones they care for. Aries is notoriously independent and will never request a lot from their companion, but they do require an equal who can hold their own space, as well as space for them when they need it. Versatility and patience are key when partnering with this fire sign.

With Aries, there is no lack of passion or romance. There is something naive and sweet about the way they jump into love headfirst without too much thought. It crushes the ram's spirit when there is too much realism. There is always a touch of fantasy in the way that an Aries loves. The ram is born with a fire that burns within them, and they apply this element to everything they touch. When they are faced with a threat to their partnership, the flames of jealousy will rear their ugly head. Aries is known to be quite covetous when someone has their eye on the one that they adore. The truth about Aries is that they are quite vulnerable when they throw themselves into love. It is their vulnerability that causes them to have a streak of red suspicion that, if uncontrolled, can cause issues of mistrust. There is no malintent behind this doubt. They just do not want to lose the love that they have sacrificed themselves for. It is the influence of Mars that makes this sign a warrior for their relationship.

Although this sun sign is intense, the way they show affection is completely pure. They are not interested in playing games and are looking for an honest and direct kind of connection. You are either in or you are out with an Aries. Their clear view on love is wise and admirable, but if it is perceived through negative eyes, it can be seen as childish and foolish. It is intense to be with someone who is as forceful and direct as Aries is, but if you cannot take the heat, get out of their kitchen.

How to Spot an Aries

Have you met someone lately with a huge smile and a forceful manner? You probably have an Aries on your hands. A ram will impulsively tell anyone exactly what comes to their mind the second it culminates. There is not a lot of filtering that happens with these folks. If an Aries gets annoyed, they have no problem letting you know, which can lead them to often regret things that spill out in the heat of the moment. When you speak to them, they will look you dead in the eye with no restraint.

Physically it is not too hard to spot an Aries. They are not the quiet ones sitting off in the corner by themselves, and you will notice immediately that they have a strong presence. Rams typically have a reddish tint to their hair and a pinkish hue to their face. These are compliments from their ruling red planet, Mars. Aries is blessed with energy for days, and they just keep going and going. Their form is solid, and their movements are so quick you would think sparks are going to start flying out of them. When they walk, they lead with their heads, much like a ram does. There is not much that is graceful about this sun sign, but they do project a scarlet aura that shows off their supreme ego.

Aries is the infant of the zodiac, and their personality as an adult still carries a childish candor. When you are an infant, you cry when you need something, and you expect to be given what you want immediately. Therefore, when an Aries wants something, they do not want it tomorrow or when you can get around to it—they want it now. This sun sign tends to receive forgiveness and compassion from people quite naturally due to their innocent and naive nature. Much like with a child, it is difficult to remain cross with them for long because they never deliberately try to make people upset. It is their lack of self-awareness that is frustrating while equally endearing. They are the first sign on the karmic wheel and are always concerned with their sense of self. Aries are naturally and unintentionally selfish, which is why they love to talk about themselves and their big plans for the future. Something impressive about them is that they can talk for hours about a subject they know very little about. Their confidence is contagious—even when they are out of their depth.

Aries often does not feel a need to ask for permission when making decisions because they are doers. In their world, asking for forgiveness is easier than asking for permission. They are known for their short fuse, but they get over things in a flash. They just simply let things go and will always apologize if they offended someone. On the other side of the coin, they will rarely accept defeat, even when it is staring them dead in the face, which can make it very hard for them to say the words "I was wrong." They have a tough and forceful behavior, but their innocence and childlike wonder gifts them, even in their later years, with the belief that magical things can always happen.

Aries are career people and, thanks to their strong cardinal modality, fantastic ones at that. Subtlety, humility, and tact are not always qualities that they possess. However, generosity, a liberal attitude, and strong leadership qualities are traits that they do. These are great attributes for being a front-runner, but sometimes they can cause friction in their personal relationships. Aries are the first to complain, but they are also the first to give liberally. Rams love cash, but they are not ones to put importance on the almighty dollar either. Just because you have wealth does not mean you will get special treatment from them; they believe in giving everyone a fair shot. They love to do people favors, especially if they are large and altruistic. Aries are nothing short of being gregariously generous, and even though they have a "me first" attitude, they can also be some of the warmest and most charitable people in the world.

There is something irresistible about this fire sign due to its innocence and lack of self-awareness. It is their naivety that mellows their aggressiveness. Aries's pureness breeds boldness and fearlessness, but it can also become a problem with trusting people too much too soon. They have a hard time remembering pain from past relationships or friendships, which causes them to make similar mistakes over and over. Regardless of how many hits they take on their journey to find love, their courage and willfulness always get them back up to continue, which is an incredibly admiral trait of this sun sign. What you see is what you get with the ram. Their uncomplicated personality makes them vulnerable, but their determination will help them get their way almost every single time.

The most lovable thing about the ram is that they will always fight for those who are less fortunate than themselves. They are born a crusader full of faith, joy, and naivety that is wildly endearing. They are strong, determined, and are wonderful at giving people encouragement in their darkest moments. They are always leading everyone to a goal that seems impossible, but for the ram, nothing is out of reach. Feed this person's ego and you will get the same in return. If you need a miracle to happen, go to Aries. They will make it come true in a fiery flash.

How to Lose an Aries

The ram lives for fiery passion, and sex is a crucial component to their partnerships. They need a mate with a high libido and the confidence to try new things in the sheets. Aries will pursue what they want and love whom they desire in a forthright manner. To some, their energy can be overwhelming, but if looked at in a positive light, it can also make one feel truly cared for. Aries's attitude is sassy and bold, and they need a partner who is willing to step up to the plate. The ram can smell fear a mile away, and they will walk all over someone if they are enabled to. Even though it may seem like that is what they want, it most certainly is not. Aries enjoys a challenge and some playful pushback, and their strong personality requires a lover who is solid enough to keep them in check.

Aries likes to be the boss, so if you have issues with giving up control, this may not be the sign for you. Aries is known for being the most courageous sign in the zodiac, and they emit their bravery throughout all areas of life, including relationships. When a ram is in love, they do anything to make it work by taking the reins. They do not really have a "go with the flow" type of personality because they would rather take the bull by the horns. If Aries finds someone trying to push them into a corner, they are not afraid to fight their way out tooth and nail to regain independence. This is why it is crucial to give the ram autonomy in your partnership and never make them feel forced to fit into a box. Accept them for who they are and what they are not, so you can enjoy their unapologetic magic for exactly what it is.

Aries is loads of fun, but if you dull their flames, they will be on the run. Not only are they down for whatever, but they are invigorated by spontaneous and impulsive escapades. Aries searches for these experiences in a partner and always seems to find an opportunity wherever they go. They love to make things happen and cannot have a significant other that worries too much about branching out and trying new things. Their crazy and impulsive life is created to discover the unknown, so their lover must be willing to create space for these experiences to happen. Encouraging the ram's passion and never holding them back is what will keep them around. Aries hates being bored and craves change to make their life worth living. This also goes for their work ethic. Aries is quite business focused, and they are always looking for ways to make money. They need a partner who is encouraging of their entrepreneurial spirit and understanding of their need to work around the clock.

Aries fully enjoys being the center of attention, so make it all about them and you will see their good side. They are confident in their own skin, in their own thoughts, and in who they are as a person. However, do not let all that confidence fool you because they also need a lot of affirmation. This is what causes a bright red streak of jealousy in every ram. They do not want to be the center of everyone's attention like a Leo but rather just need to know they are the center of their partner's universe. An Aries is protective of both themselves and what they consider to be theirs, and they always have a watchful eye on the people they love. For all their hotheadedness, they are incredibly gentle with their partner's heart, and when they feel safe, Aries expresses adoration in a childlike way.

Aries does not know how to be wrong, and as their partner, you will find yourself frequently apologizing first. Agreeing to disagree is really not how an Aries rolls, and they would prefer to cut to the chase by agreeing that what they said was correct. Aries is prime in all areas of astrology. They are the first sign, the baby of the zodiac, the first cardinal sign, and the beginning of the fire element. They are innately number one and winners at that. Arguing with a ram takes a lot of patience, tact, and compromise. They are incredibly forgiving, but they are not great at being mistaken. Learning how to create boundaries with them and conducting a healthy dialogue will keep them around. Choosing your battles wisely is crucial when in love with a ram.

Aries likes to hunt for their meals, so if they are not after you, they are not into you. It is really that simple. Allow them to chase after you; they want a prize to be won. They also know what they want, and they want it fast. If they look for it and find it in you, they will demand an intentional relationship from the start. If you get cold feet or make up absurd excuses as to why you do not want to commit, you will lose them. It is crucial to be sure you are ready for commitment when getting involved with a ram. They are not into being made into a fool in front of anyone, so if they feel like you are not in it to win it, they will be gone as fast as they came. Be prepared to fall in love with Aries because it happens quickly and easily, and when it does, you will not regret it. The trick is to not lose them along the way.

How to Bed an Aries

Having sex with Aries is like taking a shot of cinnamon whiskey; it's sweet, hot, and makes you want to come back for more. Aries's energy is bold, but there is something so innocent and naive about the way they love that it leaves the heart scintillated. They enjoy going between being dominate and submissive and are happy to take either role with pleasure. They are ruled by the god of war and will do whatever it takes to win their lover over in bed—even if it means going to battle. If you are looking for a bashful wallflower, you are with the wrong sun sign. Aries is aggressive about what they want, and they will do what it takes to gain their desires.

In bed Aries will express themselves passionately and physically. They will enjoy making their partner's wildest fantasies into red-hot reality. The ram is all about themselves, and that means they have absolutely no problem bringing themselves to climax if you cannot do the trick. They like having their way, so if they want something, they are going to get it and fast, even if that means in public. If their impulsive side takes over, all else is forgotten. Foreplay is not at the forefront of their mind because they like to get right into the action as soon as possible. Instant gratification is what this sun sign is all about.

Aries's personality is ferociously independent, so if you are not doing it right for them in bed, you will be finding your way out the door. You may be surprised at their taste of sexual partners because you would think that they would require a strong, dominant one. However, it is quite the contrary because their sweet side takes over when picking their mate. Aries knows what they want, and they know how to get it. If that thing is you, you will feel their fiery passion soon. When a quick love interest starts to lose their appeal, Aries will find someone that fits their needs emotionally and sexually. Once Aries finds their mate, they will be extremely jealous with them. If you want to see Aries's fiery temper, flirt with their partner. You will feel like a stick of dynamite just went off.

The ram knows how to please their lover in bed like no other because of their boldness and willingness, which is met with innocence and ease. Conservative sex is not how they play, and their sex drive is uncharted. Out of all the sun signs in the zodiac, it is safe to say that Aries enjoys frequent physical oneness more than any other. Their energy needs a place to be channeled, and what better way than through the aggression and purity of making love? Their innate masculine energy plays into their vigor, and for Aries, too much is never enough.

☼ ☼ ☼

ARIES & ARIES

♈ ◈ ♈

Aspect: Conjunct
Elements: Fire and fire
Modalities: Cardinal and cardinal

Aries have a way about them—their own way. Two rams will either hook horns or climb mountains, or maybe a little bit of both. Two Aries in love can make giant mistakes or giant achievements together. The choice is theirs. They both have strong egos, but they can appreciate one another in a way that no one else could. Their spontaneous energy will bring a surge of strength to the other, and it is a joy for them to find a twin with the same positive, enthusiastic, and open nature. When they first meet, they will have an instant rush of mutual admiration for each other that rarely fades.

Not everything is a walk in the park for a pair of rams. When fire meets fire, the flames are bigger and hotter. When two Mars-ruled people clash, it can be an all-out war. They will have to control their tendencies to lash out at one another. The best thing for them to do is take some time apart before they cause too much damage. They both have dominate and uncontrollable spirits, and finding each other among their endeavors can be tricky. Making time for one another will be key. The great thing about Aries is that they are over their arguments as quickly as they started them. They are great at making up for their outbursts with over-the-top compliments and generous gifts to apologize. Much like a bomb, they are quick to go off and create damage, but then it is over, and they can quickly start picking up the pieces to move on.

There will be times of domination from both, but because this is a masculine-ruled sign, the energy will be aggressive. The pair will have times when they simultaneously want to be the leader, and there are some well-needed lessons to be learned from one another here. They can run the world together if they just learn to get along. However, behind that hard ram exterior is an innocent soul that craves being taken care of. An Aries heart always has scars that no one will ever see because Aries's pride would rather protect the hurt. Of course, there is an understanding between two Aries when they are in each other's arms because they feel understood and protected, which is something they both desperately and secretively need. One place they do not mind giving up power is in the bedroom. Aries knows what they are doing when it comes to sex. Physicality will be at the forefront of their relationship in a lot of ways because there will be a lot of it. Sex is how they wake up and make up. They will both like being in charge, which can cause a few problems, but if they find harmony, it can be amazing. They will have explosive and carnal lovemaking that is full of passion and fire. If they can learn to give up a little independence, the sky is the limit for this hot, passionate combo.

When it comes to cash, they are both generous in this arena. Mars's way when it comes to money is that if it is gone, there will be a way to manifest more. They are touched by the way they can trust each other when it comes to this. They each know that the other is a boss and gets whatever needs to be done accomplished. The trust that they mutually share is the solid base of their relationship. There will rarely be any dishonesty or pretense between two Aries because of their straightforward communication. There is very little that will be impartial between them thanks to their double Mars energy. It will not be easy, but Aries loves a good challenge. They are capable of reaching pure joy or utter chaos together, and they can beautifully sympathize with one another, which is something they both desperately need. They will have to choose to continue to keep trying. There is something that is so uncontrollable about their love. It is almost like a wildfire that is too hot to be stopped. However, when something is too hot, it can burn out too fast. If two Aries in love want to last, they will have to keep their heat at a smolder to make it through the years.

Everything they do—their lovemaking, their fighting, and more—will be at 110 percent. When the going gets tough, they must do their absolute best to remember how lost they would feel without their ram counterpart. As independent as Aries is, they deeply long for a partner, but not just any partner. Aries wants a true life partner. A conjunct pair must be kind and patient with one another. If anyone can understand them for who they are, it is each other; they are one in the fiery same. The Golden Rule is something they can always come back to. If they can both live by the rule of "Do to others what you want them to do to you," they can truly rule the world together.

☼ ☼ ☼

ARIES & TAURUS

♈ ⬦ ♉

Aspect: Semisextile
Elements: Fire and earth
Modalities: Cardinal and fixed

You may think that because these two both have horns, they must share similar traits, but that is not the case with this love match. Aries is strong-minded, and Taurus is persistent. The difference is that one is an action, and the other is a reaction. Aries likes to start something, but the bull will finish it. Aries is aggressive, impulsive, bossy, extravagant, talkative, and optimistic. They love a fast-paced and exciting environment that keeps them on their toes and interested. Taurus prefers to be reserved, practical, and is careful about what they say out loud. They love stability, and their alone time provides the tranquility that they require to recharge. Unfortunately, Aries gets a bad rap for running people ragged and burning bridges everywhere they go. However, Aries can be surprisingly gentle as well. Taurus, on the other hand, gets accused of being dull and lazy, ready to smother any type of enthusiasm. But if you get to know them, they have a beautiful imagination and a warm wisdom under their earthy exterior. Aries's and Taurus's motivations and actions tend to go in different directions. However, one thing to take into consideration is that in life and in love, it is good to be with someone who possesses the qualities you lack. This is how you learn and grow. Taurus should try to be more tolerant of the ram, while Aries should try to imitate the bull's stability. This will help them grow stronger together, and strength is one thing that they both admire.

Financially these two make a powerhouse team. Taurus is wonderful at securing their funds, and Aries's energy and tireless drive brings home the bacon. Aries is attracted to the fact that Taurus is dependable in this way. When the day is done, Aries appreciates the calming and earthy energy that Taurus exudes. In this way, they can establish a free flow of give-and-take between them if they are able to learn how to blend their natures. Part of achieving that is time apart. Aries must have their night on the town, so Taurus can have their time at home alone to recharge. It is all about compromise and balance.

Taurus will never be pressured into anything quickly—ever. If Taurus says no and Aries keeps pushing, it will just make them less inclined to even consider the offer. Taurus needs to understand that Aries is not always practical, and their impulsive excitement tends to get the better of them. However, Taurus needs to let Aries express themselves without taking them too seriously. If Aries really wants something, they need to present their case to Taurus after it has been well prepared and thought out. Aries must learn how to make recommendations, not demands. Suggestions will get Aries a lot further with Taurus.

Aries loves to be near Taurus and benefits from their steadfastness, and their physicality will be satisfying. Aries is all about sex that is wild and hot, while Taurus takes a sensual and practical approach. Taurus will love the fiery dominance and confidence Aries emits. Aries is so straightforward about what they want, and Taurus will happily make space for it. Aries is ruled by Mars, the god of war, and Taurus is ruled by Venus, the goddess of love. This couple is progressive, but in the bedroom the combination of their masculine and feminine energy makes their romance feel classic.

Taurus is a fixed sign and, therefore, a creature of habit. Because of this, their thoughts and dreams tend to move in a circle, not really getting anywhere. Aries is a cardinal sign and is always moving full steam and straight ahead. With time and a gentle approach, Aries can break Taurus's circle and let new ideas into their head and heart. This change of direction will be productive and good for the bull. Taurus can help Aries find happiness as well by supporting the ram with warm patience. Taurus has the ability to create a safe haven for the ram to call home, and together they can help one another reach new heights and create a bright future that is exciting and sturdy.

☼ ☼ ☼

ARIES & GEMINI

♈ 💎 ♊

Aspect: Sextile
Elements: Fire and air
Modalities: Cardinal and mutable

The ram and the twins are an unstoppable team that is always looking for an adventure to conquer together. There is not a lot that will hold their interest for long, which is why these two are always on the move. Aries fizzes with childlike impulsiveness, and Gemini is determined to achieve complete individuality by breaking every promise of the soul. Because of this, maturity of thought rarely supports their shared actions. Together, they are a bright picture of optimism, youth, vitality, and vigor. Seeing them together is like watching two children at play. On the flip side, they can be selfish, illogical, and inconsiderate with one another. Their innocence and ignorance can be their greatest gifts while simultaneously their fall. However, if they understand that all that glitters is not gold, they can make their charming combination work.

When Aries pursues Gemini, the twins will not have any other option than to let Aries take a chance with them. Gemini treats relationships like just another gust of wind to ride until the next breeze picks them up. After getting to know Gemini for a while, Aries will realize that their charm and intelligence is something that they can learn from and apply to their own persona. Aries will keep the relationship steam going with the victory of a long-lasting love in mind. Gemini likes to weigh their relationship out with an unattached manner, never really showing all their cards. Aries loves a challenge, and they definitely get one with this sign.

Aries operates in a cardinal modality and loves to lead, inspire, and keep an enthusiastic mindset. Gemini is mutable and would prefer to relate to most things in a fun yet unpersonal manner. They are mental and communicate through reason and ingenuity. They have a way with words that makes Gemini so appealing. The Gemini method is less aggressive and more mental, but the twins are sympathetic toward the ram's more expressive approach to things. Aries appreciates the emotional freedom that Gemini obtains with their aloof and untouchable aura. Conversation is lively with these two as Aries is loud and Gemini is chatty, making them quite the spectacle in public. One thing to be mindful of is that Gemini is a flirt, and Aries is very jealous. The ram loves intensely, which is the only way they know how to love, and does not want to see anyone interested in their partner. This will usually cause Aries to grasp their Gemini tightly, which will only cause them to push their Gemini to move further away. One thing that can be assuring and healing for them is their intimacy.

Because of their differences, they feel liberated around one another. This liberation is what creates a vibe of friendship in their relationship. Gemini can create illusions of excitement for Aries, and role playing in the bedroom will be something they enjoy doing together. The twins will love the ram's intensity in bed, and Aries will love all the fantasy that Gemini brings to the table. Both possess an innocent, fun nature that will translate in their physical playtime, making their sex colorful. This keeps their sexual experiences fun and fresh, which is something they both admire in a partner.

Gemini will always drive Aries a little crazy in the worst and best ways. Aries always feels like Gemini is searching for something that does not exist because they are always looking back and recollecting on the past. What Gemini needs to wake up and realize is that Aries can be what they are looking for right now and also give them an amazing future. Having a partnership with Aries does not mean that Gemini must clip their wings and never feel the freedom of soaring. They just need to stay on Aries's flight plan by letting them drive and holding on tight. These two are both so wonderfully youthful together, and if Aries can just remember to let go of control and if Gemini can stick around and skip that next gust of wind that comes by, love can do just about anything for them.

☼ ☼ ☼

ARIES & CANCER

♈ 💎 ♋

Aspect: Square
Elements: Fire and water
Modalities: Cardinal and cardinal

If the ram and the crab are willing to take the time to translate each other's heart, this match can reach great heights. Aries and Cancer have different forces and vibrations that they move to regarding their elemental nature. Aries vibes to a feverish red-hot fire, while Cancer prefers the tepid calmness of blue waters. Cancer intuitively knows that Aries needs some of their energy to cool their heels, and Aries feels as though Cancer could use some of their fire to warm their emotions. If they can find a careful balance between their elements, they can make some lovely steam. One thing that they do have in common is that they both express themselves in the cardinal modality, which means they both like to lead. However, they just like to lead in different ways. Aries enjoys—and needs—to win. Cancer likes both of those things, too, but prefers to enjoy them in a demurer way. Aries charges full force ahead, while Cancer skims from side to side. The ram's horns and the crab's shell are equally tough, and this will cause some quarrels over who gets to be the spearhead and in what manner they decide to move. The pair must compromise by walking hand in hand so that no one is in front or behind.

These sun signs share the same goal in life both emotionally and financially, and that goal is security. However, even though they want the same things, the way they get there is quite different. Aries is more generous—and at times reckless—with money and love, whereas Cancer saves every single penny and preserves their sentiments. Aries is overall much more optimistic and positive that things will turn out just fine, while Cancer is more negative and fearful about taking big gambles. In Aries's mind, you miss all the shots you never take. Meanwhile Cancer hogs all the balls on the sideline. What they both must realize is that it is all about mindset. You have a better chance at winning in life if you go into it with the attitude that you will win, which is something that Aries can teach Cancer. Adjacently the crab will teach the ram to curb their impulsive attitude.

Aries was not born to be patient and prefers things fast and instantaneous. They choose a direction and move full steam ahead, but Cancer will teach Aries that there is more than one way to get somewhere. If Cancer is positive and humorous in their approach with Aries, the ram will be receptive. However, if the crab is snappy, Aries will not be amenable. Aries can try to boost Cancer's spirits, but when the crab is in one of their moods, it is best to let them come out of their shell on their own terms. Once the crab leaves their cavernous casing, sex is a way to smooth things over.

Their attraction will not be instant but rather something that is discovered over time. Cancer is a lot more emotional about sex than Aries is, which will take some adjustment. The crab is never one to trust instantly, but Aries knows how to make them feel secure, and Cancer senses this. In return, Cancer will assure Aries that their heart is safer with them than most other signs. While the crab tends to be a lot deeper and more sensitive about the act, they will find something refreshing about sex with Aries. Patience is not the ram's strongest virtue, but they will have to wait through periods of Cancer's moods to get to them, and in the end, it will be worth it. Cancer is an emotionally and physically sensual lover, and if Aries can give themselves completely to their moon-ruled crustacean, there will be a closeness and a deeper love and understanding between them. It is their sex that will get them through the tough times.

Cancer is ruled by the moon, which waxes and wanes, pushing and pulling their temperament in several directions throughout the month. One day they are amusing and hilariously entertaining, and the next day they just want to be left alone. Aries will have to remember on the tough days that Cancer is beautifully sensitive and that eventually they will come out of their shell. The ram has Mars, the planet of war, to thank for their own strength and aggressive temperament. Even though Aries exudes a strong impression and is known for their powerful will and bold temper, Cancer will intuitively know when to comfort them, making them feel truly cared for.

Cancer is proud of Aries's courageous mind and bright spirit, and they are not afraid to be sentimental or affectionate. If Aries moves Cancer's heart, they will see tears of tenderness from the crab. Aries needs to see these tears to know that they fondly care for them the way they have been emotionally longing for their whole life. If these two can find a way to carefully blend Aries's initiating personality with Cancer's determination, they can make anything happen. Furthermore, if they mix that with patience and love, they will make it through to the end. Look after Cancer's feelings, Aries, but do not ever let them know. Look after Aries's heart, Cancer, and let them know every day.

☼ ☼ ☼

ARIES & LEO

♈ 💎 ♌

Aspect: Trine
Elements: Fire and fire
Modalities: Cardinal and fixed

Aries are born winners, and Leos were born on top, so these two fire signs will find each other in life and in love with ease. They somehow bend their egos to be with one another because they finally see that they have found their equal counterpart. Both signs seek and demand adoration, and so they both enjoy showering each other with extravagant compliments and over-the-top gifts. Aries needs Leo's wisdom, strength, and tenderness, and Leo requires Aries's innocence, independence, and challenge. The chemistry between these two is undoubtedly magical, and everyone can not only see it but feel it. Their grand auras and fighting spirits are impossible to miss.

They are harmoniously aspected to each other by a trine vibration, which gives them a natural and genuine admiration for one another and a warm and happy love—most of the time. Leo feels a need to share their critiques and insight with Aries. This can come off as if Leo is talking down to Aries, which the ram will not appreciate. If Leo can express themselves in more of a humble way, the ram will be much more receptive to Leo's grand speeches. On the other hand, Aries feels a need to command Leo around, which will not be appreciated. If Aries can learn to ask Leo kindly, their relationship will become more amicable. Their egos are where they meet, but it's also where they can clash. These two may fight about silly things here and there, and the spats will usually be over as soon as they started. Aries can tend to be a bit immature at times, which will either have Leo laughing or annoyed. Leo can tend to get suspicious, which either will have Aries walking on eggshells or feeling adored. Whatever the case may be, the couple must watch these traits and be mindful of one another's sensitivities. The ram and the lion will fight, no doubt, but make up just as quickly. Aries's fuse may be short, but they forgive rapidly, and Leo may go into an envious fury, but their huge heart forgets swiftly. These two will tend to be even more in love after their misunderstandings than they were before. When they can find room for mutual consideration, it gives space for an extraordinary love to flourish between them. Their physical oneness is another way that they can fall deeper in love.

When it comes to sex with this pair, it is as hot as a roaring fire in the middle of July. Their lovemaking is passionate yet sweet, large yet uncomplicated. They will always have a burning romance between them that can be as simple as a loving kiss on the forehead to an all-night session that wakes the neighbors up. Their sex life is one that is envied by all others, and they create fireworks in the bedroom by mixing their hot auras. Aries loves sex with their Leo so much that they will not even want to believe they have been with anyone else. Leo will adore being at the center of Aries's attention and will appreciate the ram's audacious personality, which complements their own. Together, their oneness creates a story that is one for the books.

When Leo opens up their bold, warm heart to Aries, the ram will give all of themselves to the lion, and they both will find a safe place within their passionate and incredible relationship. In one another, the ram and the lion find the enthusiasm that they are always searching for in life. They both have dynamic personalities, and even though they are different, they blend like two primary colors into a new, beautiful secondary color that they can call their own. Aries and Leo love to manifest fiery passion together, creating a world painted with their new hue. This original life that they produce together will never be dull. Instead it will be a beautiful, bright creation filled with reds, yellows, and their new orange shade—a picture of pure joy and magical warmth.

☼ ☼ ☼

ARIES & VIRGO

♈ ◈ ♍

Aspect: Quincunx
Elements: Fire and earth
Modalities: Cardinal and mutable

The fiery ram and the earthy angel are more different than they are alike, but it is the space between their differences where the magic takes place with this pair. Aries easily becomes bored with details and nuances, whereas Virgo picks apart each point and loathes generalizations. Passion is the fuel to Aries's fire due to their trust in their emotions, whereas Virgo removes emotion and replaces it with unwavering practicality. When Aries feels something, they make it well known, whereas Virgo buries their opinion to become more amicable. These sun signs have so much to teach one another, but one thing that brings them together is their kindness.

They have an alchemic ability to see the best in each other when the world cannot. When most people describe an Aries, they will use words like bossy, impulsive, impractical, immature, and ridiculous, but through a Virgo's clear eyes, they see the ram as fresh, innocent, and honest. When a Virgo loves an Aries, it is impossible for them to view their lover in a negative way because they see the fun and eternally young soul that keeps their life so alive. Aries is ruled by the planet Mars, which is the ruler of war and aggression, yet they show Virgo their dreams, unselfish love, and soft side. Virgo is ruled by the planet Mercury, which is the ruler of cunning communication, but Virgo feels safe to tell Aries their true feelings without being judged. This earth sign makes this fire sign feel so secure that they rarely feel the need to initiate their temper, and this cardinal sign makes this mutable sign feel safe to be themselves, which is so refreshing to Virgo.

They will have to learn to let each other be themselves. When they are positive with one another, they can blend together in a beautiful way. Virgo is critical yet kindhearted, while Aries is domineering yet sweet. Virgo is wonderfully close to the one they love, and Aries would get the moon for their angel if they asked them to. Being a mutable earth sign, Virgo is a steadfast character and chatterbox, and Aries, being a cardinal fire sign, is a strong, exuberant leader. The two will have a lot of great conversations and will talk about anything and everything together. Aries will love listening to Virgo's intelligent mind, and Virgo will think highly of Aries's powerful entrepreneurial ways. Together, they can make an incredible team. Once a Virgo enters an Aries's life, Aries starts to notice that everything around gets better. There is just something in the way a Virgo takes things and makes them so perfect. If Aries can let Virgo take control in some areas and if Virgo can let go and let Aries lead a little, they will have a love and life most would envy.

In the bedroom, Aries is sizzling and wild, whereas Virgo is pristine and thoughtful. Their sex is guiltless and fun, but Aries will have to get Virgo to loosen up a bit. Virgo will love the ram's stamina and affection, but Aries will need to give Virgo time to refresh. Their sexual differences are vast, but they can make it work with care. Aries will learn to have to take it slow with Virgo and that not everything has to be so fiery and fast. Virgo requires that there first be mental respect rather than emotional idealism, but over time they will build both with each other. Aries must sympathize with the fact that it will take Virgo more time than them to open up and feel comfortable, and Aries must understand that they should not take this personally, realizing not everyone moves at the same pace. Virgo must analyze things, which Aries can take personally, but if Aries can understand that is just how their mind operates, they will start to understand their Virgo. In return, if Virgo can realize that, even though Aries may seem brash, Aries's intentions are always in the right place, Virgo will never have to guess where they stand with the ram because they will always make their intentions clear, which is refreshing.

Every time that their personalities start to clash, there is no reason that they cannot mend the problem with a little bit of consideration and a lot of love. They both find fulfillment in fixing things, and with this mindset they can get through just about any hardship life throws their way. Aries's love is sweet, and Virgo's love is pure. When Virgo lets their senses go and trusts their ram's enthusiasm is when they will start to feel closer to them. Virgo must allow their Aries to get close and open their wings to let their passions whisk them away. Aries is made to lead, to protect, and to love, and the ram's fiery passion will keep Virgo warm on the coldest nights.

☼ ☼ ☼

ARIES & LIBRA

♈ ◈ ♎

Aspect: Opposite
Elements: Fire and air
Modalities: Cardinal and cardinal

Neither one of these sun signs has felt this kind of initial attraction, ever. The chemistry between Aries and Libra is so thick and so sweet, you could cut it like honey butter. Aries has never seen such an ethereal creature in their life, and it will be impossible for them to see a flaw in Libra's perfectly balanced aura. Libra is effortlessly beautiful, superior, and bright. They check every single one of Aries's boxes, and Aries will feel as though they won the jackpot with this one. Later Aries will discover a few surprises about Libra that they were not expecting, but we will get to that later. For now, enjoy the beginning of this relationship, where everything will be peaches and cream.

Libras are ruled by Venus, the planet of love, and Aries are ruled by Mars, the planet of war. However, they are both cardinal signs, which means they both like to lead, and this is where things can get a little sticky. In another light, it can also make these two quite the power couple. There is a good chance that they will both be the boss in their careers and will love to meet up for drinks after work at a swanky bar or go work out at the gym to let out some steam from their day. A way they connect is by giving back by volunteering time to the greater good and will enjoy leading initiatives for charity. Both have a strong sense of justice and cannot stand any inequity in the world. Together, they will make it their job to fight for equality.

Libras like to take their time when making decisions, small or large, and Aries are impulsively decisive. This sort of irrational impatience can really throw the Libra's scales out of balance. Libra will have to use their charm to get Aries to slow down and see that taking the time to weigh out their decisions can really pay off. It is the Libra's charm and the Aries's sense of humor that will help them get through their differences. When Aries is angry, all they see is red, not allowing them to see Libra's side of things. When Aries cools down, they will probably feel stupid for how they acted, so if Libra can just know that their ram will come around, it will help their relationship significantly.

Libra likes to debate things to thoroughly see all sides of a topic, and Aries will love this about Libra. Even though they ultimately enjoy getting their way, Aries would be bored with a partner who just agreed with everything they said. Aries loves a challenge and excitement, and Libra will be the air that feeds their fire. This also translates into the bedroom, which is where their opposing energy can blend into one that stokes Aries's flames into a bright fire. Seeing that they are opposites on the karmic wheel, they are strongly attracted to one another and sexually merge very well. Aries likes taking the lead in the bedroom, and Libra should let them. Their love will be wild and fun, and no matter how long they are together, Aries will always be mystified by their attraction to their Libra.

Libra is a powerful sun sign, but Aries is up for any challenge. Libra will always support their ram's enthusiasm and will be interested in hearing what they have to say whenever they need an ear. The root of any issues with this cardinal pair is their intrinsic need to lead, but they will have to learn to compromise and know that it is healthy to agree to disagree on occasion. They must learn to work as equals side by side. This means Aries will need to take a seat and let Libra be the boss from time to time. Besides, it is easier to hold hands when you stand next to each other rather than standing with someone in front. The real joy in love is when someone loves you just the way you are, and that is where these two will find safety with one another.

☼ ☼ ☼

ARIES & SCORPIO

♈ ◈ ♏

Aspect: Quincunx
Elements: Fire and water
Modalities: Cardinal and fixed

Scorpios are intense and penetrating, full of confidence and totally unshakable, and Aries will love this intensity from the moment they meet them. When they start to get to know each other on a deeper level, Scorpio will share their secrets with the ram. Aries will see parts of the scorpion that they have never shared with anyone, making them feel special, and Aries likes to feel special. Scorpio loves the fresh innocence and undying faith that Aries obtains. Scorpio also needs and respects the loyalty and space that Aries holds for them. They will never be able to get enough of one another, and while Scorpio's obsession may scare some sun signs off, Aries is all about it. Even though they are quincunx in aspect, which means they have different elements and modalities, they share the ruling planet Mars, which is where a huge piece of their connection lies. Mars adds energy, physical stamina, and motivation—times two—for them and gifts them with undying passion for one another.

One thing they share is the extreme need to love and be loved in a complete and all-consuming way. They rarely do anything—especially relationships—halfway, and that will make things very impassioned between them. Scorpios are loyal to a fault, so the ram's jealous tendencies will never be a problem with this pair. They will feel secure with one another, offering equal amounts of trust. Even though Scorpio can come off as reserved, Aries needs to remember their sensitive soul is hidden behind their hard exterior. Scorpios are tender and can love to a depth that is not attainable to most. This depth is intense, but Aries does not mind the power.

Emotionally they are a great match because of their corresponding desires. However, mentally they are about as different as you can get. Scorpio is critical, skeptical, and cautious, while Aries is direct, careless, compulsive, and uncompli-cated. These mental differences will either intrigue one another, or it will break them. Before Scorpio walks into a partnership, they will have a lot of questions for Aries and put them through a few of their rigorous tests. The great thing about Aries is that they will not fall ill to Scorpio's stings or their searching ques-tions. Aries is a tough sun sign and can put up with Scorpio's complicated nature to an extent. One thing Scorpio will never be able to do is control the ram's fiery temper. After all, it is their vital spirit and independence that attracts the Scorpio to them in the first place. Scorpio will accept Aries's aggressive mannerisms, especially behind closed doors.

Things sexually are really hot and heavy with this pairing. With Aries's heat and Scorpio's passion, they can create some steamy lovemaking. Together, they feel fulfilled in this area of their relationship. Sex between them will be a very important part of their dynamic and surely a way to smooth over any arguments. With Mars as their planetary ruler, their togetherness will be erotic, fervent, and intense. Their physicality is an extremely important piece of their togetherness because it is something that ties them together spiritually.

Because Scorpio is ruled by both Mars and Pluto, nothing is ever halfway with them. They either build it up to heaven or tear it down to hell. They are devoted and loyal and have every intention of permanency if they feel like they can trust their partner. Aries oddly understands Scorpio in this way—possibly because Aries has a strength that matches their own. Aries is really no match for the Scorpio magnetism, and that's how the Scorpio can snag their ram and keep them around through the tough times. However, between the Scorpio skepticism and Aries's immature nature, there will be many days that they have to choose each other over walking away. Nevertheless, when they join forces, there is next to nothing that can get in their way. When they make wishes together, it is as if the heavens have no choice but to open up and obey.

☼ ☼ ☼

ARIES & SAGITTARIUS

Aspect: Trine
Elements: Fire and fire
Modalities: Cardinal and mutable

Fire plus fire equals more fire, and that is just what these two signs combined create. Being that the ram and archer are the same element, there is an undoubted natural attraction between them. They could be across the room or across the world from one another and somehow still find each other. Aries and Sagittarius get along so well because they have so much in common. They share an optimistic view filled with sweet innocence and a love of life. They both believe that if they wish for something hard enough, it will come true, and oddly with this pair, it usually does. There is no relationship that is ever perfect, but these two are easily able to restore harmony between each other with their bright dispositions.

It may be hard to tell them apart, but because of their ruling planets, the differences are there if you look hard enough. Jupiter causes Sagittarius to be expansive, honest, and experimental, whereas Mars causes Aries to be forceful, defensive, and fierce. Aries is much more sensitive and vulnerable to abandonment because of their blamelessness. Because Sagittarius has further evolved around the karmic wheel, they do not possess this pure goodness like the ram. Regarding the ram's innate naivety, Sagittarius must learn to never make a promise that they cannot keep and never give Aries a reason to be jealous while appreciating their independence. Aries must learn to embrace the archer's free spirit by meeting them in the fire, trusting them with every beat of their fierce heart, and remembering to have patience with them. If they can both do these things, they will have laughter and love for eternity, and their spirit for one another will never be replaceable.

They are both essentially extroverts, which can cause mistrust between one another's intentions at times, but when faith is formed in this relationship, it has the potential to last forever. The emotional stability they give one another is pure perfection, and they are a really fun couple. They are both friendly, warm, and open, which makes them feel exhilarated when talking about dreams and ideas that they have about life and efforts. They could be in a room with nothing in it and would never get bored. Sagittarius loves the childlike spirit that Aries encapsulates and wants to take the ram on every adventure through life, which is perfect for their wanderlust spirits. Traveling together will bond them, making them feel closer. Another pledge they will form is the one they have sexually. Their sex is automatic, harmonious, intense, and imaginative. They will try things in bed neither of them could have imagined because they feel comfortable and fascinated by each other. They are both into pleasing one another physically. Sagittarius will like telling Aries what they want, and Aries will like giving it to them. Their bedroom activities are fun and fiery, and they will love each other well.

Sagittarius will find something about Aries nostalgic, and Aries will find the excitement in Sagittarius that they have been pining for. Their love may get a little bumpy, but it will never be dull. They will protect one another from any outside negativity by setting their love aflame as a shield, only attracting positive and like-minded souls into their world. It is the unquenchable romanticism that makes Aries uncharacteristically empathetic, and it's their undying honesty that touches a part of the archer deep in their philosophical core and moves them to stay true to the ram. Combined, they are both explosive and compatible in the way that only two fire signs can be. Once these two have found a fiery rhythm together, there is next to nothing on this earth that will stop them. The heavens will grace their love in many ways, and the strength of partnership that they form will be impossible to break. This is their magic.

☼ ☼ ☼

ARIES & CAPRICORN

♈ ♡ ♑

Aspect: Square
Elements: Fire and earth
Modalities: Cardinal and cardinal

The ram and the goat can truly make a fascinating couple. Aries lives for instant gratification, but Capricorns do not give up anything willingly or without rigorous proof of authenticity. Capricorns are incredibly hard workers and are constantly climbing to the top, and a ram knows that the view is always better from the peak. However, you cannot reach the mountaintop without going off the beaten path. If this is to work, they will need to hold hands, pack a bag full of understanding, and bring along a canteen full of apologies for the hike. If any two signs know how to scale a mountain, it is the goat and the ram.

Capricorns place their family and friends on an important level in their lives. To make a Capricorn truly happy, Aries could invite their family on their next vacation. Aries would prefer their partner's attention to be focused on them, but spending time with Capricorn's crew is nonnegotiable. Capricorn will need to compromise and make sure their Aries gets some alone time in return. In regard to their alone time, there will need to be some adjustments in the bedroom. Capricorns are notorious for building walls around their heart and emotions that are created by doubt. These thoughts can really affect what goes on sexually, making Capricorn hold back from completely giving themselves to their partner. What Aries needs to know is that deep down Capricorn wants to let go of control, but on the outside, they play it cool. The goat's ruling planet, Saturn, constantly reminds Capricorn to keep structure in everything they do. Saturn causes Capricorn to control their urges a lot more than Aries is able, which is why they are more likely going to be the one to initiate sex with Capricorn. Capricorn must give in and let go by loosening up in bed with Aries for this to work out.

Sex is not something that should be planned or precise; it should be natural and passionate.

If they do not work things out, their relationship can become very dramatic and not even Aries's hot fire will be able to melt Capricorn's cool exterior. One thing Aries can do to ease this tension is to make Capricorn feel safe and secure. No matter how self-assured Capricorn may come off, they deeply search to feel protected in their partnership. They get worried that if they let their walls down too soon that a beautiful, fiery love may take a piece of their heart they may never get back. To get any piece of Capricorn's heart is precious, and Aries must take that into consideration when entering a union with the sea goat. It will take time and patience, which are not Aries's strong suits, but it will be worth it once obtained.

Capricorn does not care for surprises and would rather live a life that is full of what is to be expected. Self-control is their preferred method because they think that there is no one out there strong enough to catch them if they fall. However, Aries is strong, even strong enough to catch the weight of Capricorn's heavy doubts. If Aries can show Capricorn that they have the stamina to be there through the good and bad, they will reveal the incredibly tender heart protected behind those concrete walls of doubt. Capricorn only gets more amazing the longer Aries knows them. These two can develop a love they can both trust, a love that can grow, and a relationship worth fighting for no matter the friction their square aspect creates. To get to the summit of one another's heart, they must remember to have patience, to let go of the little things, and to have loads of compromise.

☼ ☼ ☼

ARIES & AQUARIUS

♈ 🝡 ♒

Aspect: Sextile
Elements: Fire and air
Modalities: Cardinal and fixed

Aries will fall in love with Aquarius as fast as lightning. When Aries proclaims their love for Aquarius, they will be expecting an immediate response, but Aquarius is rarely all in one place at one time the way Aries is. The water bearer's mind is often in the future, on a different wavelength, and possibly in another dimension. Besides, they would much rather be friends with the ram before they dive into a red-hot romance. How can people be in love when they are not even each other's best friends first? This is the approach that Aquarius takes to every partnership they enter. When and if they do become best friends, Aquarius will then decide if adding another layer to their relationship is really what they want. You see, they work at very different speeds.

Aries will be perplexed by the lack of interest that the water bearer has for them, but if they know that Aquarius is the one for them, they should give them some time. If the ram is what Aquarius's intellectual soul is searching for, Aquarius will never be interested in anything more than them. In fact, just when Aries is about to lose hope and settle for being friends, Aquarius will shock the ram, telling them that they are in love, and ask them to spend the night. It will be like a bolt of lightning that comes out of nowhere, but that is just the Uranian nature of being completely unpredictable. The fact that Aquarius made Aries wait will be frustrating, but in the long run, Aries will learn that Aquarius's slow way of falling in love eases their jealous mind. They know now what they have is genuine, authentic, and hard to get. Their love is something that was built over time, and their Aquarius will not just casually wander off into someone else's arms. Aries needs to know that their partner is all for them, and Aquarius does just that. This base of friendship that they build with one another will always be woven into their relationship no matter how long they are together. Even when people meet them, they will give off that friend vibe with one another. This also creates a safe space where they can have open communication and causes them to be straightforward with each other. There is rarely a time where they will have to play guessing games.

Their sextile vibration spills over into the bedroom because friendly and straightforward sex is how they like to play. Aquarius will not quite know what hit them when having sex with Aries, but whatever it is, they will like it. The first spicy kiss with Aries will leave Aquarius's head spinning, but once they find their feet again, they will come back with a strong force that makes the sex out of this world. Aquarius is a little out there and will love Aries's enthusiasm to try new things sexually. Aries is a lot more intense than Aquarius is, but the water bearer does not mind the heat because it will keep them interested and coming back for more. Aries must understand that with Aquarius, sex is not just sex, so

Aries needs to make it special and interesting. Sometimes the ram will feel like Aquarius is not connecting with them because Aquarius can be aloof, mostly because they have a million things planned and a million friends to hang out with. This means that the water bearer will constantly need to try to be present and connected. Physical togetherness is more important to Aries, while mental connection is more important to Aquarius. Both should take note of this and make space for one another to feel whole.

Aquarius cannot believe how much energy and drive their ram has. They are like a stick of dynamite ready to explode with just the flick of a match. There are days when Aquarius wishes that they could get Aries to slow down and join them in the clouds of their intricate mind. If the water bearer does happen to get Aries to meet them in the sky, Aquarius will enjoy it for a while but then want that fiery, impulsive partner in crime back. This keeps their relationship ebbing and flowing together, and it certainly leaves their love story consistently interesting. As they continue their rhythmic pattern throughout life, there will be times when they are on the exact same wavelength, and they will both know that they have finally found their unique beat.

☼ ☼ ☼

ARIES & PISCES

♈ 🖤 ♓

Aspect: Semisextile
Elements: Fire and water
Modalities: Cardinal and mutable

The ram and the fish's initial attraction for each other is compelling thanks to their varying energies, which captivate one another. This love match does not happen often because of their vast contrasts, but when it does, it is sweet. When they fall in love, nature is taking its course due to their inherently different yin and yang vibrations. Every fish has a choice of whether to swim up or down stream, as well as which body of water they would like to live in, and who they partner with greatly impacts these decisions. The flow of Aries's forthright vibrations is a great influence for Pisces's imaginative mind and allows them to absorb the ram's vitality, which assists in tangible manifestations. Conversely, Pisces cools Aries's flames, allowing the ram to slow down and see things with their soul and develop their intuition rather than relying on their impulses. These two are innately diverse, making it hard to stay perfectly compatible for a long time. However, they would do good to remember that it was their dichotomy that attracted them to each other in the first place. It is solely up to them if their variances will be their strength or their demise.

Sometimes Aries's strong personality can overpower Pisces's gentle nature, but Pisces usually will not complain. This does not mean that they are happy about it, though. This can be confusing to Aries because they are so used to sharing their thoughts in a bold and direct fashion. Pisces is not known to be confrontational about what they want, so the ram will need to remind themselves to check in with their fish. It is never Aries's intention to drive their lover to become complacent, but Pisces is not the type to outwardly say that the ram's thoughtlessness and selfishness is deeply hurting them. On the other hand, Pisces should understand that Aries is so busy living, being, and doing that they forget to take the time to look around to see what is wrong. Pisces will need to build the courage to tell their partner how they feel and will notice when they speak softly to Aries that they never meant to be that way and will apologize. However, if Pisces continues to be passive, they only have themselves to blame for their undoing. Aries is not as naturally intuitive as Pisces is, and they would both benefit from understanding this to bring more empathy and communication into their union.

In the bedroom, there will be a wonderful harmony between them. They step into their natural roles of domination and submission that they both enjoy. Aries is exciting and fiery, and Pisces is deep and watery. If Aries can make room for understanding and not burn all of Pisces's emotions dry, their sex can be amazing. Aries needs Pisces to be theirs and only theirs. The ram cannot have it any other way due to their intense suspicion. Pisces is compassionate and will understand that this need is derived from Aries's vulnerability, but it is still something they will have to work through. Aries must learn to trust Pisces because you cannot go through life and love always thinking that your partner is being unfaithful when they are not because it becomes exhausting. Pisces will have to work to make sure the ram knows that their heart belongs to only them, especially in the beginning of their relationship.

When you put these very different people together, one of two things will happen; they will grow to love each other more and more, or they will grow to love each other less and less. It is truly up to them to create their own ending because it is not their differences that matter but their will to make it work. The one thing they have in common that can pull them through the tough times is that they are both afraid to get their heart broken. Pisces may wonder how their brave and brash Aries could ever be susceptible enough to get hurt, but Aries's vulnerability is just as present as their own. It is just simply disguised better. It is hard to interpret Mars-ruled fear because it is so challenging for Aries's pride to allow them to be vulnerable with their partner—or anyone, for that matter. It will never always go the way it should, and there will be days with ache, but their love can turn the whole thing around if they remember that one another's heart is in the right place.

☼ ☼ ☼

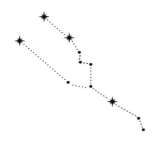

Chapter 2

Taurus

Taurus's love archetype is the sensual lover. They are a private, reflective, and strategic lover who is devoted to physical pleasure. Taurus's lesson in love is to impart that love is fortitude and absorb that love is compassion.

Element	Earth
Modality	Fixed
Polarity	Yin, negative, and feminine
Mantra	"I have."
Hue	Emerald green
Deity	Aphrodite, goddess of love
Glyph	♉
Flowers	Daisies, garden rose, foxglove, and violets
Tree	Apple
Jewel	Emerald
Crystals	Green aventurine and blue kyanite
Fragrance	Sandalwood
Body Parts	The neck, throat, larynx, tonsils, and jugular veins
Animals	Cattle
Food & Herbs	Wheat, berries, apples, pears, grapes, artichokes, asparagus, beans, cloves, sorrel, spearmint, pokeroot, black walnut hull, and blue violet

Taurus's Ruling Planet: Venus

Venus in love rules marriage and attraction and reveals the capacity for affection, beauty, and harmony in partnerships. Venus brings charm and blessings to unions, represents the colors, sounds, music, and varieties of love, and is there to provide couples with smooth sailing through stormy seas. Venus gives Taurus their desire to spend most of their time, effort, and assets surrounding themselves with beautiful and sensual things. A happy home and stable relationships are everything to Taurus.

Taurus's Mythology

The constellation of Taurus represents the bull that Jupiter transformed himself into when he became captivated by the beautiful princess Europa. The princess was awestruck by the beauty and gentleness of the white bull. As the bull and Europa relaxed on the beach, she climbed onto the bull's back, and he swam out to sea with her. He took her to Crete and revealed his true self. They had three sons together who became the royalty of Crete.

Taurus's Positive Qualities and Negative Forms

Taurus's positive qualities are strength of purpose, patience, steadfastness, and conviction. Expressed in their negative forms, bulls become stubborn, blind with prejudice, and have a lack of reason for their convictions.

How a Taurus Loves

When a Taurus falls in love and makes a commitment to their partner, they will put copious amounts of energy into their relationship. They are sensual lovers who are not only devoted to their own physical pleasure but that of their partner's as well. Venus is their ruling planet, so they naturally seek out a romantic companion to connect and share their life with. Bulls have a calm and serene façade, and there is an earthy passion that lives inside of them that few have privy to see. A romantic at heart, their true nature is tucked away and patiently saved for the ones that move their steadfast soul.

Taurus is known for their loyalty and persistence in love, which gives them an invaluable amount of devotion. They stick by through thick and thin while always thinking of their loved one before themselves, gladly making sacrifices when needed. Because of these traits, they expect a lot in return and will not settle for crumbs. They want—and deserve—the whole cake. They long for consistent romance and respect along with complete fidelity and dependability. A Taurus's intense involvement in their relationship can turn to jealousy if not checked. Therefore, they always keep an eye on their lover, and if they have a reason to suspect any disloyalty, the dark side of this usually calm sun sign will come out.

Bulls are naturally erotic and place physical oneness high on their list of priorities in their partnerships. In ways that they are unable to connect through words, they can connect through physical touch. Their senses are heightened to a degree that supersedes any other sun sign. This is why they are sensitive to certain colors, tastes, music selection, and the way material feels on their skin. Because of their intensified senses, sex becomes an uninhibited hedonistic necessity to the bull. Unifying their body with their partner is the way that they can connect and show love. The other way is with their devotion of loyalty and dedicated steadfastness. They are unshakable in the most precarious of situations, which makes them an incredible ally to have in life and love.

Taurus admires beauty in all forms, which is why many of them live a sybaritic lifestyle. A happy Taurus is one that has lots of security, especially when it comes to finances, which is able to give them the luxuries that they crave. Taurus is not a shallow or materialistic soul, but they do appreciate the comfort that money provides. Bulls are simple creatures with uncomplicated emotional natures. They want to be well fed, have a beautiful home, and a sensual lover. Their endless patience and easygoing calmness create peace and tranquility in their partnerships. It is difficult to get a bull upset, but when it happens, it will be something not quickly forgotten. The saying goes to not poke the bear, but it really should be to not poke the bull.

When it comes to trustworthiness and persistence in love, there is no one that beats the bull. They are not a difficult sun sign to make happy because of their appreciation of the simple things in life. They have a strong backbone and an iron will that gets them through the tough times, allowing space to find perfection in the imperfect. Their sure-footed and thoughtful steps are rarely flighty or built on far-fetched dreams. Taurus has a way of making an intangible and abstract emotion such as love turn into something that can be palpably experienced. Their love is like smelling freshly baked cookies, tasting the sugary graininess of a pear, seeing a multicolored sunrise, hearing birds chirp their sweet songs, and feeling the warmth of a crackling fire on a crisp autumn night. The bull's tactility is their magic in love.

How to Spot a Taurus

Most Taurus suns will resemble a bull in some way. They will be sturdy with a transparent, peaceful, and steady look in their eyes. They are graceful and move slowly, but you will see the strength in their bodies. They usually have solid shoulders and noticeable necks. Their ears tend to be on the small side, and there is a methodical way about their movement. They tend to have waves in their hair and dark eyes no matter what the color. Taureans are blessed with a sense of strength about them, and they are born with their earth element's power paired with Venusian beauty.

When you meet a Taurus, you will notice that their presence demands a sort of quiet respect. They do not require an audience like other sun signs do, but their calm and sensual aura will attract many. It is their practicality and honesty that naturally draws others to them because they are easy to be around. They know what they are, and they know what they are not, which gives them a confidence to be envied. You will never meet someone with more self-control than this sun sign. They think in a logical and practical way that ensures things are done properly and well. They do not sweat the small stuff, and they keep a level head even under the most stressful situations.

The bull is known for their love of the tangible because their senses are much more evolved than most. They relish in the beauty in simplicities and always stop to smell the roses. They have a knack for color as well, which makes them natural artists and designers. Pastels and earth tones are some of their favorites. When it comes to food, Taurus has an unparalleled sense of taste, which makes them an amazing chef, and a bull enjoys a delicious meal for the pure pleasure of it. When it comes to sound, you will never meet a bull that is not entranced by music. Many Taurean souls are connected deeply to music in more ways than one. They also rule the throat, which blesses them with velvety singing and speaking voices.

Taurus's fixed nature desires security and sanctuary more than anything in life. Success naturally comes to this patient sign because Venus showers its children with sparkling luxury and bestows their lives with splendor. Some may see this sun sign as mundane because the bull's peacefulness is as deep as a wooded pine forest, and their sensibility is as solid as stone. However, if you look a little closer, you will notice how their notions are full of brilliance and shimmer. So, if you happen to spot a soul who looks unshakable with a twinkle of grandeur in their eye, perhaps you are spotting a Taurus.

How to Lose a Taurus

This sun sign prefers to be in a state of stable tranquility, so if they find themselves frequently upset with you, they will look for greener pastures. To get a Taurus angry takes a lot of pokes, but getting a bull irritated is never an enjoyable experience. Taurus does not require that their partner be on a genius level. In fact, they value common sense over intelligence. However, if you are lacking in the rationality department, it will be met with some irritation. They appreciate a partner who has it together and can make decisions with practicality by removing emotion. This is especially true when it comes to money. Taurus loves their dollars as much as a kid loves candy, and if they feel their partner is not accountable with their funds, it will have them feeling nervous. They work hard for their income, and they require a financially responsible partner.

The bull is notoriously persistent, and some may even call them stubborn. If you try to change their mind frequently, you will feel their heels dig right into the ground. Accept Taurus for who they are because their resistance is unmatched. If you are the kind of person that likes to argue and persuade, you are up against a lifetime of unhappiness if you choose to always pick an argument with your bull. Do not argue with them unless you are ready to lose. They know what they want, and they know their argument is solid. Case closed. Taurus is slow, steady, and patient, and they do not appreciate being rushed. If you are the one for them, there is no need to push to get what you want; Taurus will come up with a stable and steady plan.

Taurus relishes in physical pleasures and learning how to consistently deliver them will keep Taurus satisfied. Taurus relishes in experiences and encounters with their partner that include all the five senses, especially touch. If you are not into that, this is not the right sun sign for you. Taureans are soft, sensual, and simple, so when they partner with someone that is over the top and tacky, it will be a challenge. Taurus is sensitive to the way things feel, smell, and look. If you keep your space looking like a dump, it will be a big turn off, and you may find yourself sans bull. Taurus also needs their downtime, so if you are the type of person that cannot find the time to relax, you may also find yourself apart frequently. Taureans enjoy being comfortable at home, so be prepared for a lot of weekends where you order takeout and eat it in bed. Rest and good food is absolutely the way to a Taurean's heart.

A Taurus is one of the most loyal and reliable partners you could have by your side. Once they choose you, they will choose you for life. They will always have your back and fiercely defend you from others. It is hard to lose them thanks to their undying loyalty and staying power, but if they are pushed, it is possible. Taurus is one of the most supreme lifelong partners to obtain in the zodiac. They are loving, loyal, trustworthy, sensible, diligent, and self-sufficient. If Taurus chooses you, do not forget how lucky you are.

How to Bed a Taurus

Taurus is everything that the word *sensual* encompasses. They are carnal, physical, and bodily. The bull focuses on the senses as a way of arousal. Do not let their slow and steady nature fool you; in the bedroom things get steamy. They will delight your body in ways you never knew existed, and soon enough you will be melting into their very comfortable bed. Nearly all Taurus suns have luxurious beds. Due to their heightened sense of touch, they require high-count sheets, feather pillows, and supple mattresses. They are also great cooks, so do not be too surprised if food is used for foreplay. Aphrodisiacs such as oysters, black licorice, and chocolate covered strawberries with whipped cream are always a good idea for this erotic sun sign. The surroundings will be comfortable, and they usually smell of earth, tobacco, sandalwood, vetiver, and vanilla.

The bull's love language is often physical touch. They love massages, cuddling, and frequent sex. They indulge in the finer things in life that appeal to their cravings. Their stamina is impressive, so you better get some rest before romping with this sun sign. They can go until the sun comes up and will leave your body satisfied in more ways than one. You will always be physically gratified after bedding a bull. There is something about their touch that is soft yet erotic enough to make you feel as though you are going to shatter. They like to make their partner wait. They know the reward of delayed gratification because they are never in a rush. They will enjoy taking their time to memorize your entire body, and you will surely love theirs, which is gifted with beauty and virility from Venus itself. Taurus rules the neck, and that will be a place that arouses them most.

They will magnetize you with their dark doe-like eyes, which have a traditional strength about them. They like to satisfy the senses of those that come into their bed by taking it slow, sweet, and deep. They are not promiscuous and will patiently wait for the right partner to come along. Being good in bed is at the top of their list of importance, but they also want someone they can see themselves growing old with. If you want to impress Taurus on a date, you will need more than good looks and witty chatter. This sun sign expects delectable food, a luxurious environment, beautiful flowers, and delicious scents surrounding them. They are not impressed with slick orators who try to impress them with cheap talk. The bull wants something a little slower, more relaxed, and comforting than someone blabbing away about nothing. They want a secure partner who has loads of sagacity, has their ducks in a row, and can keep them warm at night. This sun sign is known to be possessive at times, so make sure that your eyes and attention stay on them.

Appeal to their eyes with soft, earthy colors. Appeal to their nose with fresh flowers and sandalwood incense. Appeal to their mouth with erotic aphrodisiac foods, such as figs and wine. Appeal to their ears with the sound of beautiful and relaxed music, and appeal to their sense of touch with the feeling of your soft skin. Take it slow, and do not rush while enjoying every palpable bit of them. Do all of this, and they will soon be all yours in no time.

☼ ☼ ☼

TAURUS & TAURUS

Aspect: Conjunct
Elements: Earth and earth
Modalities: Fixed and fixed

Two bulls have so much in common, and it is in their cohesions that they will fall in love. They will both enjoy the great outdoors, appreciating fresh air while sitting on their porch and drinking rich French press coffee over a crisp newspaper. They frequently find themselves discussing the rise of their investments in the current market. They truly are such tangible creatures, and this is something that they grow close from. Two bulls will have an incredibly beautiful home filled with leather, wood, plush furnishings, and most likely a pet or two. They are the couple that has a garden most would envy, and both have quite the green thumb, as most earth signs do.

Because Taureans are naturally drawn to anything economic, they intrinsically have an excellent work ethic, and they are inclined to jobs that showcase that well. They enjoy the lavishness that the city has to offer them, but there is something deep down in a Taurus's soul that longs to be in the simplicity of nature. This pair may even decide to retire to a ranch and pick up a knack for horseback riding. Things like that come effortlessly to them. The countryside is more pleasurable to their senses than the city, and the bulls' surroundings are an important piece of the puzzle in making them happy. If they never make it out of the city, they will vacation often to escape the noise and bustle.

Marriage is something that will come so naturally between these two that, in a way, it is almost expected. However, they will not make it to the altar if their inflexibility gets in the way. We all know that bulls are famous for being very stubborn, and once they have stuck their heels in, there is usually no moving them. This will make it impossible for them to communicate, which consequently makes it difficult for them to ever get to a resolution. They are both fighters through and through, and if the argument is bad enough that they are unable to find a resolution, Taurus couples have been known to just completely walk away from relationships. They are patient, so they will take their sweet time waiting for the other person to surrender, and that does not always happen.

Sex will be something that can heal a lot of their tenacity and soften their willfulness against each other. As previously mentioned, these two are tangible souls, and their attraction will be carnal for one another. They will have an earthy and slow physical union. They will go to another physical dimension with one another just by hearing each other's beautiful and velvety voices. They will find pleasure in their oneness very much, but occasionally they will need to spice things up because they are both relaxed, languid bulls. Luckily for this pair, it will not take much more than a tender touch or a soft kiss to get things warmed up. Aphrodisiacs are something that work well, so go out for a round of oysters and finish with some dark chocolate and a bottle of red wine. You will be in business in no time.

Together, they really can have it all, and they will because they are truly a lovely match with loads of staying power. As a team, they can make a luxurious home filled with nostalgic memories, delicious dinners, and nights of sensuality. They will have a magnificent nest egg in the bank, making their retirement years potentially some of the best of their lives. These Venus-ruled creatures may just be living in a version of heaven here on earth. They will have a life full of rich love that most only dare to dream of.

☼ ☼ ☼

TAURUS & GEMINI

♉ ♡ ♊

Aspect: Semisextile
Elements: Earth and air
Modalities: Fixed and mutable

Taurus suns are quiet, steady, strong, patient, and practical people. On occasion, they can be intense, but they would prefer to remain neutral and calm. Their incredible strength and determined staying power are something to be admired. Geminis love being two different people disguised as one. They are fast-moving souls with intelligent minds that go through life with zest and spontaneity. Taurus loves peace, and Gemini loves action, so you can already see they will be a wonderful challenge for each other in many ways.

Most Geminis manage to blend their two individual personalities into one bright, brilliant, and interesting human being, which makes them reasonably honest and refreshingly adaptable. However, their ability to change from one viewpoint to another can give Taurus an uneasy feeling that they cannot quite understand or trust. Taurus's caution looks like a mental pothole to Gemini, and yet they are able to sympathize with Taurus's hesitancy to toss away security more than the bull will be able to sympathize with Gemini's need for variety. Even though they may never say it, Taurus is aware that they have something to learn from their bright Gemini partner.

Taurus would love to be able to take life more casually, throw caution to the wind, and skip happily ahead into a new adventure each day like their Gemini

lover does. Taurus wistfully yearns for the freedom of spirit that their sparkling Gemini possesses. The reality is that Taurus puts their needs before their
wants almost every time. They crave security and steadfastness above fickle
dreams, and they are determined to stick with ways that are tried and true. This
approach may seem like stubbornness, but this is where they will have to help
each other. Taurus will be there to add some gravity by bringing the twins back
down to reality, and Gemini will be there to spark some variety to bring the bull
some uplifting optimism.

Gemini has incredible powers of persuasion, but Taurus is not persuaded easily. When they disagree, Gemini is able to bring opposite opinions together and
hang them on a thread of truth that is coated with charm and logic, creating an
aura of idealism and peace on all sides. Gemini was not coined the "communicator of the zodiac" for no reason. Taurus, on the other hand, will see right
through the wit and prefer to get down to the point with cold, hard facts that are
not laced with Gemini's pixie dust. The airy detachment of Gemini can hurt and
annoy Taurus because detachment is indicative of being either rudely ignored
or condescendingly patronized—and neither of them are particularly pleasing.
They do not call Taurus stubborn for nothing.

How can Gemini make it up to their Venus-ruled lover? Stop talking so much
and touch them. Taureans' love language is touch, and physical affection will
make them melt. Taurus is a sensual lover and makes love to create delightful
tangibility. Sex is an exciting activity to Gemini, but for this air sign, sex is not
always associated with palpability. The twins enjoy sex with their partner, but
they can separate it from reality, which may throw Taurus for a loop. Sometimes during sex, Gemini likes to take a trip to space, but it would be smart for
Gemini to stay focused and present in the moment. Taurus likes to take things
slow and requires their lover to be in attendance with them from the opening
act to the finale. A Gemini wants fantasy, and a Taurus wants reality, so if they
can combine these, they will find a place to meet. They will need to take turns
in how they connect physically; Taurus can lighten up while Gemini takes sex
more seriously.

Together, these two are innately different, but together they are also a beautiful mix of earth and air, yin and yang, and fixed and mutable energy. These two
sun signs have so much they can teach one another, and it is a good thing they
have a whole lifetime together to learn. Their love story requires compromise

between them, but there is nothing they cannot do if they are really committed to making it work. Gemini loves daisies, sunshine, and soft music, and if Gemini slows down, they will see that Taurus is all those things. It will take Gemini a bit to get used to the bull's earthly intensity, but once they do, Gemini will appreciate the home base that Taurus provides. Taurus's feet are firmly planted on the ground, but if Gemini sprinkles a bit of their pixie dust on them, they can fly together. They will rise and they will fall throughout their journey, but their story will be filled with magical moments that defy the laws of love. If they can just get above the clouds, they will find the sunshine.

☼ ☼ ☼

TAURUS & CANCER

♉ ⯰ ♋

Aspect: Sextile
Elements: Earth and water
Modalities: Fixed and cardinal

Cancers are known for needing three things in life: financial security, emotional stability, and family. This list is in no order because the importance of these three topics varies from crab to crab. Taureans also highly value these things, which makes this pairing quite a beautiful match. Cancer's largest struggle in life is making a direct decision, but Taurus has all the patience in the world to let the crab take their cautious time. Crabs precariously move side to side before really taking a step forward, but once they finally decide, there is no stopping them. Taurus really appreciates that Cancer does not want to impulsively jump into things because they themselves enjoy taking their time when it comes to getting into any sort of serious relationship. There is no wild passion in the beginning but rather a slow and steady build of love, creating a solid base for their connection to flourish.

Let's go back to those three things that Cancer really cares about and explain how Taurus fits into the categories. Taurus is savvy with money, and Cancer will greatly appreciate that. Taurus enjoys items of quality, which leads them to spend, which Cancer appreciates within reason. Looking at emotional stability,

Cancer will most likely be the more emotive of the two, while Taurus is about as internally stable as they come. However, Taurus can create a safe place for Cancer to feel emotionally secure and nurtured. Lastly, when it comes to home and family, the crab is a homebody, and so is the bull. They both enjoy being in their comfort zones around family, which will bring them to desire children in their home, which they have crafted with care. Taurus has a love of animals, and Cancer has a bleeding heart, so this pair will naturally have a pet or two. They truly check one another's boxes, especially in the bedroom.

Together, their elemental combination creates a relaxed sexual chemistry. Taurus wants a love that is simple, and Cancer wants one that is deep. When they have sex, they will blend both emotionally and physically. Taurus will give Cancer sexual security, and the crab will give the bull comfort and attentiveness. They need different things, but in their case, their needs are complementary. It is a mix of sweet and savory. There is something so personal about how they make love, and it allows Cancer to feel special and safe while they create a space where Taurus feels wanted and needed. The bull's sincerity touches the crab in a way that permeates past their tough shell and into their soft soul. In return, Cancer will admire Taurus never leaving them. Together, they can effortlessly gift each other with everything they want and need.

Cancers are natural-born leaders thanks to their cardinal modality, while Taurus is stable and sturdy thanks to their fixed modality. Taurus does not mind when Cancer wants to take the lead on most things because the bull does not have an innate need to be the leader the way the crab does. However, Taurus does not really care to follow either and would prefer to move at their own pace. As perfect as these two may seem, there will be areas that need to be worked on to keep things harmonious, such as the way they communicate. In the off chance of a disagreement, they both tend to revert to being far away from one another rather than talking about the issue at hand. Bulls tend to be stubborn, and Cancers tend to be sensitive, which leads neither to act contrite. Because of the bull's doggedness, they have no problem waiting for Cancer to apologize first. If they could both tap into their logic, they could resolve their issues together in a more constructive and efficient manner.

Cancer's moods are like the moon—waxing and waning—but Taurus has all the fortitude in the world for the crab's shifting phases because they know their love is worth it. They always find their way back to each other, and it is not hard because their relationship is built on a solid foundation. Cancer's watery element is magically perceptive, and they know that Taurus is the one for them. They can feel it in their soul. After many moons of not directly asking Taurus if they would be their one and only, Cancer will suddenly feel a rush of emotion that comes over them, and they will not be able to hold back the feelings that have been bubbling up since the moment they met. Cancer will look into Taurus's soft eyes and will touch their face so gently that it will melt the bull's heart to a place of no return. At that moment, Taurus will know this is it, or perhaps, in the back of their mind, they already did.

☼ ☼ ☼

TAURUS & LEO

♉ 🖤 ♌

Aspect: Square
Elements: Earth and fire
Modalities: Fixed and fixed

Taurus requires loyalty and affection from their partner, while Leo requires compliments and admiration from the one who holds their heart. The bull is a fixed earth sign, and Leo is a fixed fire sign. They are both prime examples of their elements and modalities, which means that at times these two can become astrologically at odds with one another. Their dual fixity means that neither one of them has a strong need to lead, but they also do not like to follow either. Leo can be too self-absorbed to give their strong bull the respect they insist on receiving, while Taurus is too stubborn to give their proud lion the worship they continually seek. However, their fixed nature makes them both wonderful planners. They each possess a rich emotional loyalty, creating a pair that is able to craft a future together by organizing one another into their dreams. These sun signs are aspected in a square to one another, which means that their relationship will require a bit more work to make things harmonious, but if they are truly in love, it is nothing that they cannot conquer. If the bull and the lion can compromise, there will be giant rewards of peace and concord.

Taurus does not need as much personal glory as Leo does—or at least they would never tell anyone if they did. Taurus does not mind letting Leo get the attention because Taurus is more interested in cold, hard cash being stacked up in the bank and the appreciation and emotional peace of mind from their partner. When a Leo is in love, they will give their devotee tender and amazing care. The lion's dramatics are a lot to handle, but the bull has an iron will that is made of solid gold, and Leo likes gold. Together, these two can be a true powerhouse couple because Taurus and Leo are incredible at promoting and building things together. Leo comes up with grand ideas, and Taurus will be fabulous at contemplating the financial return of them. They are always working on building their empire together.

When a Taurus thinks of success, they think of fiscal security combined with the devoted love of their partner. To them, these two things are the most important and vital things in life, and the older they get, the more important those things become. The only thing Leo is that sure of is their own ability to make the things they desire happen. Leo's warm heart is full of nobility and spirit, which is what draws Taurus to them. Bulls are steady, purposeful, and relentless, and obstacles do not disturb or upset them as they do Leo because Taureans accept limitation and delay as part of the price they must pay for eventual success. Taureans believe that if something is worth doing at all, it is worth doing well and waiting for. Leos, on the other hand, do not believe in limitations when it comes to their plans. Their goals are way too lofty to have a ceiling, and their attitudes are hopeful and determined. They like to take chances because they know that the greater the risk, the greater the reward. This is a way that they balance one another.

Whatever their relationship lacks in agreement will be made up in the bedroom. In many ways, Taurus will surprise Leo with how erotic and sensual they are. There is not another sign in the zodiac that appreciates tangibility and touch more than a Taurus. Sex pleases every bit of them, which is why the bull is a master of senses. It is better to show a Taurus than tell a Taurus, and Leo has no problem putting on a show. The bull's strength and stubbornness melts away when they are with their lion behind closed doors. They will truly enjoy each other's company doing everyday things together as well as going out for fancy dinners at their favorite restaurants, which is pure foreplay for both. Taurus is patient with Leo's needs, and the lion is lovely to their bull for it.

Leo enjoys protecting those they love and lavishing them with gifts and grandeur. Taurus's loyal and dependable heart secretly and deeply loves how protective and affectionate their Leo is. The bull and the lion truly want their love to last and desire to make one another happy. The best way to do that will be to start listening to each other's silent, pleading hearts. The loveliest similarity between these two is that their hearts are equally loyal. When they fall on hard times, they should reflect on why they fell in love in the first place, which is one another's strength. Leo is ruled by the sun, which is life, while Taurus is ruled by Venus, which is love. Together, they are life and love. Is there anything more?

☼ ☼ ☼

TAURUS & VIRGO

♉ ❤ ♍

Aspect: Trine
Elements: Earth and earth
Modalities: Fixed and mutable

These two earthly creatures will blend beautifully from the start. Taurus is slow, steady, and sensual, while Virgo is pristine, perfect, and poised. Taurus loves all things quantifiable, and Virgo will love to keep them fresh. Taurus enjoys making money, and Virgo will enjoy making sure their finances are working hard for them. Taurus appreciates a comfortable bed, and Virgo will not mind making it. Taurus relishes the taste of food, and Virgo will enjoy keeping their bull healthy. Together, they can create one beautiful team and home.

The mundane day-to-day and conducting life in a practical manner may sound boring to some, but to these two, it sounds like heaven on earth and will be something that ties them strongly together. They do not sweat the small stuff, and this will be a refreshing break from all the pettiness they have dealt with in previous relationships. Money is rarely an area of disagreement because they are both quite frugal. The only thing that Virgo may not understand is why the house must be so lavish. However, Virgo will soon realize that their Taurus likes having comfortable surroundings, and they will benefit from this as well.

They rarely will irritate one another because neither one of these characters gets angered frequently, meaning fighting will be rare. While most would be offended, the bull will take Virgo's critical manner with the sweetest appreciation. However, Taurus needs to understand that their pristine partner is not always the angel that they may think they have on their hands because Virgo always comes with some little hidden moral quirks. It is a rare occurrence when Virgo goes against the grain, but when it happens, the stiff bull will have to find flexibility by not only seeing what is in front of them. What is important to know about Virgo is that their intentions are never in the wrong place because they have an inherently pure heart. After some time being together, they will have a few practical and warranted arguments that will allow them to understand and appreciate each other wholly. With their patience, the bull will begin to view Virgo's nitpicking, analytical approach, and critical attitude as meticulousness, intelligence, and perfection. Taurus will admire that Virgo does not let what others think sway their calculating mind.

Before they have sex for the first time, Taurus will wonder how this perfectly poised person can match their sensuality, but Virgo will undoubtedly surprise them. Virgo is full of a bright white heat that fulfills Taurus completely and brings them security because they know that Virgo's love is not the temporary type. Their sex will be grounding and powerful yet respectful with a quiet, unspoken understanding of what each other needs. They will, without a doubt, be able to fill each other's desires. Taurus does not need to hear what Virgo is thinking because the tangible Taurus prefers to feel love. However, Virgo is of a mutable modality and needs to communicate and receive feedback and praise. Although Virgo would never admit it, they are always worried if they are satisfying their partner, so if Taurus can give some affirming words to them, it would be greatly appreciated.

All in all, this match is one that is made to last. When Taurus places more importance on the bigger picture rather than the details, Virgo must remember how their bull makes them laugh. When Virgo is being hard on Taurus, the bull must remember how Virgo is the hardest on themselves. They will soon realize that there is perfection in the conglomeration of their imperfections. Between Taurus's rich humor and Virgo's articulate communication, most disagreements will end in apologies and forgiveness. They will be able to always bring the sunshine back to each other's lives when days become gray.

☼ ☼ ☼

TAURUS & LIBRA

♉ ❖ ♎

Aspect: Quincunx
Elements: Earth and air
Modalities: Fixed and cardinal

A Taurus's life without love is a muddy-colored world that they patiently live in until they meet someone that can paint their sky. That is exactly what a Libra does when you dive into a relationship with one. They have this magic way about painting the heavens cotton candy colors more beautiful than you have ever seen. Libra is as sweet as sugar, and Taurus truly enjoys every delectable bit of them. Everything about Libra's physical appearance is appealing to Taurus, which says a lot seeing as they have an incredibly high taste level. Their tangible senses are incredibly particular. Everything from Libra's creamy voice and flirtatious eyes to their delicious, dimpled smile will have the bull's heart doing flips. Libra is a charmer—there is no denying that—but Taurus may not see the storm that is brewing on the horizon. They are too busy looking at the pink and blue hues Libra painted in the sky before them. The storm Taurus needs to be wary of is Libra's unresolved thoughts toward exclusivity and whether they want this relationship forever or just for now.

Libras love the idea of love, but Taurus does not play that game and would rather play for keeps. There could be a lot of confusion for Taurus when they have been dating for a while and—after assuming that Libra only had eyes for them—they come to find out Libra is in fact dating a few others as well. Taurus will be absolutely shocked, but when they bring it up to Libra, they will simply tell Taurus that they never agreed to a monogamous relationship. Now that Libra knows Taurus wants one, they will have to think about it. It is a blessing that Taurus has all the patience in the world. Most other sun signs would be long gone. Once Libra has decided they really do want to be with Taurus and only Taurus, they can make quite the romantic pair.

They are both ruled by Venus, the planet of love, giving them an affinity for beauty and luxury. Their home will be lavish, and they will share a love for music and fine dining. In their Venusian world, experiencing the finer things is what life is all about. They will have wonderful and memorable experiences together that people only dream of. A lot of their shared life will be filled with rosy harmony, and this includes their oneness in the bedroom. Both sun signs enjoy romance in all its forms and will have little to no problems behind closed doors. They will revel being in bed with one another to have sex, cuddle, watch movies, read, and even just gaze into one another's eyes. They cannot get enough physical contact because Libra is all allure and Taurus is all sensuality. Together, their lovemaking is like something out of a romance novel.

One thing Libra will need to know if they want to keep this harmony between them is to not worry so much about what everyone else is thinking and use that energy to worry about making their bull happy. Air signs have a constant need to feel independent and free from restraints—no matter how wonderful their relationship is. If Taurus can use this astrological fact from early on, before they get in too deep, they will have more awareness of why Libra decides to go on a hiatus. Taurus can be a very possessive sign, and that is not something Libra will have an easy time adjusting to. They will need to come to a healthy agreement about what makes them both content about the independence in their relationship, or things can come unraveled.

In their relationship, there is bound to be some melancholy, but most of it will be pure romantic bliss. If Libra can put their indecisive tendencies away and realize what an incredibly wonderful match they have found for themselves, they can realize that monogamy with a bull is incredibly rewarding because they like to experience life in a similar fashion. Remembering their ruling elements is a crucial component to understanding their compatibility. Earth contains air and needs it, but air does not contain earth and does not need it. Earth is obligated to remain where it is and only moves in the event of an earthquake, whereas air moves freely above it, choosing wherever it wants to go. Libra may have some elemental power over Taurus with their charming ways, but patience is the bull's secret earthly power over Libra, which is the strongest virtue to have in life and in love.

☼ ☼ ☼

TAURUS & SCORPIO

♉ ◈ ♏

Aspect: Opposite
Elements: Earth and water
Modalities: Fixed and fixed

Taurus will never forget the first time they held their Scorpio and felt them melt in their arms. The bull will always remember the way their intoxicating scent filled them with warmth while a shudder simultaneously went up their spine. Scorpio will feel it, too, in the way Taurus touched them while staring into their intense eyes so steadily. There is something calming and grounding about the bull's energy that cools the internal flames of Scorpio to a medium heat. Bulls are solid, sensual, and strong, which makes Scorpio wild with passion and attraction for them. They see many similarities in one another and yet so many differences all at once. These sun signs stimulate attraction for one other in a way that only opposing energies can. These two are on opposite ends of the karmic wheel, which causes immense magnetism and differences between them. They can both teach each other a lot of wonderful things that they need and want from one other.

Something they must always remember is that they are both equally strong. Not necessarily in the same ways but rather in complete opposite fashions. Scorpio is mesmerizing, fair in their actions, ruthlessly protective, and always has their stinger ready for people who need to be taught a lesson. Taurus is patient, steady, and will not bat an eye even in the most stressful of circumstances. Together, they can make quite a powerful pair. The thing that will attract Taurus to Scorpio the most at first will be their palpable sexiness. There is something about a Scorpio's voice that sounds like velvet, and the way Scorpio looks at Taurus makes them feel something they have never felt before. It even makes them a bit nervous. One place they will meet eye-to-eye on early on is their sensuality. Taurus suns are undoubtedly the most carnal sign in the zodiac, and they have a need for touch in their partnerships.

Scorpio will love Taurus's practical approach to life, which is an area that Scorpio could take a few notes from. Scorpio will teach Taurus how to feel passion not just in the physical sense but in other forms, such as the spiritual, as well. Taurus naturally loves solidarity, which tends to lean them toward jealousy, and Scorpio is not a stranger to this because of their own possessiveness. The difference between jealousy and possessiveness is that being jealous is defined as being vigilant in guarding a possession, while possessiveness denotes ownership. In other words, Scorpio truly likes to own and, in some cases, control the ones they are with, while Taurus will stomp the ground if they see someone trying to take what is theirs. Similar? Yes. But the same? No. Neither one of these traits in excess are healthy in any relationship, and they should be something to be worked on by both parties.

The bull and the scorpion may spend most of their first dating days getting to know each other in the bedroom. This is funny because Taurus is not really one to rush anything, but they may not be able to help themselves when it comes to Scorpio. Taurus may even wake up next to Scorpio after a night of lovemaking after a few dates and think "This is so not like me!" Not to worry, Taurus. Even though Scorpio is the sex symbol of the zodiac, they do not take the act of oneness lightly either. When having sex with a Scorpio, you see a part of their desire that they seem to hide so well in the outside world. Oneness with a Scorpio is a place—and sometimes the only place—where they can feel vulnerable, which makes the act not just physical but also ethereal. This ancient sexual alchemy of spiritual wholeness through physical oneness will be some-thing that Scorpio can gift to the bull, and in return, Taurus will create a safe space for their vulnerabilities to release.

Scorpios are black and white, which may be a bit hard for Taurus's practical mind at times. Scorpio is either all the way in or all the way out, while Taurus tends to see the gray and even enjoys sitting in the in-between at times. Taurus does not possess the polarizing emotions like Scorpio does and can occasionally find Scorpio's extremes unnecessary. If Taurus can use their patience, and if Scorpio can mellow out a bit, they will find a common ground. Scorpio can be vicious with their words and seem so cold after their relationship seemed so hot, but if anyone can warm a scorpion's heart back up, it is a bull. Opposing sun signs always want the same thing; they just have different ways of getting there. These two will find themselves either deeply in love or in extreme dis-interest. There is rarely light flirtation or casual dating with these fixed signs. If they are pleasant, kind, and forgiving of one another, they can create an unbreakable love that others will never achieve.

☼ ☼ ☼

TAURUS & SAGITTARIUS

Aspect: Quincunx
Elements: Earth and fire
Modalities: Fixed and mutable

It is the archer's sunny aura and nonchalant attitude toward everything that will have Taurus smiling to themselves when they first meet their optimistic Sagittarius. Taurus will have serious plans in mind for their future, and they have the patience to make it happen. It is the bull's gentle understanding and steadfastness that attracts Sagittarius initially, and they will be so excited when they meet their steady bull. Sagittarius is not exactly sure what Taurus will be in their life, but they know they need to have them.

For a sun sign that prides themselves on their openness and honesty, Sagittarius is not always so forthright about their intentions when it comes to love. This is not because they want to be deceitful in any way. Instead, it is because they really are not so sure about staying anywhere for too long. Sagittarius has so many people to meet and so many things to do in their life that monogamy may get in the way of achieving those goals. Taurus has another plan in mind for the two of them, and they fall in love with Sagittarius for all the right reasons. However, no matter how patient Taurus may be, they will not settle for anything other than exclusivity. The bull demands it, so if that is not something Sagittarius is able to give, it is better to let them know now than to lead them on and lose them forever. Taurus admires forthright honesty, so the archer should never beat around the bush with their intentions. Taurus will never waste their time with someone that they believe is a flake. When Sagittarius realizes that this sun sign truly understands them and loves them wholly, along with all their character flaws, they will expand their devotion to the bull entirely. It just needs to be the right time because in the world of a Sagittarius, life is all about timing.

After the bull and the archer get to know each other further, their differences may become a bit more glaring. Sagittarius likes everything fiery and fast, and Taurus prefers things to move at a slow and steady pace. Sagittarius enjoys a good debate just for the fun of it, and Taurus would rather have peaceful, harmonious conversation. When Sagittarius rocks the boat, Taurus will usually stay calm—unless they really push their buttons. Sagittarius is quite social and frequently has gatherings, whereas Taurus would like to have quiet solitude in their nice and tidy house. These differences will cause them to spat, but if Sagittarius can save their debates for their friends, hire a house cleaner, and go out with their group instead of having them over, there will be more accord. It is all about compromise, communication, and understanding. If they do argue, Sagittarius will tend to forget about it quicker than Taurus, so the archer will intentionally have to work harder to smooth things over. Even though they have very different social needs, sex will help mellow out their disagreements.

Once they figure out how to please one other, their physical union can be a wonderful way to connect. Sagittarius's love language is words of affirmation in the bedroom because they seek spirituality and emotion when having sex with their partner. Taurus's love language is physical touch because they seek physicality and connection through contact. Taurus does not care to have conversation in the bedroom, but Sagittarius certainly will because they like to hear that their partner is pleased. If they can understand each other's different needs and make some adjustments, it will serve them both well. Taurus may not be as involved as Sagittarius needs them to be, but with a little work, they can make this relationship passionate and fun. The archer's open and honest approach to sex will excite Taurus, and the bull's sensual nature and protectiveness will make Sagittarius feel adored. Their oneness is healing for both and gives them a reason to keep trying to make things work beyond any of their innate differences.

Their archetypal energy is astrologically completely different because of their quincunx aspect. However, their matching sense of humor will be a helpful gift that will be sure to get them through times of trouble. Sagittarius is fiery and creative, while Taurus is earthy and steady. Sagittarius should not expect the bull's vigor to meet theirs and should instead see that they are a rock for them to anchor, which creates a place to call home and a spot to rest their busy head. Taurus will believe in all the archer's dreams and be a positive partner that Sagittarius can share challenges with while being independent from them when they need. If Sagittarius can take the time to appreciate everything that the bull brings to the table as a partner, Taurus can be all the things Sagittarius desires. With time and perseverance, the archer will learn that love is slow and patient and not always rapid and exciting. The kind of love that has staying power does not need to be a hot and heavy romance. Simple, practical love is just as beautiful. If Taurus can keep Sagittarius safe, Sagittarius will keep Taurus wild.

☼ ☼ ☼

TAURUS & CAPRICORN

Aspect: Trine
Elements: Earth and earth
Modalities: Fixed and cardinal

The cosmos knows what they are doing when they bring these two earth signs together. Sea goats and bulls rarely talk about their personal lives, so few will hear or know about their deeply romantic love story. If you ask them about it, you may get a grin or a shrug but never the true tale of their romance. If these sun signs are lucky enough to cross paths and fall in love, there is a very good chance that they could even be twin souls. They are both skeptical of such ideas because they are believers in things that are realistic, but deep down they can sense something is *different* about the way they feel for one another—more so than anyone before. It is as though they fall into a world together that is their own, and fate starts to unfold.

Taurus will instantly admire how practical Capricorn is and will esteem them for a multitude of reasons including their independence, their dignity, their reservations, and how they make them work for their love. Taurus does not believe in having something if it comes too easily, but Capricorn will not be able to keep themselves from the bull long—or at all. Capricorn is not the warmest person you will ever meet, but their loyalty is like no other. The sea goat is ruled by Saturn, making them as tough as steel. It takes time to break the walls down that they build so high around their very tender heart. Because of this, they use both their heart and head when falling in love. Taurus will adore all these things about them, and their natural chemistry makes Taurus work as hard as they can to win Capricorn's valuable affection. Taurus has all the patience in the world, which will work beautifully to make it past those high walls.

Taurus and Capricorn have natural chemistry that will make things go smoothly, but just like any relationship, there will be places of struggle. Capricorn is a cardinal sign, and Taurus is fixed, making the goat the leader and the bull not one to be easily persuaded, which will occasionally cause a division. Taurus is a creature of habit, so when Capricorn wants to pull the bull in a new direction, they may have to do some coaxing. Taurus is stubborn toward change because they hold value to the sentiment of tradition, making them softhearted but strongheaded. Taurus knows exactly what they want and will pursue it at their own pace. Capricorn has a hard time apologizing, but when they make a mistake, they will never do it again. Capricorn appreciates Taurus's gentle manner and sense of humor, which helps them forget their stubbornness.

Sex is robust when it comes to these earth signs. Taurus is corporeal in bed, and it is the tangible things that excite them, such as how Capricorn's skin feels, how their hair smells, and how their kiss tastes. Capricorn brings out the bull's sensual side, and they will not be able to help their earthy desires. Capricorn requires respect in the bedroom, which Taurus will gladly give them. There is a still strength and silent allure about Capricorn that Taurus has a hard time controlling themselves around. It is a delayed type of gratification that makes everything better until the very end. Capricorns are more apt to separate feelings from sex than any other sign because they are not comfortable with emotion and prefer to guard their heart. Taurus will show them that their union is steady, safe, sincere, and true, which will help Capricorn combine the physical element of sex with their emotions in a way that no one else may be able to do. Sex without love leaves the body cold, and love without sex leaves the soul empty. Capricorn may know the meaning of both, but they have finally found them together with Taurus.

In the past, Capricorn may have been called selfish, cold, and practical. In the past, Taurus may have been called stubborn, stale, and boring. However, they only put these façades up as barriers to protect themselves while placing a high value on their hearts. They both have a strong sense of security built by their shared gift of patience. Patience gives birth to a lot of other beautiful things in a relationship, such as devotion, faith, and loyalty. When you have those characteristics in a connection, it creates a strong, loving bond that nothing can break. They are not typically believers in fate, but then they meet each other and it is almost as though an earthquake takes place and every wall, barrier, and façade they ever built crumbles to the ground. They free one another in a way that they did not even know they needed, and once they start growing into one another, their years of being together will build an inseparable vow.

☼ ☼ ☼

TAURUS & AQUARIUS

Aspect: Square
Elements: Earth and air
Modalities: Fixed and fixed

Taurus characters are warm, comfortable, and classic, while Aquarius personalities are cool, unique, and out of this world. Aquarius is, by all terms of the definition, a maverick, making up the rules as they go along, and it is their assured demeanor that Taurus admires. The bull finds the water bearer honest and refreshing, but one thing that Taurus may learn is that those qualities do not mean they are reliable. Aquarius's vague, bizarre, and detached approach creates a space for Taurus's sense of humor to surface, which is a place where they will connect.

Aquarius will immediately want to be friends first and lovers second, which will be confusing for Taurus because they will hold hands, go on dates, and it will look and feel like a lot more than just friendship. Taurus must understand that no matter how lovestruck they feel, they need try to see the signs of friendship between the lines. Taurus sun signs are incredibly patient, and it takes Aquarius a long time for them to really realize what they want. Water bearers feel safer when they are free of obligation, and that is something that will never change about them, no matter how serious this couple may get.

Aquarians are a wonderful kind of crazy mixed with intelligence and fun, and there will nearly never be a monotonous day with them around. They rapidly change with the blink of an eye, while Taurus will always be the constant rock in the relationship. It may take Aquarius a while to realize how wonderful life with a bull can be, but it is impossible to ignore. Taurus is not really one for change and will constantly question Aquarius's actions, which will be a great checks and balances for them and their union. Taurus has remarkable staying power, which is something Aquarius could greatly learn and benefit from.

Taurus and Aquarius innately have a lot of differences, but if they find love between them, their mutual determination can make it happen. Aquarius has no problem settling down, but it must be the perfectly right person, and sometimes Aquarius themselves does not even know what that person looks like. They are both fixed signs, which alludes to the idea that there will be times of friction due to their lack of wanting to move from where they sit comfortably. Neither one of them are huge fans of feeling like they are being pressured into something. Therefore, if one wants something that the other does not, there could be trouble. Aquarius's eccentric energy is unpredictable and zigzags all over the place, while Taurus is slow, steady, and very predictable. Aquarius will teach Taurus the joy of being sporadic, and Taurus will teach Aquarius the pleasure in predictability. They are both okay with just letting things be and let sleeping dogs lie, which is how this relationship is going to work for them to create harmony.

Aquarius's abstract sexual desires are much different from the bull's realistic ones. As physical companions, they both need to look deeper into the situation of their sexuality, which can be glaringly different at first. Sensuality will always be more important to Taurus than the water bearer, but the bull's warm nature truly touches Aquarius. Taurus likes to keep a steady pace, and Aquarius's energy is everywhere and nowhere all at the same time. Taurus needs more focus and physical touch than Aquarius personally requires, which means Aquarius will need to slow down a bit and tap into their bodily presence in order to channel it to their lover. The water bearer's mind is constantly running off ahead into the future, but when it comes to the bedroom, they need to learn to be present. The bull will discover that new things are not always scary but can become refreshing and fun. If Taurus can get around Aquarius's quirky sexual behavior, and Aquarius can learn to streamline their energy, it may just work out. Together, with some adjustments from both, they can find a place to meet.

Taurus will love Aquarius for all their quirks and flaws, but that's only if Aquarius lets them in. For that to happen, the bull needs to let their inhibitions go and run a little wild with their water bearer. Aquarians are not meant to be tamed, and they need to run free until they find someone just as uninhibited to run with them while maintaining some perception of reality. Aquarius should merit Taurus's patience and, in return, help the bull find some freedom.

As partners they will have to figure out how to live with one foot in Taurus's steady reality and one foot in Aquarius's high vibrational fourth dimension. With love and compromise, there is nearly nothing that is impossible.

☼ ☼ ☼

TAURUS & PISCES

♉ ◈ ♓

Aspect: Sextile
Elements: Earth and water
Modalities: Fixed and mutable

It will probably be just like any other day on the day that the bull and fish meet. However, Taurus will immediately know this magical being can feel and sense things much deeper than most. Pisces's energy is ethereal and gentle while remaining effortless, which puts the bull in a delightful trance. Taurus will use their incredible patience and wit to attract the fish to dry land, which is something Pisces has been looking for to bring stability to their precarious and aqueous energy. You see, Pisces is born with rushing, fluctuating thoughts, and they are looking for an earthy partner who can slow their troubled mind. It may be their magic that initially appeals to Taurus, but they will soon discover that Pisces's most redeeming quality is the way in which they listen with compassionate intent, only furthering the love spell the fish unconsciously puts on the bull.

Through the years, Pisces will bend to make their bull happy because of their mutable modality, which is more flexible than Taurus's fixed one. However, Taurus should take heed to allowing their relationship to be one-sided. Pisces has so many dreams, which can cause their mind to wander frequently. There will be many times in a fish's life when their spirit wants to go where the water takes them. This will seem fickle to Taurus, seeing that they are a creature of routine and discipline. Taurus could not imagine a life with a such a rootless existence like the one that Pisces embraces. However, if Taurus never takes Pisces's dreams into consideration and does not even once offer flexibility, there is a high chance that the fish will eventually swim away so that they can fulfill their lifelong fantasies alone or with someone else, leaving the bull sad and confused.

Pisces will not look back once they have made this decision, so Taurus must put their stubbornness aside and never mistake Pisces's kindness for weakness. However, it takes a team effort to make this union work, and Pisces must also directly and clearly communicate what they want. Taurus may believe that Pisces needs some saving, but once the fish opens themselves up to the bull, they will realize how incredibly self-sufficient they truly are.

Taurus wants financial security, but money to a fish is not the number one priority in life. They know that it will come and go, which is a great reason to let Taurus handle the finances. Pisces do not typically put a lot of time and importance into money because they have bigger fish to fry. What Pisces lacks in financial concern, they will certainly make up for in romance. Pisces are inherently poetic, and Taurus will feel right at home in their idealistic waters. Taurus is ruled by Venus and values the tangibility of love over anything else in a relationship. Taurus is not as vocal about their feelings as Pisces is because they are not a mutable water sign. The bull's style of love is more of the sensual and physical type. The pair will find so much blending and connecting when it comes to sex. They naturally bring each other fulfillment, much like how water brings nourishment to land. There is a beautiful truth in the way that they connect because Taurus uses their physical senses, and Pisces's emotions are what guides them. Taurus loves the way that Pisces empathizes with them so deeply, which may even bring them to tears. They are easily able to meld their sexual energy together when combining as one, which feels real, right, natural, and healing.

There is always a hint of mystery to Pisces and something in their watery eyes that Taurus's concrete mind will never be sure of. Taurus will either love it or leave it, but one thing they will never do is forget it. Pisces absorbs the energy and feelings around them like a sponge, which gifts them with an immense amount of empathy and perceptiveness. This is their magic. It is the thing that made Taurus fall in love, but it will also be the thing that they will wish they could grasp. When Pisces is feeling heavy with emotions, Taurus should not try to fix or understand them but rather to create a space of support by being the rock they need. With intent, listening, and patience, Taurus can absorb the wisdom Pisces has been intrinsically gifted from being the last sun sign on the karmic wheel. Pisces is ever changing like the ocean tides, and Taurus is solid like the earth that needs the water to grow, which makes them require each other in many ways.

☼ ☼ ☼

Chapter 3

Gemini

Gemini's love archetype is the messenger of love. They are an intelligent, aggressive, dynamic, and romantic communicator who expresses words of love through storytelling. Gemini's lesson in love is to impart that love is perception and absorb that love is experiencing.

Element	Air
Modality	Mutable
Polarity	Yang, positive, and masculine
Mantra	"I think."
Hue	Yellow
Deity	Hermes, god of trade and communication
Glyph	♊
Flowers	Daffodil, lavender, and lily of the valley
Tree	Chestnut
Jewel	White sapphire
Crystals	Agate and apophyllite
Fragrance	Verbena
Body Parts	The shoulders, arms, fingers, lungs, nervous system, and upper ribs
Animals	Small birds, butterflies, and monkeys
Food & Herbs	Nuts, peas, carrots, beans, marjoram, sunflower seeds, milky oats, coltsfoot, and any vegetables grown above ground, such as tomato

Gemini's Ruling Planet: Mercury

Mercury in love rules mental activity, intelligence, reasoning, and communication. Mercury also reveals short journeys, siblings, and studies. The quicksilver planet represents thoughts, phrases, and the sound of the way you speak. Regarding Gemini, Mercury gives the twins the urge to connect using their air element for intellectual stimulation. For Gemini, ideas are quickly picked up and quickly put down, knowledge is swiftly understood, and interactions with love interests are precipitous.

Gemini Mythology

The twins, Castor and Pollux, were mothered by Leda. However, they had different fathers because, in one night, Leda was made pregnant both by Jupiter and by her husband, King Tyndareus of Sparta. Pollux was immortal because he was the son of a god and was renowned for his strength, while his mortal twin brother, Castor, was famous for his skill with horses. Pollux was overcome with grief when Castor died and begged his father, Jupiter, to allow him to share his immortality with his perished twin. Jupiter acknowledged the heroism of both brothers and agreed to bring Castor back, reuniting the pair in the heavens.

Gemini's Positive Qualities and Negative Forms

Gemini's positive qualities are versatility, mental alertness, quickness of perception, deductive reasoning, and flexibility. Expressed in their negative forms, they become restless, superficial, shallow, and unreliable. They practice double-talk and can even deceive themselves.

How a Gemini Loves

Geminis are the messengers of love who always have a clever way with words to express their sentiments and idealistic thoughts. While the twins certainly do not need a partner as much as some other sun signs, their duality longs for the spirit of a companion to make them feel whole and someone to share their brilliant mind with. Gemini tends to overthink everything, including their emotions, which is why love can feel confusing to them. Their restlessness causes them to always think of the possibilities that love can be, which keeps the way they partner youthful and childlike. They always have their sharp eyes on the future and crave a partner that can get them to slow down a bit and fall in love with the present, which requires finesse and just the right amount of pressure.

Geminis remain childlike, even in their later years, which tends to attract them to people with nurturing qualities. They look for caretaking virtues but in a way that does not smother them. The way they love is charming and delightful, and their minds sparkle with effervescent ideals of love. However, when it comes down to committing, they can talk themselves out of a relationship as fast as they can talk themselves into one. Therefore, they need a partner who gives them rope—and lots of it. Even though Gemini is a free spirit in many ways, they still have high ethics. They are ambiguous in their emotional nature because they would prefer to keep things light and airy, but their intellectual mind requires a precise amount of balanced energy from their partner to equate with their own. Gemini will never let their age get in the way of what they want, especially love. Most have several relationships until they can find the one that they want to stand still with. Therefore, Geminis usually end up with the loves of their lives because they have tried enough different kinds of partnerships to know which one is right for them. They cannot breathe when connections get too heavy or emotional, and they look for a free-flowing kind of love in their unions. Gemini's versatile mind is much like a butterfly going where the wind takes it, which is precisely how they extend their sentiments. They want someone who can help them put the faceted pieces of their heart together, so they do not feel so fragmented.

Loving a Gemini is elusive and tricky but never boring. Their mercurial nature is alchemic, and their wit is something that can get them out of the most precarious of situations. They feel most comfortable when they have an ear to listen to their ideas, and in return, they will gift their lover with their contagious enthusiasm. Their restless nature calls them toward adventure, fun, travel, and entertainment, and these are the ways to get into a Gemini's heart. The best partner for them is sociable, a great listener, intelligent, understanding, patient, open minded, and dedicated. Variety is the spice of Gemini's love life, so if they do find themselves committing, it will be with someone who is able to shapeshift through life's demands with them. What makes them endearing is their scattered yet marvelous character, which constantly lives in a state of fascination and curiosity.

How to Spot a Gemini

When you start seeing double, do not be alarmed—you are just looking at a Gemini. Now you see them, now you don't. These mercurial sprites have personalities that are incredibly changeable, and many of them have alter egos. Their expressions change, like lightning, from hate to ecstasy, intelligence to idealism, and sorrow to joy all within a mere minute. It is hard to tell where reality ends and illusion begins with these magical people. They often resemble birds, butterflies, and fairies because of their lightness and cheerful natures. They are always flitting about, sometimes with direction but usually at random, going where the wind takes them. Trying to find a Gemini is hard to accomplish because they change their jobs, home, and hobbies in the blink of an eye. They all love to read, though, so a bookstore or library is a good bet.

When you finally do catch a Gemini of your own, you will feel the electric energy that surrounds them. Their eyes move quickly and have an irresistible sparkle to them. They talk and listen fast because their sharp minds are in constant motion. They lack patience but make up for it in wit. They are alert, agile, and have a quickness about them, and they can talk themselves into and out of anything in one thought. Their marvelous duality allows them to do two things at once with ease, so they do not care for monotony or routine, finding the mundane overrated and dull. They excite and thrive with spontaneity and live life in the moment without a plan or reason. Their nature is instinctively restless, always in search of something different—not always or necessarily better, just different. Very often, the grass tends to look greener on the other side, and Gemini will forget everything they recently worked for to bet it all on that greener grass. Some will learn, and some will never care to.

Geminis operate under the mutable modality, so language is their specialty. Gemini rules speech, which is why many of them speak more than one language, and they will love to learn different dialects, which will come to them with great ease. Because of their gift of gab, they are fabulous salespeople. They have a way of spinning words into beautiful webs that easily catch their prey. They are like a walking, talking dictionary, full of intelligence and using a new word every day. They can promote just about anything and have people believing what they preach in an instant. Geminis often need to rest their busy brains more than most, but their minds tend to keep them up too late, making many of them insomniacs. Gemini's nature is always searching and impatient, so calming their nerved and twisting minds is not an easy feat. Their talents throughout life accumulate, making them multiply gifted. They are rarely overly emotional because they see life to be too short to be sad. Maybe one of the twins can be sad, but the other one will be busy at work, concocting their next great adventure to get them out of their funk.

Their energy shifts between shades of yellow, blue, silver, green, and gray. They are a breath of fresh air that seeps into your lungs and then is gone with your exhale. There may be a day that they stop and wait for you to catch up, but do not hold your breath. If you happen to spot this magical being, do not blink because they will be gone faster than you could believe.

How to Lose a Gemini

There really is no such thing as having a Gemini 100 percent because they always keep parts of their persona to themselves. Geminis notoriously have Peter Pan syndrome, which will be a trait you are either going to adore or abhor about them. This characteristic will be something that you are going to have to give them space for, or they will fly away to Neverland, and you will not get an invite. The twins are not made to be put into a category, box, cage, or container. Their soul is made to fly free, and they are not interested in a partner who tries to control them. When Gemini is in a partnership, there will always be a piece of them that needs to feel available and liberated. To experience this in a relationship, Gemini will need to find a partner who is independent from them. This sun sign goes wherever the wind takes them, rarely without a plan in place, which makes them require a type of companion who does not constantly nag them for consistency, or they will be forced to flee.

Gemini is always on the go with a new idea in their mind and a new adventure to embark on. If you cannot keep up with their antics, they will fly right past you. Every Gemini has multiple interests to please their dual personalities' different hobbies. If you are unable to find any mutual interests, you will find yourself without a Gemini. This sun sign is known to be very intelligent and can usually run circles around people. They are naturally curious characters who need communication and conversation in a relationship. Transmission in love is important to them, so being able to chat up a storm must be a part of your every day. If you cannot keep up in a discussion, they will find someone who can. Keeping dialogues fun, witty, and interesting is always important for

Gemini. They prefer to intellectualize their emotions, so if you get caught up in your feelings or dampen their fun, they will leave you high and dry.

Gemini loses interest in things very fast, especially if they do not feel a head over heels type of excitement. They want someone who appreciates them for their funky, fun, and spirited self. However, they also need someone to keep them in line in a refreshing way. They are looking for a partner who gives them a love nest they can return to while allowing them to still feel free to fly when they feel the urge. This sun sign requires a partner who is strong without being controlling. Geminis place high value on the experience over the destination when it comes to love, and they want someone who is more interested in the journey. However, the twins appreciate a partner who is opinionated and rooted in their beliefs in order to give them something to learn or debate. Geminis are spontaneous souls who are down for escapades and love keeping things fresh in a relationship. If you have a Gemini in your life, it is like catching a butterfly, and you should feel lucky. Gemini will charm you to chase them, and if you do hold them in one spot, remember that it is like holding a handful of sand. If you hold too tightly or too loosely, you'll lose them, but if you can find the right amount of pressure, you will be able to keep most of them. The other bits belong to Gemini and always will. If you find that evenness, Gemini may just stick around.

How to Bed a Gemini

The Gemini character is full of all sorts of duality when it comes to their sexuality, which makes them zesty in the bedroom. The twins obtain dual—and sometimes even multiple—identities that are all bundled into one busy body. They are smart and witted, leaving you dizzy with delight. With a Gemini in bed, you never know who you are going to ravage that night. It could be their innocent side, which will want some tender love, or the other twin could show up for a night of dominatrix thrill. However, dullness is something that is never on the menu.

Role-play is one of their favorite amusements, and they are quite good at it. Investing in some costumes and props for different nights of fun will really turn them on. The Gemini imagination is always running wild, so keeping them entertained is key. Switching up where and how you have sex keeps things imaginative for this sun sign. There is not much that they are not willing to try, but the versatility that they crave will come once they feel comfortable being vulnerable around their lover.

Gemini is not interested in a mate who is dull or unintelligent, but rather a partner in crime who is bold, funny, and smart. Divulge their brain with wild and fun topics to feed their bright and brilliant mind, and their body will soon follow. A Gemini's physicality always follows their thoughts, and intellectual conversations are a huge turn on for the twins. Tell them they are fascinating and enjoy their eclectic personalities—all of them. Gemini's love language is words of affirmation because their modality is mutable, meaning they love to talk. In the bedroom, they will have no problem telling you where and how they want it. A Gemini is anything but quiet during the act.

Gemini also requires someone who is grounded enough to bring them back down to earth on occasion. Just remember that this zodiac sign has a mind of their own, several of them, in fact, and no matter how flighty or wild they may seem, they are anything but dumb. Treat them with respect, and they will pay it back tenfold, especially in the bedroom, where they will be waiting for you with a new surprise every time. If you can remember that Gemini is not to be understood but appreciated, you will start to put their sexual puzzle pieces together.

☼ ☼ ☼

GEMINI & GEMINI

Aspect: Conjunct
Elements: Air and air
Modalities: Mutable and mutable

Geminis are the free spirits of the zodiac. Together, they can live in a land of fantasy and flight, undisturbed by the harshness of reality. Who really wants to grow up anyway? These two will go through life wanting to learn something new every day, and what better way to do that than with their best friend? The twins rarely sit and ponder their decisions because they know the enjoyable parts of life are spontaneous and unplanned. To most, this sounds terrifying, but to a few Geminis, it is just another fun-filled day.

A Gemini pair is bound to be chatty because they are both mutable signs. They are so great with words and can even make bad news sound good. They will both be talking at the same time and still know what the other is saying. They may tend to leave their listeners in a tizzy, but they both love to be heard. Just try to keep up. This may sometimes make them battle for the stage, but if they do bicker, it will never be for long. They get over things quickly because they are already moving on to the next thing before you can even bat an eye.

Gemini is the sign of the twins because in each Gemini lies two or more personalities. You can imagine how many characters you will see come out of this pair. Many of these sun signs have aliases for their alter egos, and the two of them will have several nicknames for one another. It will be exciting to see who they are dealing with that day, hour, or even minute. Because of their duality, their sex will be different and magical almost every time. There is a certain intimate understanding between one another that is wistful, fun, and light. Their physical oneness is prismatic, and when the light hits it just right, they will see beautiful colors scatter and dance across the room. What they have is nothing short of enchanting. Moreover, they will connect in an even deeper way through vibrant conversation that is filled with wit and charm. Their dual air mentality allows them to blend the swirling thoughts that mix and meld between one another's lucid minds effortlessly.

With all conjunct pairs, the lesson is to see yourself mirrored back through your partner, the good and the bad. On occasion, when they feel like they are losing themselves in their partner, they will want to escape for a while. They may even get so caught up in the moment that they leave their Gemini lover in the dust. They both must be conscientious and compassionate toward one another's need for freedom and work on not getting ahead of themselves or their counterpart. The two must hold hands through life and race across the stars together. As every Gemini knows, it is not the destination but the journey that holds value. They will have to reassure one another that they are there for each other, even while one is away on one of their endeavors. If there are times of separation, they will be brief, as they will soon long to be together. Geminis do not care for loneliness one bit and get bored way too easily when left alone for long stretches of time.

Gemini companions are as lighthearted as can be, but it takes a long time for them to really decide to give themselves entirely to another. It takes patience, trust, and a deep, connected friendship to completely be ready for huge steps in their relationship. Life for a Gemini is never meant to be lived too seriously, but marriage is a serious topic that they do not, in any sense, take lightly. They may even have to part ways for a bit because one is ready and the other is not. With time, the other twin will realize that they want to return to the quirky and magical sense of reality that only the two of them can make. They will realize that they are not like other couples, and they love that dynamic within their relationship. Most duos strive to be one with each other, but that sounds so boring to a Gemini pair. Besides, how is that possible for a couple that is made up of two people who are not even one person within themselves? It is not, and that is what makes their love uniquely free and faceted.

☼ ☼ ☼

GEMINI & CANCER

Aspect: Semisextile
Elements: Air and water
Modalities: Mutable and cardinal

The twins and the crab easily fall in love thanks to their similar childlike natures, but they will soon learn that the stars made their personalities quite different. Gemini leans into their quick mind, while Cancer prefers to use their intuition. They will come close to figuring each other out but never completely because Gemini will have a hard time understanding what Cancer is feeling, and Cancer will have a hard time understanding what Gemini is thinking. This disconnect is a theme in their love, but it is certainly not one they cannot work around.

Their auras are painted with every color of the rainbow thanks to Gemini's mercurial qualities and Cancer's fluctuating lunar moods. Gemini will jump from a bright yellow cheer to a dark purple despair while Cancer dips from a sweet lavender-hued laughter to the deep blues of melancholy. When their auras mix, it's like a never-ending kaleidoscope of emotive colors. Cancer often visits their dark despondency, while Gemini would prefer to keep things sunny and cheerful. On occasion, Cancer's pessimism will drive Gemini crazy. The twins are a mutable sign and like to talk everything out, so Gemini will get frustrated when they cannot cheer their crab up with some simple conversation. Poking and prodding Cancer to come out of their shell is not going to help the situation, but letting Cancer know that you are there for them will convince them to come around.

Gemini enjoys changing their mind as often as the wind changes direction, while Cancer's cardinal modality prefers to make things happen. Cancer has a hard time getting things to come to fruition when Gemini's mutable mind is always altering the plan. This can lead to a few problems in their productivity as a pair because Cancer has a need to understand what Gemini wants. However, most of the time Gemini does not even know what they want, which is why it is difficult for them to turn their faceted ideas into one solid goal. When Cancer gets frustrated, they will shut down. During that time, Gemini should make it a point to get to a conclusion.

These two operate at different speeds; Cancer is slow and cautious, and Gemini is quick and carefree. Cancer will feel uneasy with Gemini's tendency to be energetically scattered because Cancer would prefer to cling to one thing at a time. The twins crave duality; one twin will want to stay closely by Cancer's side, and the other one will want to do whatever pleases their impulses. Cancers are naturally adherent to the things they love. Therefore, when Cancer's retentiveness crosses with Gemini's constant need for freedom, the clash can bring trouble. If Gemini is financially unstable, it will make Cancer's clinginess even worse. However, if Cancer has enough emotional reassurance, they will not need as much financial security. Correspondingly, when Gemini feels like they are being restrained, they will push for more detachment. However, if Gemini is gifted with more autonomy, they will not feel a need to spend as much time away. Mutual respect will be what cures these aches. If they can equally give into one another's innate wishes, they can find connection and healing through physical oneness.

When it comes to sex for these two, it will be mentally and emotionally erotic. In the bedroom, Cancer supplies the sensuousness and affection while Gemini supplies imagination and variety, which will rarely become repetitive. There is something delicate and gentle about the way Cancer seeks affection, and Gemini's tenderness, sociability, and imagination are a good match with Cancer's sensitive and sexual nature. An area to work on is that Gemini will need to slow things down a bit and hold Cancer a little longer than they are used to. Doing this will make Cancer feel safe and secure. When the moon is full, Cancer will be able to mysteriously tie Gemini's personas together, leading them to a concentrated and dreamy connection. The magic of the moon will gift them with their best experiences, and they would be wise to use the lunar cycles in their lovemaking for these reasons.

Cancer loves familiarity and feeling safe with people they know and trust. When a crab is in love, they will not be easily able to toss it away. Rather, their feelings must wear away throughout the years. Gemini is marvelous at letting go because they do not have enough patience to keep people around that weigh down their light spirit. If something feels too heavy, the twins will cut them out and fly away on the first gust of wind. Gemini is not one to be tied down, but Cancer may be just the one to do it by showing the twins that the core of lasting love is patience. If Gemini can love Cancer completely, including their need for emotional affection, and if Cancer can love Gemini and all their visceral identities, they will create a sweet synchronization. Love will be the thing that tethers them together and allows them to find a peaceful, patient, and pleasant partnership.

☼ ☼ ☼

GEMINI & LEO

♊ 💠 ♌

Aspect: Sextile
Elements: Air and fire
Modalities: Mutable and fixed

When Gemini first meets their lion, they will wonder if Leo is as fearless as they portray themselves to be, while Leo will wonder if Gemini's directionless energy is trying to compensate for something they lack. The truth is that they both guessed correctly. Leos are always trying to prove themselves by projecting their nobility, and Geminis are always telling stories flavored with excitement to distract anyone from seeing that they are running in circles. That is the beauty of this pairing; they can see right through each other's expressive façades.

The twins and the lion are sextile, creating a strong bond of friendship between them. In fact, it is quite possible that they were friends before they became lovers. Despite any differences between them, they will always be able to reconnect through their amity. This pair is beautifully harmonious, and their energy flows naturally. Leo adores being front and center in the relationship, which will not bother their airy and indifferent Gemini, who is more inclined to move gracefully alongside their partner. Gemini will be the one to bring a change of scenery when Leo becomes bored and will regularly stroke the lion's ego, making Leo cherish their bird even more. Leo desperately needs to be respected, but they appreciate that they cannot fool their bright Gemini. The twins know that behind their big cat's personality is a tender heart.

When it comes to money, Gemini believes that illusion is the most dependable form of wealth, while Leo likes their bricks of gold stacked where they can see them. However, something wonderful about them both is that they become the energy that they project. It is like they say: if you tell yourself something enough times, it starts to become truth. When Leos and Geminis dream together, they eventually start to materialize and manifest almost anything they want, including income. What will hurt these two is if one does not support the other. If the Gemini does not believe that their lion is as brave as they suggest, or if Leo does not believe that Gemini's ideas will ever happen, it can tear them apart. What they must understand is that they are both artists of the imagination in their own special ways. They would do better to combine forces than to question them.

An area that differs between them is their vitality. Leo, like the sun, will have bursts of energy, but then they like to rest—a lot. They are not necessarily lazy, but they do not have a need to be moving all day long like Gemini does. Most of Gemini's physicality is also entangled with their emotions, meaning that they would prefer to run it out. Gemini is a master of words, and Leo's love language is words of affirmations (with gifts being a close second). It is Gemini's gift of charm and casualness that makes them so good with Leo, especially when it comes to activities in the bedroom. Leos are amazing coordinators and a lot more tolerant than people expect, especially with the ones they love. Organization and patience are necessities when partnering with a Gemini. The twins always want to speed through life, never concerned about the details, but their Leo partner will slow them down and show them how there is more to life than just skimming the surface, especially when it comes to sex.

In the bedroom, Leo always needs 100 percent of their partner's attention, so if Gemini is not fully committed, Leo's ego will be bruised. The lion likes the twins to make it all about them, and in turn, they will pay Gemini back with their fiery passion. Gemini brings a lot of excitement to their lovemaking with their changeable personalities. Leo may have sex with one of their personas one day and another the next. Leo has a greater hunger for romance and sentiment than Gemini does, and the twins would be smart to keep that in mind. Leo loves to rest and cuddle and will want to feel Gemini's head against their golden heart. The present is not Gemini's favorite place to be, but they must learn that is where they will need to be when they are in bed with a lion.

Gemini will find themselves in trouble occasionally, but they can always count on their brave Leo to come to their rescue. Leo takes on the role of Gemini's protector because deep down, Leo feels compelled to shield their mercurial bird. Leo will occasionally become arrogant and bossy, but Gemini's flattery and optimism have the magic to bring the lion's roar down to a purr. In many ways, they instinctively flatter each other by giving one other the things that they need. Leo bestows Gemini the royal fortification and freedom they desire while Gemini offers Leo the verbal boosts they crave, transforming them into the most majestic versions of themselves. When they combine their complementary air and fire elements, they create a balmy tropical breeze.

☼ ☼ ☼

GEMINI & VIRGO

Aspect: Square
Elements: Air and earth
Modalities: Mutable and mutable

When Gemini first meets Virgo, they will love the idea of a causal relationship. Gemini enjoys how the virgin charms them by firing up their mind in such fascinating conversation. They banter like two evenly talented opponents in a heated tennis match—with a new winner every time. Then, one day, Gemini will blink and realize that they have been together for a year or two, and something inside them will become worried about how they got so far along with someone who seems to constantly speculate everything. Gemini will realize that all the reasons they love their Virgo are also reasons that concern them.

Gemini does not possess a heavy spirit, and they prefer to not have anything weighing them down. Virgo does not require extreme variety or spurts of change physically, mentally, or emotionally. The virgin's predictability is nonexistent in a Gemini's personality, which is why the twins need it. Gemini loathes monotony yet desires a place to call home and someone to bring them out of the clouds. Therefore, if Virgo can show their appreciation to all of Gemini's personalities by offering them freedom and variety, they can help them stay nearby. For this complex combination to work, these two need to know who they are—along with what they are not—and appreciate each other for it.

Gemini is conceptual, while Virgo is concrete, so there will be many times when it will be hard for them to see where one another is coming from. That being said, they are both mutable signs and are both ruled by Mercury, which gifts them with the art of wit-filled communication. This pair is aspected by a square to one another, which, in astrological terms, is considered as a challenging match. However, they can be very beneficial for each other in many ways. The two find one another fascinating and frustrating in equal parts. Even with all their apparent variations of personality, there are also many similarities. The biggest connector between them is their intelligence. They are both brilliant and thrive off intellectual debates while enjoying their morning coffee.

Even if the relationship between the twins and the virgin may have not started off very seriously, Virgos rarely take a relationship lightheartedly for very long. If Virgo senses that Gemini has no intention of ever taking the relationship where they want it to go, they will end things neatly and swiftly. In their search for love, Virgo seeks perfection. Geminis are endearingly discombobulated, so the virgin will need to get past the idea of a "perfect partner" to see the gem that they have right in front of them. Virgo must remember to not sweat the small stuff and look at the big picture if they want this to work. Gemini will find themselves frequently talking fast to get out of hot water, but one way they can make it up to their angel is in the bedroom.

When it comes to intimacy, Virgo requires evident affection, and Gemini requires sparkling variety. There are a lot of differences between them sexually that they will have to figure out together, but next to nothing is impossible for these two intelligent creatures. Gemini is so changeable that Virgo will have a hard time finding the security they require, which can cause them to be guarded toward their Gemini. Virgos are critical of others, but they are always the hardest on themselves, which will cause them to think that they are not able to connect because something's wrong with them. What Virgo should remember is that Gemini is inherently ever changing, and their mind is rarely completely present. Gemini must realize that their Virgo needs them—all sides of them—to be present, especially when in the bedroom. Gemini's body always follows their mind, and Virgo will have no problem using words as foreplay. They will have intellectual debates that will continue in the bedroom. Virgo can be rigid when it comes to sex at times, but they just need someone to break them free from their ruminating thoughts, which should not be too difficult for Gemini. If Virgo can learn to let go, their physicality will be lite and fun. Neither one of them is overly emotional, so there will be a simplicity with their oneness that they will both appreciate. However, they must be very careful that their connection does not become too shallow. They must both try to go a little out of their comfort zones to show some depth, or the relationship may never flourish.

Virgo really does adore Gemini's quirks and flaws, even if they may pick at them from time to time. Virgo will never be bored, and Gemini will never have to worry about the details. Virgo will take care of all the logistics and little things that Gemini tends to miss, and Gemini will fill the relationship with color Virgo could have never imagined on their own. There will be plenty of tough days for these two, but there is always a rainbow at the end of the storm. Love is compromise, and these two can tell you all about it.

☼ ☼ ☼

GEMINI & LIBRA

♊ ❖ ♎

Aspect: Trine
Elements: Air and air
Modalities: Mutable and cardinal

The twins and the scales have so much in common that you may even think that they are the same person at times. However, for all the things they have in common, they have equal amounts of differences. They share the mentality of two air signs, which brings harmonious vibrations between them, and thanks to their trine aspect, their blending of energy tends to make things easy for them. Gemini is a lot quicker than Libra, both mentally and physically, because of their ruling planet, Mercury, but Libra has a stoic way about them that gives Gemini something to hold on to. Libra loves to be taken care of, and Gemini will gladly run around for them, succumbing to their airy requests. In return, Libra will fill their life with divine Venusian gifts of love and beauty. This constant flow of give-and-take births a space that blesses them with magic.

Geminis innately want to be a million and one things in their lifetime, and this trait would drive most people completely wild, but Libra supports their imaginative mind while gently keeping their dreams on track. Libra is fabulous at seeing all sides to everything, so when Gemini comes to them with one of these wild ideas, Libra will not be dismissive. Instead, they will look at it from all sides with them. Libra will teach Gemini practicality, and Gemini will teach Libra how to dream. Gemini has so many beautiful worlds that they flicker between, and they will want to share them with their Libra.

When Gemini's nasty twin shows up one day—most Geminis have one—Libra will be able to charm them with ease. The tough twin will break promises that the nicer twin made, but Libra will somehow understand this while treating it like a fun game to play. Because of their duality, Gemini is never completely attainable, making them a constant challenge for Libra, which is something that this sun sign needs. Geminis are eternally children, and children need boundaries. If they are left to their devices, they will run wild, but if you are too strict, they will rebel. Gemini needs an iron fist in a velvet glove, and that is precisely how the Libra leads.

These two primarily live in their heads, and it is where they like to spend most of their time. When it comes to sex, it will be lite, airy, and enjoyable. They do not get fiery like the fire signs, emotional like water signs, or even contextual like earth signs. Rather, their lovemaking is uplifting like a cloud floating on a summer breeze. Sex is important to them, but their mental connection is what truly bonds them. They will take turns ruling the bedroom, but seeing that Libra is the cardinal sign, chances are it will most likely be them. They will find so much fulfillment and peace when they blend their bodies because they are magnetized by one another, and their sex is something truly delightful. The way they enjoy one another is slowly, and then all at once.

Geminis do not typically set marriage as a goal for themselves. However, when Gemini meets Libra, that whole mentality may change very quickly because they will realize that they like everything about Libra more than they have ever liked anything about anyone else. Once Gemini starts falling in love, their bright personality will make Libra want to be even better for them and their relationship. Gemini is so many things all wrapped up in one person, and the twin's interests push Libra into new frontiers they never even thought of exploring. For this reason, travel will be something they truly love together. Discovering new worlds will be part of the journey that makes them fall even more in love.

Gemini will drive Libra wild on several occasions. However, Libra will never want to leave because there is beauty in the outrageousness that they cannot get enough of. It is Gemini's innocence and sunny nature that makes it easy for them to forgive, even when they mess up. Gemini needs Libra's strength, and Libra enjoys being relied on in this way. Libra may not even know why they fell in love so hard for this wild child as much as they did, but love does not always require an explanation—it is an abstract emotion. Gemini is a conceptual soul, and it is in their faceted mind that Libra's indecision will be mellowed because they know they have found the one that will be everything they have ever dreamed of in a partner. Gemini will teach Libra to adapt to life's ever-changing roads ahead, but Libra will be the one to choose which path to take when there is a fork in the road. Together, they will have a marvelous journey.

☼ ☼ ☼

GEMINI & SCORPIO

♊ ❤ ♏

Aspect: Quincunx
Elements: Air and water
Modalities: Mutable and fixed

With Gemini, it is always two against one, but Scorpio prefers to have more of the players on their side. Therefore, from the beginning, this love match can get tricky. Their quincunx vibration will be steamy, intricate, and take effort from all parties. Gemini is scared by anything that may lock their free soul down, and Scorpio likes things to be promised. In Scorpio's world, promises are always meant to be kept, but with Gemini, the change of the wind can bring out the other twin, and they made no such promises. Scorpio's intensity and permanency will feel intense and may even scare off Gemini at first, but there is something mysterious about the scorpion that will keep them hooked. Gemini is excellent at figuring out puzzles, and the more complex it is, the more intrigued they become. The twins are in for a treat because Scorpio's enigmatic nature comes in countless pieces.

The scorpion can handle whatever the twins throw their way because Scorpios can handle pretty much anything. Scorpio will be the intense one, which is their natural state of being, while Gemini believes that life is way too short to go around being so serious all the time. Gemini does not have to always know where the journey is going to lead them, and they truly enjoy the ride in every aspect. Scorpio is ruled by the planets Mars and Pluto, which rule war and death, while Gemini is ruled by Mercury, which rules communication. Gemini's quick wit will save them from Scorpio's stinger on several occasions, but if they can combine their forces, they can be quite the powerful pair. Gemini is a brave soul and will enjoy teasing their arachnid, but they must remember there is always a line that they should not cross when it comes to making a Scorpio upset. It will not take too much time to find out exactly where that line is, so adjustments can be made.

Scorpios naturally lean toward monogamy, but Gemini's dualistic nature enjoys variety. Gemini always ponders what their life would be like in various outcomes, sometimes forgetting to live in the present. They will always long for their freedom, whether they are with someone or not, and this may make Scorpio's possessive nature flare. Scorpio likes to keep the ones they love as close as possible, but when Gemini feels restricted, they want freedom even more. Gemini finds jealousy to be a waste of energy and is too lighthearted to be bogged down with such worries. Gemini will not take Scorpio's jealousy seriously the first time, and seeing that they are a mutable sign, they will probably make a joke about it. This can go one of two ways. Scorpio will laugh it off and realize they are right, or the stinger will come out and Gemini will never joke about their feelings without a lot more thought attached. The latter is the more probable outcome, so thought before action will do the twins well.

Because of their quincunx aspect, they do not have anything in common in regard to their modality or element, making them fascinated by one another. Their attraction may certainly have them finding each other in bed sooner than later, but they will quickly discover that the way they look at sex is very different. Scorpio sees sex as a channel to connect spiritually with their partner, and it is not a pastime or a game to be played. Gemini believes true connection is through the mind and that sex is simply a physical act to be enjoyed. They will have to meet halfway here, and if they do, it will be fireworks. Scorpio loves sex, and with Gemini, they get to connect to their many sides, which they will find riveting. Even though Gemini is not as much of a sexual prowess, Scorpio will find a way to pull it out of them, making them insanely attracted to one another. Their oneness is an unusual combination of Gemini's interesting and changeable aura and Scorpio's intense and penetrating depth. This cosmic cocktail is what gives them such a unique hold on each other.

Gemini is so curious about Scorpio, and that curiosity lingers in their relationship, giving them a way to understand Scorpio's deep feelings. Gemini may feel like they will never be able to solve Scorpio's puzzling nature, but how does someone solve a jigsaw puzzle? One piece at a time. There will be many days when they want to connect to one another but find it too difficult to do so. Their saving grace in these circumstances will be breaking down barriers and talking to one another, which is not easy when Scorpio is in a deep emotional state. Nevertheless, Gemini is a great communicator and will spearhead the tough conversations. If Scorpio can absorb Gemini's bright-eyed optimism and soften their poignant nature, it may lighten them up to a point where they find themselves growing wings to soar next to their mercurial partner. Wouldn't that be something spectacular?

☼ ☼ ☼

GEMINI & SAGITTARIUS

Aspect: Opposite
Elements: Air and fire
Modalities: Mutable and mutable

Sagittarians are not always as boisterous and obtruding as astrology stereotypes them to be, and some are surprisingly timid and introspective. However, every Sagittarius speaks with blunt honesty when their opinion is asked because all archers gaze at the world through the calculating eye of truth. This genuine energy is what attracts and retains the indecisive Gemini into their life like a butterfly into an invisible net. To catch a Gemini's attention is no small feat, and to keep one is near impossible. But for the hunter of the zodiac, it will be done with little luck and a lot of ease.

Sagittarius is a dual sign, half horse and half human, and there are two distinct types of centaurs. There are those who take after the front end, or human half, and those who take after the rear end, or equestrian half. Gemini is also a dual sign, symbolized by the twins. They are multiple in personality, various in word and action, and numerous by nature. Even though these two sun signs sit on the opposite ends of the karmic wheel, they have much in common such as their honesty, youthfulness, refreshing candor, wisdom, and wit, which are paired with a bizarre combination of awkwardness and gracefulness.

Gemini is air, whereas Sagittarius is fire, and these two elements brilliantly mix most of the time and obscurely at others. Gemini can inflame Sagittarius into action in both negative and positive ways because air fans fire into higher flames. This makes Sagittarius feel like they can burn bright around their Gemini, but too much of Gemini's airy detachment can push Sagittarius into a frenzy or blow their fire out completely. On occasion, Sagittarius can make Gemini feel smothered because fire has the ability to burn out the oxygen in the air, making it impossible to breathe. What they must do with their complementary elements is find a balance so that they can create a nice warm breeze.

They are slightly envious of each other because each possesses qualities the other does not have but would secretly like to develop. Gemini needs the archer's high motivation, ideals, warmth, enthusiasm, and sincerity. They also wish for the Sagittarian's ability to travel over more terrain mentally, emotionally, and geographically. Gemini admires the way their archer can shoot for the stars and reach them with their arrows that drip in luck. Sagittarius longs for Gemini's cool poise and charm, their talent for keeping their foot out of their mouth, how they remain relaxed and detached in the face of most disturbing situations, and especially for their verbal competence. When they get together, they have two choices. Each can admire the opposite traits of the other and try to imitate them to grow and mature spiritually, or they can fear and envy the opposite qualities, and try to put one another down, robbing each other of all pride in doing their own thing.

They both vibrate to the mutable modality, frequently spurring one another into conversation. However, they may not actively listen to each other, even if they may appear to be. One is only waiting for the other to finish talking so they can put across a contradictory opinion. A dramatic disagreement between them can get noisy, and typically one of the two will completely subdue the other. The subdued one will seek freedom from such restriction at the earliest opportunity, sometimes even permanently. To avoid this, active listening will be something they should both work on. For when Sagittarius listens to the twins' fantasies and Gemini supports the centaur's realities, their worlds will collide, making something extraordinarily their own.

Their sex will heal most of their differences, and they will have no problem telling each other what they want in bed. The twins and the centaur have instant sexual compatibility because they tend to be scintillating rather than somber and daring rather than craven. Because of their opposing nature, their attraction for each other is strong and inevitable. They have this intrinsic need to become one with each other because of their polarity and can achieve this for a time through their lovemaking, which is delightful. Once they are physically finished, they continue connecting through conversation until the sun comes up. This part of their relationship will keep them tied to one another.

The glittering Mercury-ruled Gemini and the altruistic Jupiter-ruled Sagittarius get along exceedingly well—most of the time. According to ancient legends, the gods feel a special affection for their Sagittarian children, watchfully protecting them from those who would harm them. This is the basis for Sagittarian luck. Mercury bestows on Gemini children quick wit, swift intellect, and cleverness—sometimes too much for their own good. Sagittarius is fiery and enthusiastic, while Gemini is light and cool. However, the essential and basic natures of Gemini and Sagittarius are alike in that they are both sunny, cheerful, and optimistic. If they nurture the love they have for one another's similarities and combine it with their fascination and mutual respect for each other's differences, the sky is the limit for these two.

☼ ☼ ☼

GEMINI & CAPRICORN

Aspect: Quincunx
Elements: Air and earth
Modalities: Mutable and cardinal

Capricorn is made from pure lucidity, and Gemini is made from unalloyed illusion. The twin's energy makes the sea goat buzz, and Capricorn's earthy presence makes Gemini feel like they can stand still for a little while. Capricorn loves trying to figure out Gemini because they are like a beautiful puzzle that they cannot quite seem to put together, but Capricorn's practical mind must understand that Gemini is not one to be solved or pinned down. Gemini is not meant to be kept in a cage—no matter how bad Capricorn wants to keep them still. Confining them would be like gilding a butterfly. Unlike Capricorn's steely nature, the twin's spirit is as light as a feather. One may wonder how these two could ever truly work with such vast differences, but it is their differences that make them good for each other.

Both Gemini and Capricorn cherish their loved ones and money, but Capricorn takes these two topics much more seriously, which is why it is very important for Gemini to keep strong ties with Capricorn's family and finances at the forefront. Gemini keeps most of the relationships in their life casual, and they typically do not make plans unless they must, which is why the twins will usually end up where the sea goat takes them. However, Gemini should make it a point to tell Capricorn that it is important for them to spend time with their crew too. Capricorn is a climber, and Gemini is a floater. Capricorn analytically plans out a path in their life so they can get to the highest point the fastest, and Gemini has more of an approach of letting the chips fall where they may. Capricorn works very hard for every dollar earned, and once that dollar is made, it, too, has a safe strategy to capitalize gains. Gemini, on the other hand, is not necessarily bad with their money; they just do not have the focus to care as much. Gemini likes high-risk, high-reward investments that would make the sea goat sweat. Gemini knows that money will come and go and to not fret about something that they do not have a ton of control over. The two will need to make a compromise with their cash, either letting Capricorn manage everything or getting separate accounts.

Sexually and emotionally, they will long to be understood by one another, but thanks to their quincunx aspect, their attraction will be scintillating. Gemini is playful, and Capricorn is sensual, and with some time, they will feel more connected than ever when they share their bodies with one another. Sex will be a bonding and healing place of refuge for them if there are any discrepancies. With patience from Gemini, sex will become an important way for Capricorn to express their feelings for them. The twins use a mutable modality to communicate, which means they usually have no problem talking about anything, but Capricorn is much more reserved with their sentiments. When Capricorn's walls come down during intimacy, the sea goat may feel freed to really convey themselves, which Gemini will treasure. This makes their relationship special and private. We live in a take it or leave it kind of world, but their relationship will start to weave them together in a way that allows for solidity and compassion.

One way to keep their relationship fresh is travel. This is something that will consistently bring them closer together, and Gemini will be the best version of themselves during their adventures. Capricorn does not have as much wanderlust as Gemini, but if they have luxurious and comfortable surroundings, they will be able to relax and let go to truly enjoy one another. Capricorn will take pleasure in experiencing this mysterious sprite's love and admiration along with how Gemini is several souls in one perfect package. Gemini brings a new and fun perspective to Capricorn's usually gray life, sprinkling in laughter, color, and kindness, which are things Capricorn's heart has needed for so long. In a complementary manner, Gemini so desperately wishes for something solid and steady to come home to and someone to keep things in order, which the sea goat will dutifully provide.

A Capricorn is about as stable as one gets, and Gemini will love their natural tendency to lead the relationship in the direction they want. Gemini likes a partner that can take charge while still allowing them to have freedom. As mercurial and ever-changing as Gemini is, Capricorn may never truly understand them, but they know they never want to lose them. Capricorn is patient and stubborn, so if they want this air sign, they will create the perseverance needed to make it work. With enough time, Gemini will realize what a godsend this earth sign is in their life and how they bring a sense of balance to their mind. They may even start to notice how nice their life is with Capricorn around once they learn to stand still. Love has a way of softening the hardest hearts, but it also has a way of slowing down the busiest of bodies.

☼ ☼ ☼

GEMINI & AQUARIUS

Aspect: Trine
Elements: Air and air
Modalities: Mutable and fixed

Aquarius is truly a misunderstood creature, while Gemini always feels like no one can deal with their many personas. Then they meet each other, and it is as though the clouds part in the sky, and they can finally see what was clearly meant for them. There is a certain instantaneous comfort and awareness in their love that allows them to be anomalous together while understanding each other in a quirky and unusual way. They can feel a frequency in the air that no one else seems to pick up, and together they find each other in a faraway world that is their own strange reality. Their love story is always unique and is anything but empty; it is filled with a lot of friends, acquaintances, trips, and parties. There is rarely a dull day with these two because they are constantly entertaining each other's minds with ideas, stories, and friendly repartee.

In this partnership, Aquarius is a bit wiser and more spiritual than Gemini. This is because of their planetary rulers, Saturn and Uranus. Gemini is a lot more fun and spirited than Aquarius is thanks to their witty ruler, Mercury, calling the shots. They bicker like siblings, but their spats are rarely serious and almost comical to watch. One thing Aquarius would be wise to understand is that Gemini rarely means what they say. Their sarcasm can sometimes bring Aquarius to split, which is the furthest thing from what Gemini ever actually wants to happen. Aquarius has very high expectations for the one they settle down with, and sometimes those expectations are ridiculous and quite impossible. The water bearer's outward attitude may seem cool, calm, and collected, but inside they are praying that their expectations will eventually be met in one way or another. Geminis have their own idea of the truth, and it is not quite the same as the water bearer's. To the twins, the truth has so many ifs and what ifs. Their mind is so faceted that just about anything could be the truth. Truth will be an area that they will conflict on, but if Aquarius can remember how Gemini's mind works, they may have a little more empathy toward this issue.

Aquarius is a fixed sign, which means they tend to be quite stubborn, and they have a way of doing things that no one else does. Aquarius is on a search for the truths of life, but they do it with a completely open mind. They are extraordinary people that can truly imagine the unimaginable, which makes them a mix of fact and fantasy. Geminis obtain a child's soul, no matter what age they are, and there is true curiosity and enchantment about them. With these facts in mind, when you mix these two air signs together, they do wonders for each other. Geminis are the talkers, and Aquarians are the thinkers. Together, this couple creates a beautiful puzzle that only they can solve. They are too complex for most to understand, but neither one of them has ever been worried about the opinions of others.

Their physical union is one that is well matched, so when it comes to sex, their insecurities melt because they find fulfillment in a way that they have never experienced with anyone else. Because camaraderie is the essence of their alliance, their lovemaking is friendly and playful, making each other's heart flip in the best way possible. Sex is not the most important thing in their togetherness because mental stimulation takes the number one spot. Whether they unite physically every day or occasionally, sex to them is merely a physical act. More importantly, they create correlation through communication, which is how air signs significantly link, channeling love through their minds and souls. They then use their physical bodies as a secondary tool for connection.

Once these characters cross paths, friendship will be at the core of their union, which they will be able to fall back on during tough times. There is an air element alchemy that unmistakably links each other's hearts together like a holographic string that is only visible if the sun catches it just right. Gemini has many sides to their personality and so does Aquarius, which they both express in different ways. Their love is not necessarily simple, but it is always interesting and surely magical. The way they move through life together is airy and mystical, and their auras combine into a myriad of rainbow colors. This state of being that they create is unique to this sun sign combination and impossible to have with another soul. They know this, which is why they will never feel the need to be with anyone else.

☼ ☼ ☼

GEMINI & PISCES

♊ ♡ ♓

Aspect: Square
Elements: Air and water
Modalities: Mutable and mutable

Pisces may seem naive to many because of their sweet and self-sacrificing personality, but they are a lot wiser than most give them credit for. Pisces will do what it takes to get what they want, and the same goes for when Gemini catches their eye. Astrologically speaking, this match is not always the easiest because of their square aspect. Knowing this, Pisces will have to make a tough choice to either leave or choose to continue to sacrificing small things for the big picture. Pisces will not only have to capture but also keep the Gemini that they love, which is never an easy feat. In many ways, Geminis are like sand. If you hold them too tightly, they will slip through your fingers. Pisces must find a balance when it comes to the twins if they want them—both of them—to stick around. Luckily Pisces was born with incredible intuition to know when to pull back and when to take a step closer. It may not happen at the times they desire, but the fish is smart enough to know how to do it. To many outsiders, it may seem that Pisces sacrifices too much to keep their Gemini around, but Pisces knows exactly what they are doing.

They are both mutable signs, which gifts them with the ability to talk for hours on end about new ideas and dreams that excite their souls. Neither one is ever deeply concerned with money, so the fact that Gemini may change jobs at the drop of the hat will not worry Pisces as much as it would most sun signs. Pisces swims through life and Gemini floats through theirs, which sounds different but is experienced similarly. With their mutable flexibility, they always find a way to work it out, and they will enjoy watching one another use their different brands of magic to come to solutions in life and love.

One big difference they will need to see eye-to-eye on is how they spend and use their time. Gemini is busy doing, and Pisces is busy being. Pisces believes and knows that life should not be rushed and that there will be plenty more hours the next day, whereas Gemini cannot get things done fast enough. The twins use their double energy to move from project to project, job to job, and place to place, making Pisces's head spin. At times, Gemini will see Pisces as slow and lazy, and Pisces will see Gemini as an anxious busybody. The best advice is to spend plenty of time apart doing the things they enjoy at the pace they want—without any judgment attached.

Gemini is smart and clever but also blind to Pisces's mystifying strategy, and they will love how easy things seem to be with them. However, Gemini should take heed to not mistake Pisces's benevolence for feebleness. If the fish becomes fed up with their antics, they will swim away and never seen again, and Gemini does not like to be left alone for too long with no one to talk to. In their times of discord, Pisces's eyes will look deep and lost, while Gemini's eyes will be quick and searching. With understanding and adjustment, they can find each other where the water and air meet at the surface. As different as these two are, they have their similarities. They appreciate privacy, freedom, art, and music. Neither really are ones for routine, and it is in the unpredictability of their relationship that they will find their special style of love.

One thing that will always make them feel closer is the physical chemistry that they share. Gemini's flighty nature may be hard for Pisces to adjust to, but the fish will teach the twins a way to connect to their vibrations that is deeper and gentler. Pisces's intense emotional sexuality brings Gemini discomfort, while Gemini's aloofness hurts Pisces. Pisces needs to move slowly and work toward adding in emotion, and Gemini needs to allow themselves to emotionally connect. They must begin to sexually understand each other for this to work, but once they adjust, their sexual energy becomes magical. They can create a powerful and bonding experience that will teach one another different dimensions of love through sex. However, they must grow a strong base first so that they have a better understanding of each other's needs before reaching ecstasy. Patience is key.

One thing that will always keep Gemini's interest is how naturally charming Pisces is. The fish is an enigma to Gemini's clever mind, and they love the challenge that Pisces unknowingly possesses. Pisces enjoys Gemini's attention but will rarely ask for it directly. Pisces adores Gemini's clever ideas, which seem to pop up out of nowhere, and will find their life so much more fascinating with Gemini in it. There are many sides to the twins, but Pisces's favorite side is their inner child. The delightful mystery, guileless games, and feathery communication between them is what keeps their love fresh and fun. Pisces's deepest desire is to feel needed, and Gemini's greatest wish is to feel heard. This is the reason these two find one another and, against the astrological odds, stay together. They finally discover that the missing pieces of their greatest desires live in one another, which is always something worth fighting for.

☼ ☼ ☼

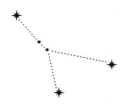

Chapter 4

Cancer

Cancer's love archetype is the loving nurturer. They are a sensitive, enigmatic, reflective, and deliberate lover who encourages growth and development. Cancer's lesson in love is to impart that love is affection and absorb that love is autonomy.

Element	Water
Modality	Cardinal
Polarity	Yin, negative, and feminine
Mantra	"I feel."
Hue	Silver
Deity	Selene, goddess of the moon
Glyph	♋
Flowers	Lilies, magnolia, and white rose
Tree	Maple
Jewel	Pearl
Crystals	Selenite and moonstone
Fragrance	Gardenia
Body Parts	The stomach, diaphragm, chest, breasts, and lymph system
Animals	Crabs and other crustaceans
Food & Herbs	Cabbage, turnips, milk, fish, tarragon, saxifrage, chamomile, ginger, angelica, red clover, dandelion root, and fruits and vegetables with high water content, such as watermelon

Cancer's Ruling Orb: The Moon

The moon in love rules emotions, empathy, receptivity, and subconscious needs from a partner. The moon reveals the feminine energy in natal charts and is also linked to our mother and how we viewed and felt their energy. This orb in love represents the emotional needs that you desire from a partner, and it goes through phases that are as changeable as your own emotional needs in a relationship. The moon is also representative of how we set up our home and how we pass on lessons to our children. Regarding Cancer, the moon represents this sun sign's touching response to life and love through sentiments. The sun is concerned with action, and the moon is concerned with reaction.

Cancer Mythology

Cancer the crab was sent to harass Hercules while he was on his second of twelve labors. As he battled the Lernaean Hydra, a serpentine water monster, Juno sent Cancer to nip at the hero's heels. Juno disliked Hercules because he was a product of one of Jupiter's affairs. The crab was eventually crushed beneath Hercules's feet, but Juno placed Cancer in the heavens as a reward for its faithful service.

Cancer's Positive Qualities and Negative Forms

Cancer's positive qualities are imagination, determination, tenderness, sensitivity, care, and caution. Expressed in their negative forms, they become stingy, irritable, melancholy, clingy, timid, possessive, and moody.

How a Cancer Loves

A Cancer in love is experienced as a nurturing, tender, caring, and committed partner. However, it takes quite a bit of convincing before they come out of their shell and hand their gentle heart away. Crabs approach love in an indirect manner to make sure that they feel safe to share their sentiments. Rejection to a crab is damaging, so they protect themselves by moving sideways many times before moving forward. Self-preservation is a necessity to a Cancer, and they do their best to protect their soft centers by snapping their pincers loudly to scare off anyone who dares harm them. They hide their pain and fear behind their claws, which only allows those who have the patience and understanding for these lunar-lead creatures to enter their hearts.

Cancer's need for roots and security is what gives them comfort and joy. There is a sort of continuity when partnering with a crab that makes it easy to love them. They are gentle, subtle, and imaginative. They take a long time to take a leap forward, so when they do, you will know that it truly means something. They are looking for a companion with a warm heart and a compassionate soul because they themselves offer up so much instinctual understanding of how life can throw curveballs, which creates heartache.

Cancer takes love seriously and their promises to the grave. They value family more than everything, so if you are theirs, you will always be number one on the priority list. They are innately drawn to the financial and emotional security that a partnership brings. Their desire for security is a main reason for their initial caution when entering a union. This sun sign partners with intent in every sense and will give their lover the moon and stars. In fact, Cancer shines the brightest when their significant other is having their darkest days. They are incredible companions to have during the tough times and can use their kindness and sympathy to heal their beloved's woes. They are uncannily gifted at knowing what their loved one needs without them ever having to say it.

Because of their cardinal nature, Cancers are shooting stars when it comes to work. Most have no problem climbing the ranks and making money to bring home. Cancers easily become attached to their surroundings—both at home and work—which is why they have great longevity in both these areas of life. Their habitual behavior is what gives them their security and comfort. Much like a tree, once Cancer plants themselves, they plan to be there for good. When something is not working, they will not simply toss it away but find a way to fix it. Their sentimental nature does not allow for giving up on a whim. They are wonderful problem solvers, especially when it comes to their relationships. They integrate themselves into their unions, which is why they will cling onto them, nurturing and saving them in any way.

When a crab is in love, they will make their partner feel like they are the only person in the world, and they would much rather stay in to have a popcorn and movie night than go out for drinks on the town. They relish being in the comforts of home while surrounded by their loved ones because this is where they find value in their lives. They do not enjoy change, but if looked at in a positive light, this characteristic can be admired because it brings longevity to love. Cancers are not meant to be adjusted but adored for the complex and emotional creatures that they are. There is a translucent, pearlescent beauty to their character that does not sparkle or shine but rather glows with a kind of magic that only the moon is able to bestow upon its Cancerian children. If you are lucky enough to have one, consider yourself blessed by the cosmos.

How to Spot a Cancer

There is something about a full moon that brings a Cancer out of their shell. So, if you are looking for one, check to see if the moon is complete and head out to see if you can spot one for yourself. At night, under the moon's gleam, you can see their ever-changing moods. There is a mystery that lies in their beauty that is silvery and magical—a consistent inconsistency. They are born with a wonderful sense of humor, and their laugh is like a loon's, haunting and strange. Cancers do not desire to be in the limelight and prefer to be noticed when they want to be. They may not pursue attention, but they certainly do not mind it either. Cancer hides from many things in their shell, but appreciation and admiration are not two of them.

Physically there are two types of Cancers. The first type are the baby-faced, round-eyed Cancers, which look like their ruling orb. The second type has smaller eyes that are spaced out with a bit of a frown to them. Their bodies are usually either heavyset or long and wiry, resembling a crab. All Cancers are blessed with impressive features that help express the array of moods that they so deeply feel. Cancers are downright dreamy, and it is easy to get lost in the stars with them. They are resilient yet get snagged in their own fears and doubts that they have within themselves. When they can overcome their insecurities is when they really shine. Their emotions are raw and beautiful, and there is an honesty and vulnerability about them that is nurturing enough to make you feel right at home.

People gravitate toward them with their problems because Cancers are wonderful at gathering information, absorbing emotions, and reflecting on the issues at hand. Due to their wary nature, they are hard people to catch as your own because they move cautiously into relationships. However, once they do move forward with someone, they rarely let go, using their claws to hold on tight. Cancers are some of the most giving and tender people you will ever be blessed to meet, and when they are moved by something, they will use their cardinal energy to be an advocate and defender. However, it is their home where they really shine; it is where they dream, live, love, and feel safe. They are incredibly sentimental and tend to hold onto everything that ever meant anything to them. Their walls are usually covered with photos of their nostalgic memories, and there is often something delicious being whipped up in the kitchen. Acts of service are their love language because it is in their nature to nurture. Due to their tender touch, they are also known to have a green thumb and find a love of gardening that comes naturally to them.

The crab's heart is soft and sweet underneath their hard exoskeleton. At first, their sensitive nature is covered up by the colors of the moonlight reflecting off their shell, shimmering hues of blue and silver that are wonderfully brilliant. Their emotions are powerful, but their loony sense of humor and raucous laughter cover it up so you cannot see. Be patient and look deeper, and you will find a secret place in them that is madness and beauty all mixed in one. It is a place that not many are privileged to view, so allow their waters to wash over you like the waves on the sand. Let go and immerse yourself in their lunar magic.

How to Lose a Cancer

Cancer has three priorities, and one of them is emotional protection. This sun sign's sense of humor is loony and wonderful, and they are quite sensitive to how people perceive their humor, so make sure to let them know you adore this about them. The crab's hard shell covers their sensitive emotions, and they require a partner that they are able to feel vulnerable with. If they think you are too rough around the edges, they may assume you will not be healthy for their emotional well-being. Cancer is incredibly intuitive and intricate, and if you patronize them for these gifts, they will hide their true feelings from you or even shut down on you altogether. When Cancer wants to be alone, let them have their time to recharge. The crab can tend to have cranky moods. This can be frustrating, but if you give them some time to cool off and think, they will come back ready to resolve. However, if you try to settle things before they are ready, they will revert even further into their shell. If a Cancer starts feeling safe enough to ask you to go on adventures, dates, and outings with them, do your best not to say no. It takes a lot of courage for them to ask, so seriously consider joining them.

The second priority for them is financial security. If someone tends to spend more than they save, they will make Cancer nervous. Cancer will potentially be unable to see a future with someone who is fiscally reckless. They like to take the lead with finances to know that everything is safely in the bank, which gives them a sense of security. Cancers are one of the most underrated signs in the zodiac. Yes, they have a watery, emotive nature, but they are also cardinal by birth, which means they are the boss. They make incredible leaders that are not only amazingly intuitive but also great at forging a way forward. They enjoy being the front runner, so if you only chalk them up to their emotionality, they may very well retreat.

The third priority—and possibly the most important one—is family. If you are not willing to put family first, this is not the sun sign for you. Cancer requires time before they walk into love and make you a part of their family. They need all of their boxes checked and security built before they show their delicate emotions or take any big steps. Cancer will put you through many tests before you become their kin. They are secretive and hide sides to them that not many get the privilege to see. So, if they let you in, take it seriously, or they will skitter across the beach in the moonlight, never to be seen again. Love them the way they deserve, and you will receive copious amounts of sensitivity, tenderness, and compassion along with stability, security, and a sense of family.

How to Bed a Cancer

There is something about a Cancer's touch that brings scintillating chills to your skin. They are strong yet sweet, hard but wholesome, and moody while somehow calming. They are like the moon in so many ways, but as we all know, the moon has a dark side. There is something silvery, opalescent, and glistening about them, and they possess an immortal energy that encompasses a deep sexual power.

They enjoy submitting to their partner, but if the mood strikes, their cardinal nature has no problem taking control. Cancer's temperament is like the waxing and waning moon; there will be days when they will have undying passion, and there will be days when they are as cool as the other side of the pillow. The love of a Cancer is not eccentric but rather rich and wholesome. It is not exotic but rather nostalgic, and it is not detached but rather profound. There is something innocent and nurturing about the way they love that can soften the hardest of hearts.

If you wish to give a Cancer the complete experience when making love, it is crucial that you remember to take not only their physicality into consideration but their emotionality as well. Physically Cancer rules the chest and breasts, which will be places that arouse them most. Emotionally Cancers are beautifully sentimental and sensitive, making them excellent lovers but also making them vulnerable to hurt. Taking this into consideration and being supportive and empathetic of their ever-changing emotions will make them open up sexually in ways that you could only dream of.

Cancers love their home and will love having you in it. Being comfortable in their surroundings will bring a hidden side of them out into the light, allowing them to loosen up. Being comfortable is an important piece of their intimacy. They have a need to feel safe and protected with the one they are sexual with before they can release.

Cancers shine like moonlight at night, and their lunar magic is laced into their sexuality, making you adhere to their every whim. Their silent strength weakens any barriers, and your heart will, somehow, inevitably be theirs. It is the Cancer's goodness that will consistently make you want to devote yourself completely to them sexually and emotionally. You are officially under their lunar midnight spell.

☼ ☼ ☼

CANCER & CANCER

Aspect: Conjunct
Elements: Water and water
Modalities: Cardinal and cardinal

If two crabs can both muster up enough courage to come out of their shells, they will discover soon that partnership is something that they both want. This sun sign truly loves protection, which is why a union between them will typically form quickly once they are able to move forward. While commitment is known to scare many, the crab makes it a central theme in their priorities. Tradition and homelife are at the core of importance to this water sign. Their love of family, finances, and a future together are at the forefront of both their minds. Together, they can be a powerhouse couple, but it is their moodiness that will tend to cause stormy waters times two. Sometimes there will be a reason for the melancholy and sometimes not. They will have to learn to live around it because they will both be fluctuating. At times, one will even be sensitive about the other being emotional. This can lead to a bit of a flood, but to them, it makes perfect sense. If they can remember to come up for air, they can weather one another's storms because they understand each other in a way that most cannot.

A Cancer couple enjoys playing guessing games, which can either be fun or harmful. They are not inclined to share every emotion, desire, or feeling right away. Instead, they will often conceal longings, even when it comes to sex. When the games are over and they can show their hands to one another, their sex will be satisfying and saturated with a feeling of security. The first few times they make love to one another, there will be a lot of shyness that both need to overcome. Then, just like the moon, they will go into a phase of wanting a more open and deeper sexual connection. Infidelity is very rare with these two, so once they join, it usually remains permanent. If the security is there, of course. If one of them starts to lose their sense of security, either financial or emotional, it may not work.

Cancer is a cardinal sign, which means they will both like to lead. They should work as a team to figure out where one another's talents will bring them the security that they desire. There will be days when they both want to be the captain of the ship, but they will have to compromise here and figure out a good system to allow both to have some capacity. These two will typically want children, and their family years will be the best of their lives. These golden years make it hard for them to let their babies go, but they will always make it a point to keep their children close. Their kids are a glue that keeps them together because they both shine as parents, making an excellent team in this area of life. They can create a beautiful home together because they never let their priorities stray. Fiscally this pair is brilliant because finances are so important to them, but it would not be a bad idea if they kept some money separate from one another so that the Cancer claws stay at bay. Money is a big issue for this sun sign, and they may not always see eye-to-eye when it comes to how to spend it.

Cancers can keep a secret, but they do not like secrets being kept from them. The key with this match is to have them both show one another their soft sides and keep the claws closed. Only then will they have the opportunity to see the beauty of what happens when they open up and become completely honest with one another. The littlest things can make a Cancer worry for no reason, so reassuring each other on a consistent basis is crucial to happiness for both. Two Cancers have a great shot of finding contentment in love and in their home. They just need to remember to keep their temperaments cool, treat each other with respect, and understand that their concerns are coming from a nurturing place. Under the moonlight, they can create a glittering silver magic that only two crabs are capable of.

☼ ☼ ☼

CANCER & LEO

Aspect: Semisextile
Elements: Water and fire
Modalities: Cardinal and fixed

Cancer is the moon, and Leo is the sun. They do not share the same sky often, but when they do, it is really a sight to see. It is a fact that the moon cannot shine without reflecting the light of the sun. Therefore, Leo will be the light in this love story, and Cancer will periodically mirror Leo's energy, waxing and waning throughout the months. This will allow Leo to experience themselves in a way that they have never been able to with another partner, which is what makes this pairing one to consider. The crab and the lion are both powerful in very different ways. Cancer is hauntingly alluring, and Leo is gregariously royal. Cancer has a goofy sense of humor, and Leo has a roaring laugh to accompany it. Cancer is naturally domestic, and Leo comes equipped with a heart of gold. There will be things they must give up to make their love to succeed, and there may be a few more sacrifices from Cancer than Leo.

Cancer has a lot of deep emotions that wax and wane, moving like an ocean tide that comes in and out throughout the day. Leo's naturally conceited personality will have a hard time acknowledging all of Cancer's changing emotions, which will often have Cancer feeling lonely or crabby. Leo must understand that a lot of Cancer's woes will disappear the more acknowledgment Leo gives them. Cancer must understand that Leo's arrogance comes from self-doubt that Leo's pride would never let anyone see. They tend to misunderstand each other quite frequently, especially in the beginning of their relationship. It takes a lot of patience for the crab and lion to trust each other and understand one another's innate differences. This pairing is a tricky combination of fire and water that is going to take a lot of compromise. However, it is one that can be done if these two are totally committed to working around anything. Their journey will include a lot of learning, laughing, and maybe a few tears along the way. It is not going to be a piece of cake, but it will make them both better in the long run.

Cancer is yin, but they are also a cardinal sign that likes to lead, which can make them quite bossy. Leo is yang but has a fixed modality, which makes them like to stay in one place. Their polarizing energy and conflicting modalities will have them running into a few hiccups. Leo likes to win the battles, but Cancer likes to win the war. This energy also plays out in the bedroom where their attraction ebbs and flows throughout their relationship. Physically Cancer is poetic, perceptive, and deep, while Leo is fiery and intense yet still and serene like a hot summer's eve. Mixing their bodily energies creates quite the concoction. Whenever you mix fire and water, it can get a little tricky, but if done properly, it can create a lovely steam bath. Leo is often demanding in the sheets, but if they become a little more delicate about their requests, their sex can be scintillating. Leo is intense, and Cancer is deep, which is a good combination to hit the sheets with. Cancer may cry after they make love, which will throw Leo for a loop, but when something is truly touching, they are known to cry tears of joy, which is nothing for the lion to fret over. Just wipe Cancer's tears away and kiss them on the forehead, and the crab will be back to their loony selves in no time.

There are many times when Cancer will seem so helpless to Leo, but as time goes on, Leo will learn that Cancer is a lot stronger than they tend to lead on. Cancer has so many secrets that Leo finds out throughout the years, but Leo only has their one. The lion's soft heart underneath all of their boldness is their secret; it is their vulnerability. Because they work so hard at hiding their own heart, Leo does not always know the right way to Cancer's tender core. One way to each other's heart is spending some time alone together, getting away from everyone and everything. When Cancer has Leo all to themselves, they will start to see that Leo's gregarious personality pretends to be a lot bigger than they actually feel. Cancer will finally realize that their partner is just looking for approval—especially theirs—but that they do not want to ask for it. When Cancer comes to this realization, their eyes will fill with tears of compassion and understanding, which will never seem to go away. Crawl out of your shell, Cancer, and swallow your pride, Leo, so you are able to meet each other halfway in one another's arms—where water and fire defy the elemental laws and blend.

☼ ☼ ☼

CANCER & VIRGO

♋ 🤍 ♍

Aspect: Sextile
Elements: Water and earth
Modalities: Cardinal and mutable

The first time Cancer meets Virgo, they will immediately notice the sharp mind behind their clear eyes. Virgo will immediately feel understood and somehow comforted by the nurturing vibration Cancer emits. Virgo is ruled by the restless planet of Mercury, and Cancer is ruled by the ever-changing moon. Together, they will understand one another's uneasiness when entering a partnership of any kind because they both have reservations about giving their hearts away. It is in this commonality that they immediately find sanctuary with one another.

Virgos are notoriously single, while Cancers are in a constant state of working toward gaining a future spouse, family, and finances. Virgos are often afraid of losing their identity in a partnership, but there is something about the crab's lunar magic that draws them in. Some Virgos go willingly down the path of marital bliss with their Cancer, and others have the urge to fight it. What the virgin must understand is that they will lose their status of singularity but gain an incredible companion that not only makes a wonderful parent but also an incredible partner through thick and thin. If Cancer keeps it cool and understands that Virgo needs their alone time and if Virgo understands that Cancer needs quality time, this water and earth sign can do beautifully together. Their balance of love is much like when waves hit the shore. There will be patience required from both parties before they understand how to ebb and flow with each other and create a rhythm that is uniquely their own.

There will be days of tug-of-war between the crab and the virgin. One minute Virgo will be saying "goodbye," and the next they will be calling to come back. Most Cancers are laser focused on their careers, which will be a great distraction from Virgo's indecisiveness with their partnership. Virgos also come equipped with an incredible work ethic, and this will be a wonderful way to find independence in their relationship. The two will love coming home to talk about the things going on at their jobs. They will like waking up together, getting ready for the day with some music on, having their morning coffee, and then going their separate ways, knowing that they will be coming home to each other every night. They will find this autonomy in their partnership, and it will be the glue that holds them together. Having their own lives, along with the one they have with each other, will only make their love stronger.

Physically they are a beautiful match, and there is something serene about their sex. Virgo will need to learn to open themselves emotionally and must control their tendency to be cool with the crab. Cancer requires words of encouragement from the virgin. When Virgo can finally open up emotionally, they will absorb Cancer's lunar magic like the earth absorbs rain. Virgo is a mutable sign, meaning that they are wonderful with words, so if Virgo can choose to speak encouragement rather than analytical assessment, they will soon win their crab's heart. However, if Virgo decides to be critical, it will hurt Cancer into a retreat, which will send them into their shell and frustrate both parties. Virgo must learn that there is a time and place for certain criticisms to be made, and the bedroom is not one of them. Cancer must have patience and teach Virgo to make love with their heart instead of their head. Sex is not supposed to be perfect; it is supposed to be natural and even a little messy. These two would be wise to use Cancer's ruling orb, the moon, to bring magic to their union. On the next full moon, they should try to harness the lunar energy to deeply connect. There is something so enchanting about the way moonbeams shine on a Cancer's skin that makes them glow. There is a softness and fostering manner about Cancer that Virgo will not see until they start viewing them through their heart and soul.

When Virgo starts to really trust Cancer, they will see their delicate side, which is so beautiful and bright. If anyone can make it through a lot of changes together, it is these two. If they can go hand in hand through life, they will have so many beautiful things to show and teach one other. There may have been partners before Cancer that Virgo could not stand still with long enough to catch their breath, which made them realize that they would rather be alone. However, there is something about Cancer that makes them feel a calmness they so desperately need. It is within this serenity that Virgo wants to stay still for a while because Cancer's cool blue energy feels like home. Together, they form a dimensional relationship with multiple layers that only they will ever understand, which is just how they like it.

☼ ☼ ☼

CANCER & LIBRA

♋ ♡ ♎

Aspect: Square
Elements: Water and air
Modalities: Cardinal and cardinal

Love has a way of softening the hardest hearts or, in this case, the hardest shells. Cancer will instantly worry about Libra from the first day they start showing them their vulnerability. This is because Cancer cares so much—sometimes too much. Libra is ruled by Venus, the planet of love, which will harmonize beautifully with Cancer's ever-changing moods and make them feel emotionally secure in a way that they desperately need. The beginning of their love story will be a fairy tale filled with devotion and tranquility. Regardless of their differences, Libra will be tempted by the idea of marriage, which Cancer will gladly oblige. If Libra is evolved and in the right place in their life, they will make the decision to take the plunge with their watery-eyed crab, and this pair will have a sort of love that is straight from the heavens—one that even the angels envy. However, if Libra is not ready, they will drag this relationship through the mud of indecisiveness, which will be a treacherous roller coaster of emotions.

The crab and the scales have vastly different approaches on how to handle things both outside and inside their relationship. Cancer tends to take a more pessimistic approach, and Libra usually takes a more positive one. Eventually they will start to rub off on each other. Libra will become less gullible, and

Cancer will become more optimistic. Just as Libra needs to be in the right place for their fairy-tale ending to come true, Cancer does too. The crab needs to be emotionally stable enough to open up and not go into the relationship with fear and worry, automatically assuming that it will fail. Cancers can be their own worst enemy in this sort of way, but deep down they anxiously want to be vulnerable to give their love longevity. Cancer will need their Libra's charm and balance to help them get there.

Once Cancer does get there, they may become emotionally possessive, which brings us back to Libra being ready. Libra, like all air signs, loves freedom, so when they are out of sight, Cancer might think that their Libra is no longer thinking of them. Cancer must understand that Libra's element needs times of intermediate space and that when they go get some air to breathe, they are not plotting ways to leave forever. Libras enjoy missing the person they love, which gives themselves new space to love them even more. In Libra's case, absence truly does make the heart grow fonder. The sooner Cancer understands this, the sooner their possessiveness will fade, and it is then that Libra will want to make things happen. Ultimately they want the same things, such as marriage, love, and protection. It is how they get there that can be the challenge. The stars will need to align just right, but if they do, it is worth all the effort.

There are very few situations where these two could not mend their love, and one way that they are able to do that is by making love. Libra is wildly romantic in bed, and Cancer will relish every bit of it. They have a gentle lust for one another, and the anticipation of experiencing Cancer's soft side is enough to drive Libra wild. They know that there is more to Cancer than what they show on the surface, and they want to understand their silvery moonlit magic. Together, their hearts will feel full when they are physically one, and their gentle passion and trembling anticipation for each other is laced with peace and contentment. They can rediscover themselves through their physicality, which is enlightening and healing.

Their differences glare when it comes to the idea of permanency in love, but if they can formulate a way to adjust their styles to work cohesively, they can find a peaceful compromise. They are not familiar with the idea of conceding due to them both being influenced by the cardinal modality. They both want to take the lead, but if they can hold hands and operate together, as a team, they will find their stride. Libra must use their diplomacy to see all sides, and Cancer must use their intuition to find the best solution. If there is ever a separation between them, they will find their way back home to each other by remembering why they fell in love all over again. The trick for them is recognizing signs of discord between them before they are too far down the road of discontentment. If this is a leap that they are both in the right place to take, Libra can give Cancer the gift of emotional security, and the crab will give the scales the gift of trust. Their sentimental and imaginative natures will make all their dreams come true. Between Cancer's loony humor and Libra's charming smile, they can find sunshine among the gray days. Besides, they have the angels fighting for them to make it, and that, in itself, is a reason to keep their love alive.

☼ ☼ ☼

CANCER & SCORPIO

♋ ❤ ♏

Aspect: Trine
Elements: Water and water
Modalities: Cardinal and fixed

These two water signs will love each other from the start, regardless of whether this relationship starts as a friendship or a hot and heavy union. Scorpio will enjoy Cancer's tenderness, thoughtfulness, and the emotional safety they provide. Cancer will find refuge in Scorpio's passion, emotional depth, loyalty, and how they are always there for them when they need it most. Once these two start a union, it will most likely be forever because the crab and scorpion take their relationships very seriously. It will be rare that either one of them gets tired of the other because they have similar habits and comparable morals, which tie them strongly together. They will make a stimulating pair thanks to their cardinal and fixed modalities. Cancers are natural-born leaders, while Scorpios do not care to follow, but what is magical about the crab is their gentle approach in using their intuition rather than force, which coerces the guarded scorpion into feeling secure in their union.

Scorpio tends to be more confrontational than Cancer because of their traditional planetary ruler Mars's fearless approach. Cancer is ruled by the moon and, therefore, is gentler and more reserved, weighing out every possible outcome before making a final decision. This will be something that Scorpio can learn from because at times their decisions can be fueled by passion rather than logic. Inversely, Cancer's waxing and waning lunar caution can be way overboard, and Scorpio will teach the crab to fearlessly listen to their intuition rather than worry. When they do get in a rare argument, Cancer will be the one to initiate fixing it with their incredible sense of satire. The boiling anger that Scorpio possesses will vanish with Cancer's wit, which lights their world like the moon brightens up the dark sky. As long as the jokes are not directed toward Scorpio, the humor will be healing. Conversely, when Cancer gets in one of their cranky moods, which happen as often as the phases of the moon, Scorpio will have a way of coyly approaching them to pull them out of their funk.

Scorpio is intensely private, and Cancer is not one to put their business all out on the table either. Because of their discreetness, they will trust one another, and together they will enjoy sharing their lives as well as their deepest feelings and secrets. Of course, their discretion can bleed into their relationship, which can cause problems, especially for Scorpio. The two need to understand that some things are better left unsaid for the health of their relationship. Scorpio is a master of getting things out of people one way or another, and this will be extremely frustrating for Cancer. The crab may even retreat into their shell for a few days, which will then upset Scorpio even further, creating a vicious circle. However, their sex will bring healing and smooth over their quarrels.

Cancer and Scorpio will undoubtedly have incredible sexual chemistry because of the level of depth that they can achieve with one another. Sexually Scorpio is intense, and Cancer is perceptive. They enjoy the reassurance and security they feel when they become one, which is too deep and passionate for words to describe. They may even find themselves in tears because they have desired to feel this way with someone their whole lives. They understand that controlled passion is not passion at all, so when they are with one another, it is a freeing feeling of body and soul. The depth of two water signs connecting is a blessing in this way because their affection and intensity becomes transcending. When they are apart for too long, it can cause immense heartache, which is why they should work on the few things that cause them to separate. However hard things may get, their love for one another will prevail.

Cancer will love Scorpio's possessive way of caring for them because no matter what age they are, they enjoy being babied. Cancer has one thing in the zodiac that no other sign possesses, which is a hard exterior that protects them from Scorpio's stings. The crab will be able to forgive the scorpion because they obtain a true understanding of their emotional depth. They recognize that Scorpio's passionate outbursts come from a place of complication. After Scorpio is done with their tirades, Cancer will gently kiss them with understanding and then the tears will come. They will hold each other tight, and quickly Cancer will make a joke that will bring Scorpio to laughter. Cancer gets Scorpio like no one else can, which is what brings that level of safety they both desperately need. Cancer's nurturing ways make Scorpio feel like they have finally found a home. Scorpio becomes exhausted of always wearing their protective exterior, which gets heavy over time, but once Cancer is securely theirs, they can take off their shield and feel the freedom of vulnerability. They will never have to worry whether or not they will find a relationship that is as profound as they dreamed because they are both swimming in the deep end, and the water is just fine.

☼ ☼ ☼

CANCER & SAGITTARIUS

♋ 🫶 ♐

Aspect: Quincunx
Elements: Water and fire
Modalities: Cardinal and mutable

These two do not naturally have a lot in common, so most will wonder how they ever ended up together in the first place. The reason lies in the magic of the stars. Sagittarians are incredibly attracted to Cancer's lunar mysticism thanks to their quincunx aspect. Cancer has a crazy pull on the archer that even they do not understand. Centaurs are a naturally curious sun sign, and they find crabs mysterious, which gives them a primal urge to figure them out. Cancer will cast a moonlit spell on Sagittarius, which makes the archer dream of them when they are apart. Sagittarius will then put on their rose-colored glasses and jump right into Cancer's cool blue waters without a care in the world.

Once they swim around for a while, Cancer will want to anchor down, which will scare Sagittarius to their core; the idea of being tied down anywhere goes against their philosophy of how to live life. The archer has giant goals and ambitions for themselves, and ties would be restrictive and binding. Suddenly their magical Cancer starts to feel like a ball and chain, threatening to take away their freedom and individuality. Cancer finds ties to be cozy, familiar, and comforting, which, in turn, makes them feel safe and protected. While Cancer understands that the unknown can be exciting, they value the security and comforts of home. This also includes financial security, which is another thing they will have to work through together. It is not that Sagittarius does not make money. They just have a hard time holding on to it thanks to their overly generous Jupiterian nature. Archers also place the value of experiences over material items.

Because of these differences, this relationship usually works better when Sagittarius is a little older and has had a chance to sow some of their wild oats. If these two do end up together at a young age, the archer may leave a time or two, coming back because of the pull Cancer holds over them. However, if they truly want this to work, they are going to have to fight through the tough stuff and come to fair compromises. Throughout the years they will figure out how to do it if there is enough love between them. Sagittarius may settle in the suburbs for Cancer if they can take some trips throughout the year. In turn, Cancer will subtly lead the centaur to a home built on a foundation filled with intimate love. It is in that intimacy that they will heal any discord when they find themselves in troubled waters.

Sagittarius must learn how to let their actions speak louder than words in the bedroom because Cancer experiences things emotionally. Cancer wants to escape with their partner in a deep way through physical connection and tender sentiment, not impulsive fierceness. Cancer requires a bit of finesse, and Sagittarius will aim to please, which will comfort and flatter them. When they adjust, their sexual chemistry is a blessing to their relationship. Sagittarius is fiery and passionate, and Cancer's mystery will have them burning even hotter. There is a stillness and sweetness about the crab that melts the archer's large heart. Cancer works slowly and gently while still approaching their lovemaking in a strong way, showing Sagittarius that a whisper can prolong satisfaction and make it greater. Cancer's dreamlike qualities sooth and cool Sagittarius in ways they never imagined.

When it comes to conversation, Sagittarius will do most of the talking thanks to their mutable modality, but together they will have a wonderful sense of humor. It pays to have Sagittarius think before they speak so that they can take Cancer's sensitive nature into consideration. The crab's poignant spirit can overwhelm Sagittarius, and even though the centaur never means to hurt the crab's feelings, they have a habit of putting their foot in their mouth. Cancer should keep this in mind before calling it quits. Thanks to their cardinal modality, Cancer would like to lead, and no matter how much Sagittarius talks, Cancer will want to get their way. Sagittarius should let Cancer do the leading so they can do the talking.

Over time, their love will only grow more intensely. Cancer will deeply respect Sagittarius's courage and honesty while trusting them with their sensitive heart, and Sagittarius will appreciate their cautious Cancer, who saves them from mistakes they would have made. They will learn to trust each other, which is the strongest blessing a partnership can have. Throughout the years, Cancer will get Sagittarius to realize that home is where the heart is, and Sagittarius will help Cancer realize that there is more to life than the cookie-cutter standards that society holds us to. There is a whole world out there that Sagittarius wants to discover, and they would prefer to do that with Cancer by their side. Together, they will come up with a version of reality that has a little bit of both of their wishes. Then they will be able to live their happily ever after.

☼ ☼ ☼

CANCER & CAPRICORN

Aspect: Opposite
Elements: Water and earth
Modalities: Cardinal and cardinal

The crab and the sea goat are 180 degrees apart on the karmic wheel of life, meaning there will be times of immense joy and times of opportunity for growth in their partnership. If they are on their best behavior, they can be an unbreakable match. Cancer is ruled by the moon, which represents dreams, change, movement, memories, reflections, softness, and dependency. Capricorn is ruled by Saturn, which represents realities, stability, caution, patience, determination, hardness, and self-sufficiency. Capricorns, by nature, are somewhat cold and suspicious, but sensitive Cancer can provide a healing space of comfort, love, and understanding for the sea goat. Like all opposing blends, a choice must be made by Cancer and Capricorn as to which of these competing forces—the moon or Saturn—will become the dominant energy of their association, or their love life will become a battlefield.

Their opposition can cause their relationship to be complicated, but nothing gained easily is worthwhile, which is a motto they both live by. Opposites are strongly attracted to each other and naturally complement one another. Each has what the other needs, wants, and desires and is, therefore, secretly anxious to acquire the qualities that their partner obtains. The crab and the sea goat each possess what the other lacks, so if they can be generous to one another, they can find mountains of happiness. The trick with this opposing partnership is finding a balance between their hot and cold natures. Cancer is the hot summer, and Capricorn is the cold winter. If they can compromise and meet each other halfway between their seasons, they will accomplish a temperate spell of their own.

Cancers require emotional security, a peaceful relationship, and a partner to sympathize with their deep—and sometimes moody—emotions. Capricorn is intensely ambitious and genuinely values comfort and security, which makes this sun sign truly able to fulfill all of Cancer's deepest wants and needs. This is one thing that will hold them together, and it attracts them initially. They also share a strong attachment to their families, which will be their glue in many ways. Cancer's devotion to home and family will please Capricorn, who is equally loyal to family ties. Family will be the number one factor in all their decision-making, which is why marriage is common for this pairing.

Both Cancer and Capricorn vibrate to a cardinal modality, meaning they like to lead. The sea goat prefers to lead discreetly, and the crab tends to lead in subtle ways as well. Their mutually shared leadership motivation may be hidden when they first meet, but it will not take long for them to figure it out. It can be difficult when there are two cooks in the kitchen, but learning how to support each other is key. Capricorn has loads of strength and determination, and Cancer is incredibly sweet and inspiring. They are both very hard workers, and their careers will be a big part of their lives. Many of these couples will meet at or through work. It is not uncommon to find these two sun signs building business empires, collecting antiques, or actively engaging in politics. This is a couple often found in bookstores—as the owners, of course—and in banks, sitting on the board of directors. They have similar views when it comes to money, and both enjoy saving it to spend on investments and things for their home. They are both CEO material, and that also translates into their oneness as well.

Sex between these sun signs is deep, steady, and sensual. Their physicality makes the world seem like a more beautiful place, and it enriches their relationship immensely. Cancer quenches Capricorn's every thirst, and Capricorn is always there for Cancer as their rock. Their love for one another passes the test of time due to their opposing nature and undying attraction to each other. This will make them both feel safe, which helps them become vulnerable with each other. Being that Cancer is a water sign, they often possess a power to come in touch with their emotions while having sex more than Capricorn can because of their water element. Capricorn has a strong sex drive that Cancer will be more than happy to please, but Cancer will bring the sensitivity and imagination that Capricorn lacks into the bedroom, which will make for a beautiful paring and bring oneness to a level that Capricorn never dreamed of. Their physicality with one another will create a robust and affectionate bond.

Their inherent traits are neither similar nor dissimilar. Rather, they are complementary of one another. They both lead indirectly while hiding their tender cores, creating a quiet and steady suspense between them that they can strongly feel. Cancer's laughter is contagious and irresistible, and there is something about the crab's sense of humor that softens the sea goat, making their disciplined emotions begin to warm. The crab feels a powerful magnetic tug, telling them that they have finally found a safe home that is protected by their tough yet loving sea goat. Together, through love, compromise, family ties, and a lot of work, they can solve the riddle of opposing love.

☼ ☼ ☼

CANCER & AQUARIUS

Aspect: Quincunx
Elements: Water and air
Modalities: Cardinal and fixed

Aquarius is an air sign and symbolized as the water bearer, the mystical healer who bestows water to the land. Cancer is a water sign that longs for a partner like Aquarius to bear them. Because of their different alchemy, they will constantly challenge each other in strange ways, yet they are oddly intertwined due to the magnetic vibrations between their ruling planets, the yin moon and yang Uranus. When they meet, they will both see something in each other's eyes that the other needs. Aquarius will be in a sea of people when Cancer first meets them, and the crab will quickly learn that Aquarius has a lot of friends that they hold in the highest regard. Everyone is an Aquarius's friend, including the one that they love, so they will convince Cancer to join their posse, which is where Cancer will have to start if they want to win their heart. Aquarius is slow to fall in love, but when they do, the friendship aspect of their relationship will never fade.

Just as Aquarius feels strongly about friendship, Cancer feels strongly about family. While Cancer does not necessarily live in the past, they are an innately nostalgic soul that likes to visit it frequently, and Aquarius may not understand this. Aquarius is always looking to the future, and they may feel like Cancer needs to grow up and grow out of this. In fact, Aquarius almost feels as though Cancer wishes they could be a kid again, and well, they probably do. Cancer is an emotional and imaginative creature that likes to reminisce and visit sweet memories in their psyche. At times, Aquarius makes Cancer feel like they need to swallow their moods, which Cancer experiences as cold and heartless and can resent them for. It is not that Aquarius lacks sympathy. Their heart does have feeling. However, Aquarius tends to scatter their emotions thinly across a broad set of issues instead of concentrating them on one idea or thought. When Aquarius realizes that they are hurting the one they love, they will try to make it up to their crab in any way they can, and Cancer should give them credit for trying.

These two are a diverse and modern couple. They are both incredibly changeable, and no one will ever know what is next—not even them. A predictable world is not one that they live in because they both have wild imaginations and change their moods with the blink of an eye. Aquarius loves to reinvent who they are and what they will look like, and Cancer is able to relate, seeing that their emotions are incredibly unpredictable as well. Cancer likes that the water bearer is zany, different, and interesting because it keeps them on their toes. Cancer loves that Aquarius vibrates on an unexpected wavelength that they themselves would have never experienced. The day that Aquarius met Cancer, they knew that the crab needed their energy to bring a splash of color to their bluish gray life. Cancer likes to be the leader, but Aquarius has no interest in being told what to do. They would rather follow their own winding, twisting path, not caring if it was the "right" way or not.

They give and receive love in very different ways, which is something they can learn and absorb from one another. Cancer's emotional expressiveness and deep sexual desires may scare Aquarius away while simultaneously intriguing them. It is not that Aquarius is afraid to feel; they just find sex with Cancer to be emotionally over the top. Once Aquarius realizes that the crab needs these sentiments to feel close to them, Aquarius may bend, but it will take them some time. One thing that will connect them sexually is that they are both interested in various forms of the whimsical and far out. This will be a shimmering link between them that will bring a colorful ecstasy of passion that is known only to people who invite their imaginations into their sex lives. Cancer's lovemaking style is classic, while Aquarius's is innovative. Combined, their sexual alchemy is intoxicating to one another. They also bring their humor along, making their sex a mix of folly and release. It is unique, unpredictable, deep, and fulfilling.

Their powerful chemistry is what draws them to each other from the beginning, and no matter how much time goes on, Aquarius will seem elusive and just beyond Cancer's grasp. As time passes, Cancer's cardinal energy will sweetly take over, and the crab will rule the way astrology intended them to. It just takes time, love, and a lot of patient understanding. Cancer will learn that there is no use trying to confine Aquarius's air essence into a neat little box. The sooner Cancer understands this, the sooner a beautiful harmony will come between them. While they are moving through life, the water bearer will have to remember that it is okay to stop and look back with their crab on occasion. Then they can convince Cancer to catch up to them by explaining that they can see a bright star on the horizon. The star is their future, which is a brilliant beacon of family, friends, and love.

☼ ☼ ☼

CANCER & PISCES

♋ ♡ ♓

Aspect: Trine
Elements: Water and water
Modalities: Cardinal and mutable

Even when these two are physically apart, they are still together because once they meet, there will be an inseparable bond tied through the stars to one another's watery soul. If they ever do part, they will never completely lose one another, which makes most wonder why they would ever separate in the first place. The first reason is that Cancers love security—both financially and emotionally. Pisces has the emotional part down no problem, but the financial part is a maybe that depends on where Pisces is in their life's journey. The fish prefers to live in their dream world, but sometimes they never turn their dreams into reality, which Cancer will struggle with. The crab wants a place to call home, a family, and a good savings account for rainy days. Pisces is generous (sometimes too generous) with their money, giving it to friends and family whenever they are in need, and this will make Cancer worry because they like to pinch their pennies.

The other struggle comes from the fact that they both have incredibly deep and morose moods. Pisces is like a sponge and absorbs any of Cancer's pain, so if the crab starts making their fish sad, they will be two very somber sea creatures. Cancer does not absorb things the way Pisces does because their shell bounces the feelings back, not allowing any of them past their exterior. Therefore, when Pisces is having a down day, Cancer may retreat to preserve themselves. They both need to learn how to bring each other up and out of sadness for this relationship to be successful. The gifts they have that can help with this include Pisces's empathy and Cancer's humor. Once they learn how to do this for each other, they will be one another's strongest companions.

Cancer requires their partner to nurture them in many ways, and they will find that their Pisces is full of tender love and care. Pisces is an unselfish sun sign, so putting Cancer first will be easy for them. Pisces will wear many hats in this relationship. They will be a friend, confidant, lover, and emotional springboard, creating a healing space for Cancer. Pisces will delicately kiss all the crab's fears, burdens, and scars of the past, healing their worried soul. Cancer feels safer with Pisces than possibly anyone they have ever met in their life. Cancer is a worrywart, and odds are Pisces will not understand why the crab concerns themselves about things that they have no control over. To Pisces, that is a complete waste of energy, and the fish would prefer to keep their spirit serene and let the higher powers take care of things. Pisces is quite fabulous at finding the best in everything, even if it does not appear to be as shiny and wonderful as most people would think. Pisces will assure Cancer that they have all the potential in the world, and they mean it. Pisces has an uncanny way of just knowing things because their intuition is one to truly be reckoned with.

Cancers are gentle and quiet, but they work hard. They will make Pisces feel safe emotionally and financially. Cancers are intelligent and have a hilarious sense of humor that will make the fish laugh on a regular basis. This is something Pisces's soul needs. Cancer is the perfect blend that Pisces always dreamed of, and it makes their eyes well with tears of joy when Cancer knows what they need without words. There is truly a bonding magic about being with someone who can anticipate your needs and feelings.

Sex is a natural part of their relationship that will heal their love when troubles arise. Pisces's spirituality and Cancer's emotional sweetness make their union truly unique. Pisces has an innate longing to feel needed, and Cancer does that in many ways because they really do need them. These two will quickly become each other's favorite person in the world—and for good reason. When these two make love to one another, it will be something of great beauty and depth. They wholly become one person physically but also spiritually as well. They will long for that closeness again immediately after separating because they are beautifully in tune with one another, and their love feels new and fresh every time, even after decades of love.

With this pair, it will seem as if they always know each other's secrets and are able to make one another's wishes come true. It will feel as if they know each other's body and soul even better than their own, and their monogamy will be too magical to become bored of. When Pisces is lost in their mutable sparkling imagination, Cancer will sprinkle their cardinal moon dust on them to make their dreams into reality. When Pisces gets stuck in the reefs of missed opportunity, Cancer will swim along and help them find the right direction. With Cancer's help, Pisces can travel through the mystical waters of life and merge their wonderful world with Cancer's. When Cancer is working to make things happen, Pisces will remind the crab to not worry about tomorrow because their love will last many lifetimes.

☼ ☼ ☼

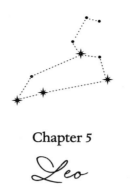

Chapter 5

Leo

Leo's love archetype is the creator of love. They are an inspirational, aggressive, dynamic, and fervent lover who brings magnificence into love through passion and creativity. Leo's lesson in love is to impart that love is pleasure and absorb that love is humble.

Element	Fire
Modality	Fixed
Polarity	Yang, positive, and masculine
Mantra	"I will."
Hue	Gold
Deity	Apollo, god of the sun
Glyph	♌
Flowers	Sunflower, marigold, and hibiscus
Tree	Palm
Jewel	Ruby
Crystals	Carnelian and tiger's-eye
Fragrance	Neroli
Body Parts	The heart, back, and spinal cord
Animals	Lions and other cats
Food & Herbs	Meat, rice, honey, saffron, peppermint, rosemary, rue, hawthorn, mugwort, turmeric, and tropical fruits, such as coconuts, bananas, and pineapples

Leo's Ruling Orb: The Sun

The sun in love rules physical energy and character. In partnerships it reveals father figures, men, and masculine energy. The sun represents the life force of the physical body and is at the center of everyone's chart. Its placement is what flavors a large majority of your personality, and it is one of the most important factors when looking at overall compatibility. The sun rules Leo, which gives them a grand aura and bright personality. They have dominating characteristics that exude power in a life-giving way. Leo is a fixed fire sign, just as our sun is a fixed star, and is wonderful at feeding warmth to people's egos through encouragement.

Leo Mythology

In mythology, Leo was depicted as the Nemean lion, who was killed by Hercules during his first of twelve labors. According to myth the Nemean lion had an impenetrable skin. Hercules got around this potentially serious obstacle by wrestling the lion and strangling it to death. He then removed one of its claws and used it to skin the animal. From then on, Hercules wore the skin of the Nemean lion as protection.

Leo's Positive Qualities and Negative Forms

Leo's positive qualities are warmth, generosity, nobility, strength, loyalty, leadership, and gentle tenderness. They possess the protective energy of someone strong defending the weak. Expressed in their negative forms, they become arrogant with false pride, vain, bossy, conceited, and unrestrained.

How a Leo Loves

The way a Leo loves is passionately and creatively, bringing a gold munificence to their romance while displaying the brightest aura in the world. Seeing a Leo in love is like staring at the sun, and their joy is contagious when romance is coursing through their blue blood. Lions are naturally altruistic and always believe in fairy-tale endings. Their large hearts contain copious amounts of fervor and power toward the ones they adore—as long as they are being fed the attention and accolades that they desire. They require loyalty in complete totality and wish for the fire of their love to have bright flames of enthusiasm. Therefore, they expect a lot from their partners but are incredibly generous lovers in return.

In astrology Leos rule the heart and spine, and they are strongly connected to their heart chakra, which is located at the center of the spine at heart level. The heart chakra acts as the individual's center of compassion, empathy, love, and forgiveness, which are all themes in how a Leo selflessly loves. This sun sign can warm the hardest of hearts and make them unhurt, unstruck, and unbeaten. Leo follows their heart over their head in most cases, and they do not hide the way they feel. Their sincerity and benevolence make them wonderful companions, which is why many are attracted to them. However, they are not afraid to ask for what they want, especially from their partners.

Leos naturally dominate any relationship that they are in and will not even be aware of it most times, which can be unpleasant. However, their enthusiasm and gregariousness make it easy to quickly forgive them. Leos are not afraid to roar from the mountaintop to profess their love and wear their partner proudly on their arm. They genuinely enjoy spoiling with gifts and tokens of appreciation. The way they love is by creatively producing a beautiful fairy-tale world to live in, as though it were out of a movie. When Leo is creating this utopia for themselves and their partner, some of the details can get lost, but if their partner can have one foot in reality, all will be just fine.

Leos are incredibly protective over the ones they love due to their chivalrous nature, and they will gallantly fight for glory and loyalty. Even though these sun signs are innately royal, they will gladly sacrifice themselves in the name of love. Leos pride themselves on being a step above the norm in everything they do, and the way they love is no exception. They have larger-than-life ideals and want a devotion that is total and epic—a relationship that most could only dream of. Because of their fixed modality, Leos are determined and headstrong and will not settle for anything less. Therefore, if they do find what their hearts desire, they will go to the ends of the earth to make them theirs. For all their drama and excitement, they have an ability to show affection like a child, which is refreshing and delightful.

Life will never be dull with this regal creature thanks to their relentless pursuit of excellence. If you can find it in yourself to allow them to be the center of your universe, you will not be disappointed in the way you are repaid, and life will be filled with gilded glitz and glamour. Every day will feel cinematic in regard to the people you will meet, the parties you will go to, the surprise gifts you will get, and lavish dinners you will receive. An enchanted life with a Leo is not so far fetched. There is nothing petty about the way a Leo lives or loves, so when they invite the one they want forever into their life, their story will be filled with charm, drama, passion, and thrill. The way a Leo loves is experienced like the sun's golden rays warming your skin after a cold night. The reverence of a Leo to the one they adore is nothing short of opulence.

How to Spot a Leo

Leos are undoubtedly the easiest zodiac sign to spot. Maybe it is the way their grand aura greatly projects and easily fills a room or the way their larger-than-life personality commands everyone's attention, or maybe what really gives them away is their large Cheshire cat grin that can heat you from the inside out. Whatever it is, their love of life is insatiable, contagious, and bright, giving them a distinctive glow to their face. Somehow the sunshine always seems to be dappled through their sizable mane. Most Leos have a wild head of hair with a bit of curl or kink to it. Some Leos are blue eyed, but the majority have brown eyes that are often round, laughing, and soft. They say that the eyes are the window to the soul, but Leo's eyes are the window to their oversized heart.

Leos have this way about them that is engaging and inspiring to everyone around. They are strong, dignified, and determined. They always walk proudly and talk with grace and intensity. They naturally attract a crowd of followers, subjects, friends, confidants, and lovers. It is rare that you will ever see these characters out on their own. As a result, it is also uncommon to find a Leo sans a lover for two reasons. The first is that they are an incredible catch, and the second is that they prefer to go through life with a king or queen at their side. The sun forgets to shine when their love life runs dry because romance instinctively runs through their veins.

Lions cannot help acting superior or dramatically. It is simply in their noble nature. They are royalty and prefer to be treated as such. It would be impossible to ignore them in a group of people because they stand out immediately. Take a minute to stop and notice the strong effect that they have on everyone; it is truly fascinating to watch. It is impossible to talk to a Leo, or even stand next to one, without finding yourself pulling your shoulders back and standing up a bit straighter than you normally would. Yet, to win them over is quite simple: compliment them.

They love to be leaned on and looked at as a source of strength. They will always be an advocate and defender of the underdog whenever they are given a chance. They feel called to help the needy and fight for the helpless. They are courageous in this way, never stopping until they have fulfilled their conquest of justice. They have an energy about them that is experienced like the protection of an older sibling. Yes, Leos do love the finer and more extravagant things in life, but their hearts are also wonderfully generous and beautifully charitable.

These royal cats are fiercely loyal friends and extraordinary lovers, and their vibrant personality will be adored by many. If you can look past their superiority and ego, you will see a golden heart that brims with love, bravery, and benevolence. So, if you happen to notice a character with an imperial disposition that has a grand glow of yellow, gold, and orange rays dancing around them, you may just be among royalty—a Leo that is.

How to Lose a Leo

Leos take a lot of pride in the way they present themselves, and they need their partner to do the same. They are the royalty of the zodiac and want to be treated as such. Leos do not appreciate their partner making jokes at other people's expense, especially their own. If you act like a joker, they will find someone else to court. If you embarrass them in front of others, it may just be "off with your head." Leos love attention and adoration, especially with a crowd. They like to be in the action and require a partner who is dazzling when it comes to being in social settings. That is as long as you are not more impressive than them, of course. If you are constantly trying to one-up a Leo, you are not going to make it far with them. They do not appreciate someone who is always trying to dim their light; they prefer to radiate positivity and need someone on their same wavelength.

Leo requires a partner who can keep up with their bold and fiery auras and support their larger-than-life personality. They need a fan for their flames and someone who keeps life exciting. If you are boring, they will look elsewhere for a good time and a partner who can keep them on their toes. Confidence is key with this sun sign because they project their big personalities, which requires their lovers to hold their own. That means confidence on the streets and in the sheets. If you seem insecure and unsure of yourself, you will be a pretty big turnoff for this sun sign. Lions like to hunt for their dinner, so if you make yourself too easy to obtain, they will think that just anyone can have you, and

Leos are not into just anyone. Compliments will get you far, but insincere accolades and "game" will get you only as far as they can throw you. Drop the act and take the time to truly admire something about them that makes them feel special. They are smart enough to tell if you are not genuine from a mile away.

If keeping a royal happy seems difficult, that is because it is. However, they repay their partners for their efforts tenfold. Leos like to provide and like to be provided for. They are by no means shallow, but rather they appreciate artistic qualities and bold visions. They are the only fixed fire sign in the zodiac, which means they are proud and often willful. They seek stability and do not like to be met with resistance. Leos have big plans, and they need a partner who is supportive of their dreams. They desire a fairy-tale type of romance that is filled with large gestures of love and valor. They need a king or queen by their side who is always down to rule simultaneously. If you are not up for the challenge, that's okay. There are plenty of others in line for the throne.

How to Bed a Leo

Bow down because you are in the presence of true royalty. A Leo's fiery, regal aura is enough to make your skin tingle with delight. This is not a sun sign for the faint of heart. They ooze sex appeal and are strong, powerful, and magnetic. The lion shines like the golden sun, and they want to hear about it too. They love being center stage, and compliments will make them purr. They are the kings and queens of the jungle—as well as the rulers in the bedroom. Their touch is warm, and their hearts are made of pure gold. Being deemed fit to bed a Leo is not an easy task, but if you make the cut, it can be done.

Leos love the company of many people, so if you are looking for one of these majestic creatures, you will find them right in the center of a group of people, laughing and dancing. They love activity and entertaining surroundings. While it is true that this sign loves admiration, loyalty is a requirement. If they bestow their allegiance upon you, it will be hard for that bond to be broken. If you want to date royalty, you must be royalty. Measly attempts will not be sufficient for this imperial sun sign. Leos never mean to make anyone feel like they are less than them, but Leos inherently are a step above the rest. These are cold, hard facts, but you will soon understand that Leos are anything but cold. If you can spoil, compliment, and caress them—cherish and admire them—then you have a shot of winning their heart and hand. And if you are lucky, they will bring you to bed, which is where the real fun begins.

Leo's dramatic sexual nature and loud roar are provocative in the bedroom, and they could even wake the neighbors during their late-night escapades. Sex with a Leo is one rowdy ride. Leo's bed is typically luxurious with silk sheets surrounded by gold trinkets and candles with tropical scents. Leo loves dancing, so a striptease could very well be part of foreplay. Leo is known for their wild mane, and hair pulling could also be a turn-on for them. Leo's sexual character carries a bright, spicy propensity. They confront their sexual efforts with loads of scintillating passion, a strong ego, and a dominating attitude. Dramatic sex is a necessity in their love life. Leo rules the heart, which is where their desire originates, and this makes their sexuality thrive with magnitude and carnality. Leo is proud and dominating, but they also carry a heart of gold. Their sexual energy indicates a colorful and fiery enthusiasm that enjoys pleasure in every imaginable way.

Leo is a fire sign, and this element is known to have powerful and hot sex. They have the stamina to last for hours due to their undying fervor. Working on your cardio before going to bed with a Leo is always suggested. Otherwise, keeping up with the energy of a lion may leave you winded. Make the sex all about them, and they will gladly return the favor. Sex is about pleasure to a Leo, so do not over complicate it with too much emotion. Leos are proud, so if you ever bruise their ego in the bedroom, you may just see their claws come out. They are willing to try everything under the sun, but just make sure you approach them with new ideas and suggestions in a fun and relaxed way. They will scream with dramatic delight if you are able to pleasure their own fantasies as well. Acquiring a Leo is not an easy task, but if you can do it, you will get a taste of the finer things in life and in the bedroom. Walking around with a Leo is like walking around with a celebrity. Everyone wants a piece of them, and you will feel so lucky that they are all yours.

☼ ☼ ☼

LEO & LEO

♌ 🫀 ♌

Aspect: Conjunct
Elements: Fire and fire
Modalities: Fixed and fixed

All hail the most royal couple of them all—the lion pride is here. Two Leos create a loving and protective relationship that is filled with loyalty and devotion. Their outgoing personalities will attract many, and both have loads of friends and acquaintances that will fill their majestic court. They are a warm, generous, bright, and loving couple that exudes an energy as bright as the sun. Together, they will have heaps of happiness, which they will perpetually share with each other, brightening one another's lives on the darkest of days. Their story is truly an enchanted fairy-tale story filled with drama and adventure.

The clouds will only roll in when they cannot share the limelight. They equally need attention and will have to learn to share the spotlight for their adoring fans. Their friends get addicted to their fun, warm, and bold personalities, so they will need to make it a point to schedule alone time for one another. If they forget to do this, they will never end up having any time to gain a deeper and more intimate relationship. Leos are always performing, joking, and entertaining their admirers, and they often feel that they do not have time to humble themselves to a more serious and personal level. Therefore, it can even be hard for two Leos to communicate the way they feel because they fear that they may not be worthy of their Leo companion. What they must remember is that a healthy and whole relationship consists of being vulnerable with one another, and that means admitting flaws, feelings, and mistakes. Humbleness can be hard for the regal lion, but there is also something freeing about it, which will, in turn, bring them closer to their counterpart. They should both keep in mind that humility is better than a lifetime of loneliness. Physical oneness is one way for them to build their bond.

These two fire signs might not get much sleep in the bedroom, and odds are their sex will be something that no earth, air, or water sign could ever fathom. There will be loads of passion, affection, romance, and joy in their lovemaking. They will worship and admire one another just like they should. Leo rules the heart, and when you have two hearts as beautiful as theirs, sex will be as rich as red velvet cake. The way they make love is warm, lovely, and simply perfect. There is no romance sacrificed with two Leos behind closed doors. The way they connect is filled with theatrics and over-the-top spectacles. These sun signs love to break up to make up, and there is something about the drama of it all that makes it exciting. In their rich passion, they are able to renew their connection over and over again.

When two Leos link their lives, there will naturally be some power struggles. They innately need to be respected and obeyed, which is great when they are both on the same page, but it is troublesome when they are not. Like with all conjunct couples, the lesson is to see the best and worst of yourself reflected back by your partner. These cats will start mirroring each other, making it easy to see where the flaws are and area of opportunities lie, so they can adjust and become the rulers they were always meant to be. They like to live big, and they want someone whom they can do that with, and who would be better to rule by their side than another royal member of the court? The trick to their harmony is remembering that they need to share power because they are both completely capable and noble. If a line is ever crossed, they should call a truce, rather than go to war, to keep peace in the kingdom.

Sometimes pride can be a problem with this sun sign, and there will be days when they mutually hurt one another with their supremacy. It can be hard for them to take their crowns off and humble themselves, even with each other. However, they are both incredibly warm, caring, and deeply forgiving once they pledge their allegiance. They must remember to love one another consistently, compliment each other daily, make love frequently, and not overlook scheduling quality time for just the two of them. They should recognize and be grateful that they met someone that encompasses beauty, boldness, and a heart of gold as they do. Once a benevolent balance is found, they will live happily ever after and reign together. After all it is their kingdom, and we are all just members of their court.

☼ ☼ ☼

LEO & VIRGO

♌ ◈ ♍

Aspect: Semisextile
Elements: Fire and earth
Modalities: Fixed and mutable

It is the way that Virgo looks at Leo that will send a chill up their usually warm spine. Virgo has a cool glance and beautiful eyes that are so clear that Leo will feel as though they have become see-through. Virgo's features and energy are composed and tranquil, putting Leo at ease. Virgo is too polite to criticize Leo, but they can see right through the lion's vividly colored personality. Virgo is so gentle, courteous, and endearing that Leo admires them, and Virgo makes Leo feel worshipped, which is the perfect distraction from all the Virgo editing that the lion knows is going on.

Virgo will enjoy Leo's bold and warm personality, but at first it will feel like they are drinking from a fire hose. However, with some time and observation, Virgo learns that, much like themselves, Leo possesses introspection and self-discipline. Virgo will be obliged to tell Leo how strong and smart they are, but they will also have a knack for criticizing as well. Leo should not take it personally because Virgo criticizes everyone, including themselves. The critiquing remarks will be the one thing that Leo will not appreciate. They prefer to focus on the positives, especially when it comes to themselves. Leo can teach Virgo to quit being so hard on them both, but if Virgo cannot do this, they may lose their lion for good. However, with Leo they usually will see the good in them, and Virgo will, uncharacteristically, be very tolerant of the lion's flaws. Virgo is subtle, and Leo is not, so the lion needs to be careful not to overpower their virgin by checking in with them to make sure they are doing well. It is easy for Virgo to adore Leo's sunny and generous nature, and Virgo will learn that there is not one bit of insincerity in Leo's actions, including the actions in the bedroom.

When it comes to sex with these two, Virgo is cool and Leo is hot. This pair will need to use their whole hearts to achieve fulfillment, but it is certainly possible. Leos are passionate lovers and are sexual, erotic, and a load of fun in bed. Leo will make Virgo feel more relaxed with them than ever before, but for this to work, Virgo will need to warm up a little bit to match Leo's spicy and wild sexual behavior. There is something natural and cozy about their romping that will have Virgo's naturally cool nature thawed out in no time. Virgo's pureness is a total turn-on for Leo, and the virgin's responsiveness and gentle nature will only help that more. Leo's mind and heart will open to Virgo, showing them the best side of their regal nature. Leo physically puts out so much energy, while Virgo mentally uses a lot of energy, which will have them sleeping a lot. This equates to frequent opportunities for lovemaking.

When they do make it out of the house, Leo will love to show Virgo off, especially how smart they are. Leo is proud to be with an intellectual. Leo has a lot of friends, which Virgo can find overwhelming, but there is nearly nothing Virgo's sharp mind cannot handle. Virgo will not put up with rudeness of any sort, so Leo should be mindful about bringing their pristine partner around any friends that would give them a hard time. Leo is grateful for Virgo's editing nature because in many ways they become a better person when Virgo is around. Their composed sweetness and fascinating personality are calming gifts to Leo, while the lion's bright personality and optimistic look at the future are their gifts to Virgo. Leo has a way of reminding Virgo that constantly striving for perfection is an imperfection in itself. It removes the charm of contrast and all the exciting textures formed by light and shadow from life, leaving only a flat, dull, and unexciting existence. Leo adds so much sparkle and color to the Virgo's monochromatic comfort, which makes the virgin realize that flawlessness is not always necessarily equated to happiness.

Virgo is sure to grow more tenderly tolerant of Leo's independent, impulsive temperament as they become more familiar, and if Leo is patient, they will notice that Virgo takes a shy pride in their beauty and accomplishments. The love between Leo and Virgo is like a flame that burns slowly but steadily, growing brighter every year if it is carefully tended to and shielded from the wind. Virgo's spirit lives in a peaceful stillness, whereas Leo's spirit lives in a wildfire. Virgo's energy can be a cool and restful place for Leo, while Leo's vitality can melt the ice around Virgo's heart. The lion can come to learn that Virgo can be incredibly kind and touching. Their actions come from a place of sincerity, which is worth its weight in gold, and Leo loves gold. When things start to feel a little too uptight and stuffy, it will be up to Leo to impulsively throw open the windows so the sunshine can pour in and give their love a livelier feeling. With collaboration they can make this unassuming love last.

☼ ☼ ☼

LEO & LIBRA

♌ ✦ ♎

Aspect: Sextile
Elements: Fire and air
Modalities: Fixed and cardinal

Leos have a spicy nature that is mixed with a healthy splash of bossiness. Libras have a sweet nature and always come packaged with a dash of indecisiveness. Leos enjoy being seen, while Libras enjoy a good debate. Leos create the fire, and Libras contribute the air. Their combined elemental energy results in a fair amount of warm-to-hot conversational breezes between them. Leo downright loves admiration, but what this royal sun sign will have to learn quickly about their Libra is that they take a long time to make up their mind on just about anything. Leo should understand that Libra requires intelligent discussion to get to conclusions in life and in love. If Leo can handle that, it will create a lovely relationship. Balance, peace, and harmony are a holy trinity to Libra's idea of a perfect partnership. Fairness is also a sacred virtue to Libra, which Leo will appreciate and admire.

There will be an extravagant amount of communication on various levels between them, and a genuine amity will flourish. Harmony between them will be easily achieved more so than with other sun signs thanks to their friendly sextile love aspect. This sextile vibration blesses them with a nearly unending stream of opportunities for friendship and alliance. When they join forces, Leo and Libra can achieve almost anything from a successful love affair or marriage to a sound friendship or business venture. Their elements give Libra the power to flame Leo into a brighter torch, and Leo can then light the way of Libra's cardinal direction, which both will greatly benefit from.

Libra possesses the instinct for knowing exactly how to handle Leo's ego, and this instinct is called flattery. Libras rarely command but rather coyly suggest. Leo has no idea that they are being swayed because they are unable to see past Libra's charm. There are times when Libra's continual optimism irritates some, but Leo adores it. They both also share a deep need for creative expression, preferably in the arts, but they can both be just as happily occupied running an empire as well. Each of them is more content when running the show, which can cause tension. Libra likes to be in charge because they are a cardinal sign of leadership. Leo likes to be in charge because, well, how can royalty not be in charge? Lions were not born under the cardinal modality, but they were born under a fixed one, and when you have a "fixed egotist," it adds up to the same thing as a leader. If any of Leo and Libra's basic needs are denied by the other, Leo can become unhappy and arrogant, while Libra can become cranky and argumentative.

Libra will have to remember to give Leo an adequate amount of respect and admiration, which is not always an easy task. Still, Libra can turn on their charm to accomplish it. No one can pay a compliment more sweetly than Libra, and no one can appreciate it more than Leo. Together, they can tend to be extravagant and lean toward luxuries, which they will both work hard to acquire. Libra admires Leo's courage and willingness to move mountains to make their life amazing and exciting. Leo demands happiness from life and love, while Libra expects it as only natural. There is a difference between "demanding" and "expecting." Not much, but a difference.

Both Leo and Libra love grand gestures of sentiment, such as gorgeous gifts, dozens of roses, and fancy dinners. They both appreciate romance, and neither of them lacks any. Sex is nothing short of splendid with these sun signs, and Libra will be able to fulfill Leo's junglelike desires with ease and pleasure. What may come as a surprise is that Libra's sex drive will be higher than the lazy lion's, so Leo had better keep up with Libra. This pair's oneness is pleasurable and almost always followed by a good nap. There are not two sun signs who love to nap more than them. It would be wise for them to invest in a nice comfortable bed—it will get a lot of use.

These two will enjoy looking at each other's attractive features and listening to one another's lovely voice. Leo will love kissing Libra's dimpled smile and heeding to their musical expression. Libra always smells sweet, and their intoxicating aura will be of cotton candy hues. Libra will adore Leo's wild head of hair, their joyful laugh, and the way they can fill up a room with their bright and golden aura. These two will never lose interest in one another as they always seem to find something fascinating to talk about. Libra has loads of wisdom to share, and Leo will always make them feel like royalty. The sun-ruled Leo will loyally protect, and the Venus-ruled Libra will charmingly sooth. This pair is galactically harmonious, and just by being together, they brighten the skies. The things that they are able to manifest are marvelous, and so off they will go into the sunset together, making each other's dreams come true.

☼ ☼ ☼

LEO & SCORPIO

♌ ◈ ♏

Aspect: Square
Elements: Fire and water
Modalities: Fixed and fixed

Scorpio is not a person who is easily wooed, but somehow Leo can charm them in a way that has them feeling a little nervous. Scorpio will wonder how Leo can so shamelessly wear their confident ego because that is something Scorpio would never do unless they knew they were around people they could trust. Of course, this huge aura and confident attitude are what will draw Scorpio to Leo. Leo is attracted to Scorpio for the opposite reasons, admiring their quiet, steady, magnetizing, and enigmatic nature, which makes Leo wonder what Scorpio knows that they do not. Leo sees that this sun sign will not make things easy for them, but the lion is always up for a challenge. There are a lot of assumptions that they will initially make about one another, which gives this pairing allure.

Leo's ability to spread warmth and light up a room has Scorpio smiling. Scorpio is a water sign and cannot easily warm a crowd quite like a fire sign is able to; it does not matter how hard they try. Scorpio's emotions are far too deep to let as many people get close to them in the way that Leo allows. When the scorpion falls in love with the lion, it will be expressed in a deep and passionate way, which may come as a huge surprise to Leo. They will be bickering one moment, and the next Scorpio will have Leo pinned against a wall in a deep kiss. Leo may not even know what hit them, but once Scorpio is in, they are *all the way* in. There is no gray area with Scorpio, so if this is what Leo wants, they must play for keeps. If Leo leads them on to believe that they want to be with them and then changes their mind, they will feel the poisonous sting of Scorpio's wrath.

Leo loves to be adored, and this is something Scorpio certainly knows how to do. However, Leo loves to be adored by everyone, not just their partner, even if it is completely harmless. This will not fly with Scorpio; they are very possessive of the one they love. Scorpio does not seek the same type of attention that Leo craves, and they will not always understand why their admiration is not enough for their partner. Scorpio is a secretively sensitive soul, and this will hurt them immensely, pushing them into a frosty silence, which will enrage Leo. The lion will want to verbalize the problems, but if Scorpio is truly hurt, they will retreat from them. Scorpio is much better at seeing themselves from within and figuring out how to fix things alone than Leo is. However, Leo is much more forgiving than Scorpio. They both operate in the fixed modality, which makes them both stubborn, but if they work at finding compromise, things between them could balance out rather well.

Sex with this pair can go one of two ways. It can either be fiery hot or freezing cold. Leo finds Scorpio a challenge because no matter how silent they are, their vibrations are sensuous, intense, and controlled. Leo must use every bit of strength to hold back their desires for Scorpio until they give the green light. Scorpio loves to tease, and Leo loves when Scorpio makes them crazy with anticipation. The buildup is all part of the fun, and Leo is here for it. Scorpio finds Leo warm and tropically erotic. Leo is self-assured in the bedroom, and their confidence is a huge turn-on for Scorpio. Leo will want Scorpio to tell them how great they are in bed, which may be a little awkward for them at first, but there is nothing Leo loves more than a compliment. Scorpio loves nothing more than to know that their partner belongs to them—all of them. Leo must have a deep understanding of this desire. If Scorpio feels like they are in a constant competition for the one they love, they may act out of hurt or anger and could try to get even, creating an unhealthy and viscous cycle. There are concessions to be found between these two, and they require a lot of understanding and acceptance of each other's differences.

Leo will bring sunlight to Scorpio's darkest days, and Scorpio will give Leo a deeper look at life and love. Scorpio is not an ordinary soul, no matter how reserved they may seem, and once Leo peels more and more of their layers back, they will see that Scorpio is quite extraordinary. Leo will need to learn from Scorpio's all-or-nothing attitude, and Scorpio will need to learn that companionship is more important than getting their way all the time, which will, in turn, have them finding themselves alone. Their different views on life and love cause a divide of confusion at times, but true love acts as a glue. For love can tame a lion's roar and act as the antidote for a scorpion's sting. Compromise is the answer for this challenging yet exciting love match.

☼ ☼ ☼

LEO & SAGITTARIUS

Aspect: Trine
Elements: Fire and fire
Modalities: Fixed and mutable

Leos are utterly fascinated with Sagittarians. It may be their guiltless charisma, their insanely good sense of humor, or their combination of wisdom, generosity, and independence. Sagittarians value honesty and integrity, and they contain a naive faith that matches Leo's. Lions are noble, loyal, and just as idealistic as Sagittarius when it comes to most things. The first few months of their love story will be filled with fun games, the two making the rules up as they go. Leo will do their best to impress their Sagittarius, which is totally unnecessary because the archer has already fallen head over heels. Sagittarius will leave their lion little crumbs of affection, all the while being sarcastic, until one night they will touch Leo gently on the arm, look them right in the eyes, and sincerely make a proclamation of their love and adoration. Leo will be so deeply touched, and the rest is history. Behind Sagittarius's loud, sarcastic, and wild nature is a very sensitive and vulnerable creature who wears their heart on their sleeve and wants love just as much as anyone else—no matter what they lead you to believe.

Sagittarius's blessing and curse is that they put it all out there, and they need to be conscientious about poking too much fun at their royal highness. Lions love fun and games, but when they are constantly being teased as though they are a sibling rather than a lover, they may come at Sagittarius with their claws. Leos want to be treated like royalty. They are sleek and graceful, sunny and warm, and wise and sensible. But something to remember is that they possess a very sensitive ego and a very high sense of pride. Sagittarius is the bravest and most courageous sun sign in the zodiac, which Leo admires greatly. The archer will enjoy spoiling their lion and conquering any problems that they face together. Sagittarians are gallant and will gladly give their Leo the respect they deserve while never looking down—or up—to them. Instead, they will see them as their equal, which is exactly what they both desire in a partnership.

Being that these two signs are mutually the element of fire, they both tend to be quick to anger. A fight with a Sagittarius usually ends as soon as it begins, thanks to their mutable modality, and words of fury are soon to be replaced with apologies and heartfelt regret. As a fixed sign, Leo is slower to forgive and forget, but Sagittarius's humor will most likely get them out of just about anything. These two will have no problems with synergizing in the bedroom, and their fiery attraction for one another is undoubtedly passionate. Their physical connection ebbs and flows between refined tenderness and raw desire. Once they have loved each other completely and have truly given themselves to one another, next to nothing will break them. Even if a disagreement between them has Sagittarius saying harsh things, leaving their Leo in a fiery rage, they will quickly miss their boldhearted lion. There is nothing strong enough in the archer to resist their lion because they will terribly and fondly miss their sunshine and warmth.

Leos must not command but guide, while Sagittarius must not tease but love honestly. When these two courageous and generous sun signs can cooperate and have patience with each other's need for independence, it will never rain on their parade. Somehow, throughout all the games, Leo knew the whole time they were meant to be because they could see it in their witty and dancing eyes. Sagittarius sees that their lion is special because there is something about their golden heart and warm aura that makes everything glow. These two may start out playing games with each other, but their relationship will grow into affection, respect, admiration, and something that cannot be replicated. Sagittarius will teach Leo that there is so much to discover in life, and Leo will follow them into the unknown, keeping their wanderer's heart safe. If you can keep a Sagittarius's heart safe, they will hand you the world on a gold platter, which Leo will cherish. Their relationship will be filled with laughter and adventure, and if they ever need to play games again, they will play them for fun.

☼ ☼ ☼

LEO & CAPRICORN

Aspect: Quincunx
Elements: Fire and earth
Modalities: Fixed and cardinal

Leos are convivially confident and put off an energy that they always have everything figured out. That may be so until they meet their Capricorn mate and look into their steely eyes, so stern yet shiny, twinkling with subtle humor. When Leo falls in love with them, they realize that they really do not have it all figured out, and Capricorn has a lot they are able to teach them. Leo would never admit this to anyone, of course, but in their heart they know. Leo cannot decide whether Capricorn makes them feel like they are dealing with a parental figure, a teacher, or that kid at school that used to pick on them. How could this soft-spoken creature remind them of these authoritarians? It softens the blow when Capricorn sweetly confides their opinions to Leo, making them realize there is a soft side to the sea goat.

To Capricorn there is something cozy and protective about Leo that makes them feel safe enough to tell Leo anything, and Leo should be deeply moved because Capricorn does not trust many. But if Leo is not actually listening to Capricorn when they are putting their thoughts in the open, Capricorn will be deeply hurt and build a wall around their heart not even a bold lion could knock down, creating a quiet and frosty energy. Those steely eyes will turn into bullets, and Capricorn's soft gaze will become a sullen stare. Leo will try to humor them, but the sea goat will not have it, leaving Leo to feel rejected and humiliated. Capricorn is extremely self-protective and has the common sense to withdraw from an approaching battle before their relationship is seriously wounded. Leo should thank Capricorn for knowing when they should take time apart to think things through, and instead of blaming Capricorn for retreating, Leo should use the time to take a long, hard look at themselves. Capricorn desires to be secure and loved, which is something Leo deeply understands. Capricorn is just not—and will never be—as open about their need for it.

Leo's sunny disposition and confidence will melt Capricorn more often than Leo guesses, and it will inspire them by lifting their gloom more than they admit or show. Capricorn will listen attentively when Leo talks about their giant aspirations and future ambitions because Capricorn admires any kind of determination. The bigger Leo's goals are, the more Capricorn will support them while lending their practical advice. Leo should appreciate their sensible take on things because Capricorns have a marvelous knack for turning dreams into reality.

One area of contention for this imperial pair is finances. The simple solution is for the lion and the sea goat to keep their financials entirely separate. Forever. Capricorn should be free to save and invest their money as they please, and Leo should be free to be generous, buy extravagant gifts, lose money on a business venture, and win cash in Vegas if that is what makes the lion happy. Money can murder romance by causing arguments, so they must learn that cash is merely an illusion they will have to put second to prioritize their love. Once they come to this conclusion, they should ignore the topic and never discuss it unless necessary.

Another thing that these sun signs see through different scopes is sex. Capricorn will most likely be too bland for Leo's spicy taste at first, so the lion will have to work to season the sea goat up. Leo loves to be the center of attention, and Capricorn may not know how—or even care—to make them feel like the center of the universe in bed. However, if Leo can tone it down and Capricorn can warm it up, they can make this work. Leo must have patience and wait for the gradual release of Capricorn's restricted emotions through learning to trust that their walls will come down. If this happens, sex will possess a new meaning for both. Few things, if any, will be more pleasing to Leo than knowing they have won this sun sign's secret sexuality. Leo now has a piece of Capricorn's intimate self-treasure that they have gifted to no one else but them.

Capricorn should never drown Leo's enthusiasm and generosity with pessimism, sadness, or caution, and they should never wound Leo's pride with criticism as it will make them feel rejected. Leo should be kind and respectful to Capricorn's friends and family and be gentle with their quiet heart. Leo must understand that Capricorn's conservatism comes from an inner fear of loneliness. Just like Leo, Capricorn needs sincere compliments and appreciation as well, even though they pretend to dislike sentiment and affection. Overall, Leo's nobility is what Capricorn loves most about them. Leo's generosity and forgiveness softens Capricorn, and eventually these traits will diminish their caution. If the lion can find patience, their questioning will decrease as Capricorn's trust grows. These two may not have a whole lot in common, but they can grow with one another, which is what is exciting about this match. Capricorn needs Leo's warmth and courage, and Leo needs Capricorn's motivation and stability. Their unique assets combined as one makes them unbreakable.

☼ ☼ ☼

LEO & AQUARIUS

Aspect: Opposite
Elements: Fire and air
Modalities: Fixed and fixed

Leo is rarely surprised or caught off guard, but the water bearer will throw them for a loop. Most people would adversely react to Aquarius's eccentric behavior, but Leo is way too proud to let them know that they are ruffled by them at all. Instead, the lion acts as though they do not even notice the Aquarian's odd behavior. Leo just observes, digests, and then pretends like nothing is strange about them at all, which is hilarious considering just about everything *is* strange about them. This dynamic between them has onlookers usually in stitches; this sun sign combination is joyously hilarious in their opposition.

The reality of the situation is that Aquarius surprises Leo every day, whether Leo decides to show it or not. Aquarius was made to break rules, and there is nearly nothing predictable about them. Aquarius also finds Leo fascinating and appreciates that they are not easy to shock. These two sun signs both vibrate to the fixed modality, but Leo's energy is much more mellow than the water bearer's high-frequency vibrations, which will typically have Leo lazily following Aquarius's electric flow. Aquarius is traditionally ruled by Saturn, which gives them a cooler temperature, but they admire Leo's warm and sunny attitude.

On a good day, the couple is playful and affectionate, especially in bed. Their sex is fresh, tropical, and fun. They feel restored after a good romp because it is simply such a good time for them. Aquarius is so cool and detached, and Leo is warm and boisterous, making their opposing forces magnetically attracted and keeping each other wanting more and more. Leo loves to be the center of Aquarius's attention. On a bad day, they can tend to be at odds due to their opposing polarities, and while they both do not like to lead, they also do not like to follow. For lack of better words, they are both stubborn, so when they get into it, neither one of them wants to budge.

One of those topics of annoyance is that Leo is always so concerned about what is good for themselves, while Aquarius in concerned about what is good for the greater. Aquarius can view Leo as selfish, while Leo can see Aquarius as too worried about people that are not even worth their time. They will have to meet in the middle here. Leo must understand that water bearers are naturally humanitarian and will have to set their arrogance aside to allow Aquarius to fulfill their own needs. Aquarius must learn how to tame their frenzied nature and take time to think before acting. Leo will teach Aquarius how to slow down, and it would not hurt if Aquarius could remember to stroke their lion's ego occasionally. Leo not only appreciates compliments but needs them.

It would be good for them to remember that they are each other's mates, not each other's opponents. Because they are of an opposing aspect, they want the same thing but have different ways of getting there. Remembering this during a disagreement will benefit them greatly. Sun signs that sit directly across from one another on the karmic wheel have an instant attraction, and this is especially true in the case of Leo and Aquarius. When it comes to their different natures, they need to remember to not envy one another but rather imitate the things that they lack. Because fixed signs do not enjoy change, reflecting one another's strengths is harder for them to do than cardinal or mutable modalities. However, if they put the work in and choose each other every day, they can acquire one another's gifts, which would truly bless this pair. That is what the lesson of opposition is all about: not fighting but blending. What these two need to stay away from is constantly trying to top one another, which will take consistent effort.

When things are good, which is often, these two will love to carry out grand gestures and scintillating surprises for each other. They both love a change of scenery, so they will certainly make travel a big part of their relationship. Aquarius's many friends will absolutely adore their regal Leo, but Aquarius needs to remember to focus their attention on their partner, so Leo feels like they are their number one. Together, these two will have a glittering magic between them that will not fade with the passing of time. Aquarius's Uranian quirkiness will always keep Leo excited, and the lion's sunny warmth will keep Aquarius toasty, even on the coldest nights. It is hard for Aquarians to say yes to forever, but if they let their Leo sweep them off their feet, they will rarely feel trapped. Leo just wants to admire Aquarius for who they truly are, and that is exactly what the water bearer needs. Fire needs air to burn strong, and Aquarius feeds Leo's flames in many ways. It is not what people say that matters but what people do, and this pair always holds true to their promises.

☼ ☼ ☼

LEO & PISCES

♌ ♡ ♓

Aspect: Quincunx
Elements: Fire and water
Modalities: Fixed and mutable

Leo's energy is yang, and Pisces's energy is yin, making their dynamism unique, which helps them acquire a balance in their blending. Pisces is sentimental, perceptive, and sensitive, while Leo is courageous, direct, and independent. These are things that they can teach each other, and the way they can find harmony is by creating as much balance as possible. Leo can be exasperatingly regal one moment and intensely loyal the next, and Pisces should give Leo an inch but learn to never let them have a mile. Pisces will love Leo's happy-go-lucky and warm personality, but they will show their icy side if Leo tries to pry out all their secrets or inflict on the times Pisces needs to be alone. Pisces is gentle and will enjoy treating their lion well, so Leo should work on not scolding them too often in fear that they may swim away and look for a partner who is easier to deal with.

Leo is fire, and Pisces is water, and when you mix these elements in equal amounts, you get steam. However, if one element is stronger than the other, it will take the other element out. This brings back the importance of finding balance within their relationship to make it work. Pisces would be smart to run things from behind the scenes, which they will be able to do with their ethereal charm. The fish may find it exhausting keeping up with how their lion expects them to be, but Leo's adoration of them will keep them going. If they do get into an altercation, Pisces will just passively disappear, leaving Leo to roar by themselves. If Leo hurts Pisces to a point of no return, they will swim far away, leaving Leo alone and confused. In Leo's mind, they were just expressing their boisterous feelings. Tenderness and empathy will need to be learned by Leo, and strength and resilience will need to be absorbed by Pisces because escaping is not always the answer.

Pisces will not mind too much that their Leo is a little bossy and demanding, but they will need to learn how to stand their ground with them in a soft way, or Leo may very well take full control of this relationship. There is something about Pisces that enjoys succumbing to their partner, but they need to make sure they do not lose themselves in the process. Leo will be so romantic to their fish, and in return they will make their lion purr. Astrologically the lion will rule over the fish, but Pisces does not mind if they are left to their own accord, freely swimming in their own waters. However, the two should be careful with too much time away from each other. While most couples find that distance makes the heart grow fonder, this pair will find that distance makes the heart disinterested.

This pair enjoys a good nap together because Pisces loves to dream, and Leo just plainly needs their rest. Because of their shared love of the bedroom, extracurricular activities will naturally take place. Leo will find Pisces's tenderness incredibly attractive, while Pisces will appreciate Leo's romanticism. Leo will get jealous and protective of their fish if anyone looks their way, which is bound to happen on occasion because people are naturally drawn to Pisces's dreamy mysticism. Pisces finds Leo's need for admiration comical and endearing. There is no doubt these two will have other admirers. Leo is royalty and many want to be part of their court, and Pisces is a dreamy, empathetic listener that everyone enjoys being around. If they make a commitment to each other and stick to it, they can become quite the fairy-tale couple. They must learn to give one another love and admiration mixed with a little bit of freedom. If they can do this, they may just get their happily ever after.

Leo has a lot of pride, and when someone hurts their large ego, Pisces will be able to sooth them with their gentle waters. There will be days when Pisces possesses very little confidence, and Leo will be able to brilliantly boost their spirits. They both obtain true magic to strengthen each other's weaknesses, which will bless them with the beautiful balance they are trying to achieve. The lion will always be the leader because that is what will work best, but in return, Leo will protect their fish, and Pisces will admire this quality. On the days when Leo's head needs a break from wearing their heavy crown, Pisces will gently remove it from their head and remind them that there is still beauty to be found in life's unexpected gray days. This is where this pair's connection is: behind the velvet curtains and in their quiet moments.

☼ ☼ ☼

Chapter 6

Virgo

Virgo's love archetype is the healing lover. They are a cautious, contemplative, calculated, and communicative devotee who mends and repairs love to create alignment. Virgo's lesson in love is to impart that love is evident and absorb that love is contentment.

Element	Earth
Modality	Mutable
Polarity	Yin, negative, and feminine
Mantra	"I analyze."
Hue	White
Deity	Astrea, goddess of justice
Glyph	♍
Flowers	Morning glory, forget-me-not, and freesia
Tree	Oak
Jewel	Blue sapphire
Crystals	Peridot and clear quartz
Fragrance	Vetiver
Body Parts	The large and small intestines and the pancreas
Animals	Dogs and domesticated pets
Food & Herbs	Nuts, peas, carrots, celery, beans, marjoram, aniseed, caraway, milk thistle, hops, yellow dock, balm, bittersweet, and any vegetables grown below ground, such as celeriac

Virgo's Ruling Planet: Mercury

Mercury in love rules mental activity, intelligence, reasoning, and communication. Mercury in the sign of Virgo reveals day-to-day tasks, health, and well-being. The quicksilver planet represents the thoughts, phrases, and sounds of the way you speak. It also shows the way you communicate with your partner. Mercury delights being in the sign of the virgin because it is both exalted and domicile when here. Mercury regarding Virgo is intellectual, analytical, and critical. Virgos relish in connecting through mediums such as the written arts and reading. Being an earth element, Virgos appreciate the tangibility to things, as opposed to Gemini, who enjoys the mentality of things.

Virgo's Mythology

The constellation of Virgo is said to be Astraea, the Greek goddess of justice, innocence, purity, and precision. Her name means "star maiden," and she was the daughter of the Titan Astraeus, who was the god of dusk, and Eos, who was the goddess of dawn. According to mythology, Astraea ruled on the earth alongside humans during the Golden Age, which was a period of peace, harmony, stability, and prosperity. Her constellation is depicted holding the scales (Libra), which are seen next to Virgo in the sky.

Virgo's Positive Qualities and Negative Forms

Virgo's positive qualities are clarity of thought, tastefulness, courteousness, service to others, practicality, self-awareness, and being true to themselves. Expressed in their negative forms, they become critical, cranky, timid, pessimistic, weak, and fault finding.

How a Virgo Loves

There is a certain way in which a Virgo's love brings you out of the clouds and back in touch with earth. A Virgo's values lie in work and nature, so the way in which they love is incredibly tangible and grounding. A Virgo's passion in love is devotion and unification through determination, solid happiness, and simplicity. Virgos do not tend to truly grasp how complex love is, which is why their expectations are hard to meet. They need a secure partner who is appreciative of what they are and what they are not. Virgo is born knowing all that glitters is not gold, which makes them value a sturdier and rock-solid type of love—a love that withstands the test of time.

Virgo likes to look at the facts through their crystal-clear eyes rather than through the delusion of rose-colored idealism. They are never really interested in dramatic displays of affection, but that does not mean that they do not love with great conviction. Their love is practical, grounded, and earthy. The virgin expresses their sentiments through acts of service, being attentive, and being useful in whatever way their loved one needs. Their flavor of romance is not sugary sweet, but rather it is naturally flavored, making it genuine and easy to digest.

Virgo idealizes the one they love because they do not fall in love easily. They are born with a discerning nature and require high standards for the one they relinquish their independence for. In fact, they are known to be the singleton of the zodiac, only settling down with their idea of the perfect one. In their heart, they would rather be alone than be with the wrong partner. Therefore, when they give their heart away, they give it all because they are with their one and only.

The virgin can be an incredibly sensual and loving partner by adapting to what their loved one needs. Once a Virgo has found their soul mate, they will go to the ends of the earth to make them happy. This sun sign is incredibly devoted and dutiful and will be there through the good times and an incredible support through the bad. Virgo's dedication is hard to match because their practicality allows them to remove emotion when needed to be the rock in their relationship. Virgo can acknowledge both the pros and cons while continuing to hold onto their values about love. This is what makes a Virgo's admiration simply beautiful.

Once this angel's heart is captured, all the feelings that they have kept hidden under their earthy exterior are lavished upon their life partner. They are loyal and nurturing as well as wonderful storytellers, creating tender and memorable moments with ease. Virgos will do the most to cherish the one they admire by going out of the way to make their union work and sparing nothing to keep their love alive.

How to Spot a Virgo

It is quite simple to spot a Virgo. They are rarely voluble, and they never make a lot of noise. They could very well be the loner quietly reading a book in the corner of the café or the one picking lint off their perfectly pressed pants. Virgos are the type to kindly inform you that you mispronounced a word or sweetly notify you that you have a little parsley in your teeth. They are gentle and attractive with chiseled, innocent faces, and they always seem to smell faintly of soap. Their minds are continuously thinking, and everything they do has a methodical pattern to it. On the surface, you will see someone who is as neat as a pin and as cool as a cucumber, but if you look into their beautifully clear eyes, you will see their minds are busy measuring everything around them.

Virgo eyes are always so bewilderingly clear that you can see your reflection in them. They sparkle with intellect and clarity of thought. Their expressions are peaceful, pure, and will fool you into believing that they do not have a care in the world. Their features are attractive and delicate, and they have an air of graceful charm about them that is easy to be around. Virgo is meticulous about the way they look and present themselves and often conservative in the way they dress. If it looks like they just got out of the shower, it is probably because they did. They take more showers than anyone you will ever know. They are also religious about their skin-care routine. To a Virgo, cleanliness is next to godliness.

They are not ones to be spotted at a party; most Virgos would prefer to skip the large crowds. If you are looking for these perfectionists, you will have a better time finding them hard at work. They are born with an innate sense of duty, so work life suits them well. They tend to tackle more than they can manage, but they always find a way to figure it out. Even though they seem relaxed on the surface, they are constantly worrying about something. They are the nervous Nellies of the zodiac.

Virgos are natural healers, making them wonderful nurses, caretakers, nutritionists, personal trainers, physical therapists, and more. They are efficient, analytical, and sympathetic, making them perfect for uncovering strange illnesses, as well as mending and repairing to create alignment in others. On the flip side of that, they are incredibly critical. There is no harder critic than Virgo. However, if you try and criticize them, it may not be warmly accepted. You see, Virgo will never receive reproach from someone that they have not already given themselves times ten. They are fabulous at staying self-aware and keeping themselves, and others, accountable. Virgos are critical, yet they are equally kindhearted.

Virgo is represented by a virgin in a field of wheat, a dove, and an angel. However, at their highest state of enlightenment, they become Vulcan, the creator of lightning. Behind their purity and purpose, there are bolts of electricity in their mercurial minds and rolling thunder in their earthly blood. Therefore, the aura of Virgo is hot and bright white. When a Virgo looks up at you from behind their tortoiseshell glasses and gazes at you with their crystal-clear eyes and you feel a little jolt run through your body, remember you are in the presence of Vulcan.

How to Lose a Virgo

Virgos are the singletons and loners of the zodiac. They will wait for their perfect person to come along and will gladly stay single until that happens, never settling for less than what they know they deserve. When they finally do commit, they go all in. They will not want to spend too much time apart from their partner because it takes forever to find them in the first place! Virgos are naturally critical perfectionists, but when they give their heart to someone, they become completely faithful and servient. If you get selected, it would be wise to do what you can to keep them in your life. They do not get close to many.

Virgo has their life together just about 99.9 percent of the time, so they do not need someone telling them what to do or how to do it. They want a stable and supportive partner. If you complain about everything this perfectionist does, they will start feeling defeated. They tend to be hardest on themselves, so they need genuine praise from their significant other. This means they need positive boosts, not someone breaking them down. Virgo likes to feel needed, so if they believe there is not a place for them in your life, they may look elsewhere to find validation. They enjoy their routine and live and breathe by their schedule. It helps them to have a partner who supports this about them but is also able to break them out of their shell to have some fun. Virgo is a busybody and workaholic that needs a reminder to relax and slow down. Having a partner that is able to help them do this is key.

Virgos are all about maintaining everything in a tight order, so if you are a mess, they will tend to react quite critically, which is why they need someone who has it together. Doing little things around the house to help out will be appreciated more than you know. Acts of service are their love language, and they cannot be with a lazy slob, or they will likely lose their cool. They like to keep everything clean, including their dialect, so if you curse like a sailor and talk like an imbecile, they will find it distasteful. Virgos are known for their outstanding intelligence. Therefore, they enjoy and require aptitude in their partner more than any other trait. Their minds need a playmate to enjoy intellectual debates and discuss intricate topics with. They are a mutable sign, meaning that good conversation is a huge must in their love life.

Virgos are incredibly resourceful and do not like to waste anything. If they find you to be a wasteful person, they will be displeased. They require a partner who contributes, rather than one who expends. They can handle a few quirks here and there, but if you are a hot mess, it will be too much for them to handle. They are not asking you to be the most beautiful or stylish, but they do require a partner who takes care of themselves, their hygiene, and the way they present themselves. A Virgo knows well that perception is reality. Virgos require complete loyalty, and many virgins only have one true love of their life, so do not screw it up by screwing around. Remember that an angel waited for you and, out of all the mortals they ever crossed paths with, chose you.

How to Bed a Virgo

Virgos take care of their partner at home and in the bedroom, and they do it well. You may laugh when you refer to them as an angel because most of them are anything but. However, there is something innocent and virginal about them—something clean and pure. Virgos tend to take very good care of themselves physically, which only makes their attractiveness stronger. They have a white-hot energy that is magnetized to dark things. Opposites attract, and Virgos are no exception to this rule. You may look at this clear-eyed analytical who seems so innocent, and think they will be boring in bed. Your assumptions are incorrect. They have tricks up their sleeves that will strike you like a bolt of lightning.

Virgos are perfectionists, so if you can handle some sexual critique, you will get along just fine. While they are extremely critical, they are also kindhearted. It takes a while to get in, but once you do, you will find that Virgos are wonderfully close to the ones they love. Being a mutable earth sign means they are sexually steadfast and enjoy using words as foreplay, which will make for a lot of dirty conversation. Virgos are traditionally not an emotional sign, and they will not cry tears of joy after you give them the best sex of their lives. They have better things to do than cry in the bedroom. They are analytical and intellectual, rather than idealistic and emotional, and they would rather direct their energy into other places than into sentiments. Virgos are as cool as the other side of a pillow and have self-control like no other, and it is because of this incredible discipline that most have some rules when it comes to sex. Their lover will have to follow them if they want to play along. Virgins have secret dark fantasies that will sometimes not match what they are getting in their actual sex life unless they are able to find the right partner to help them release their inhibitions.

Once a Virgo enters your life, everything around you seems to start getting better. There is something in the way they take control that makes everything flawless, and they intend to create a perfect sexual experience for their partner. Virgos see it as part of their job to make their lover's wildest fantasies come true, and they figure if they can give them every twisted desire imaginable, they will never need to look elsewhere. They enjoy keeping their other half neatly in the palm of their hand. Virgos like security, and they have no problem gaining it by using sex to maintain a firm grip on their partner. Not so angelic anymore, huh? It is true, though. Virgos see sex as a way to retain their partner, and they will acquire any sexual skills and will try anything to make bedroom play more blissful. If they really love you, the sky is the limit on what they would be up for. They're willing to be dominated, tied up, and experimented with. However, they also find intelligence incredibly sexy as well.

The older and more mature they become, the more sexually comfortable they are in their skin. They can trust their partners more when they learn that sex is not a task of emotionless control but a mixture of physical and emotional oneness. When you look into a Virgo's very clear eyes, you will start seeing a very faint halo form above their head. Virgos are earthly angels with a little wicked twist.

☼ ☼ ☼

VIRGO & VIRGO

♍ ❤ ♍

Aspect: Conjunct
Elements: Earth and earth
Modalities: Mutable and mutable

Two Virgos would never imagine rushing into any kind of relationship too quickly. In fact, they may not even have a care in the world about being in a relationship when they first meet each other. They are both so picky and must analyze every little detail about one another before really making an educated decision about being in a relationship. After all their careful calculations, they will realize how perfect they are both individually and together. And as most know, Virgos love perfection.

Initially they will ignore one another's advances, either by sticking their nose in a newspaper or keeping themselves busy in the garden. However, once they realize that they could be an amazing pair, it will not be too long until they will give into what they really want, and the anticipation will make it all the more worth it. What they must remember is that making mistakes together makes them stronger. Together, they can learn that life is not meant to be spent fretting over insignificant matters, ignoring temporary troubles, or keeping their sights on what is to come. When they have combined their likenesses, they can open their minds and tune in to each other's resolute callings. There will be spells of coldness, naturally, but they both must make an effort to bring some warmth to their love.

Their sex may be a little rigid and controlled at first, but with a little time, they will start to see things steam up. They need to leave their cool and controlled attitudes at the door to be able to really fulfill one another. Sex is something that innately they can see as taboo, but they can learn that together it can be a perfect and fulfilling experience, leaving them feeling whole instead of empty. They will learn more and more about each other through every experience, only bettering and deepening their sexuality. Some may wonder if two Virgos have any sex life at all considering they are both the sign of the virgin, but that train of thought is ridiculous. They absolutely are sexual beings. Every sun sign simply looks at sex and physical experiences in a different light. A Virgo experiences it in more of a pure way, and there is absolutely nothing wrong or unsexual about that.

These two angelic souls will run into a few problems, as all couples do, and they will mostly revolve around two things: imperfections and criticism. No one is perfect, but no one really appreciates receiving criticism regarding those imperfections. It is in a Virgo's nature to analyze and criticize any flaws that they see, and most of the time, they do it because they want to fix the flaw. However, when two people are criticizing and analyzing each other all day, when is there time for love? Virgos are way too smart to let little things get in the way of harmony in their relationship, so if they can work to cut even half of the critical comments out, that would be a good place to start. Just remember one thing—it is all about the delivery. Virgos have a wonderful sense of humor and clarity about them, and they should utilize this gift if something needs to be communicated. Any criticisms will come out a lot softer and be received with more of an open mind when coming from a place of love and candor.

Virgos are always searching for a level of excellence that does not exist here on earth, but if they are seeking love, they must keep in mind that there is no love that is perfect. If they can accept this and understand that love is about accepting every bit of the other person, along with approval of themselves, they can find what they are searching for. No one is born on the earth as a perfect person—not even these two—but there is a solace in finding someone that just gets you, and that is what they will find in each other. Together, they will discover a partner who loves a perfectly clean house, intelligent conversations, working in their garden together, and reading the newspaper in the buff. These two beautiful and clear souls create a love that emits a pure white energy in a way that only the love of two angels can.

☼ ☼ ☼

VIRGO & LIBRA

♍ ⟡ ♎

Aspect: Semisextile
Elements: Earth and air
Modalities: Mutable and cardinal

Libras are soft, charming, lovely, harmonious, and graceful. When Virgo sees their dimpled face and silky hair, they will be reminded of a painting that they saw at the Louvre, untouchable and perfect. However, as Virgo gets closer, they will see that Libra has cracks in their canvas just like everyone else. Virgo's eyes sparkle like the sunlight dappled on the forest floor, and their energy is refreshing, cool, and pure. Libra needs their Virgo's calmness in more ways than one. However, after some time spent among their Virgo's world, they will see that there are storms on the horizon that brew beneath their angel's perfect façade.

Virgo has a lifelong quest to serve others—even more than they serve themselves—with the hope of improving the world. Their mission in life is to bring order to chaos and confusion, so they enjoy clarifying mistakes, whether those mistakes belong to a stranger or their Libra partner. No one is spared from a Virgo's critical eye, which is why Libra should try to not take this personally. It is a Virgo's duty to follow their analytical compulsions. Most of the time, Libra's diplomatic mind will see that their intentions are pure and their heart is full of compassion. However, if Virgo does not give the affection and attention Libra craves and deserves, their scales will be thrown off balance. Libra can help Virgo here in many ways by melting away their tendency to worry by charming them to float away with them among the pink clouds. A surefire way to relieve Virgo's stress is sex.

Their chemistry is not fast and intense but soft and sweet, and they will both be content with their sexual encounters. Libra can be overly romantic, which may be a turnoff for Virgo at times and can even overwhelm them when they first meet, leaving them to doubt how genuine Libra could truly be. Once Virgo sees that Libra's romantic gestures are straight from their Venus-ruled heart, Virgo will give in completely. Lovemaking with these two is relaxing for both, and there is a lovely gentleness between them. However, Libra should keep any critiques to themselves because Virgo does not have the patience for any such sexual nitpicking.

If adjustments need to be made, it will have to be done in an ambiguous way with coy suggestions through physical display rather than direct verbal requests. Virgo is brilliant at reading between the lines and will appreciate the sensitivity.

One thing they will both love are their careers. Libra is a cardinal air sign, and Virgo is a mutable earth sign. Libras are born to lead, and Virgos are born to work, so there is a very good chance that work will be a focal point in this love story, and it could even be where they will meet. At work Virgo is the talkative Casanova, and Libra is the even-keeled supervisor. At home the roles reverse. Libra becomes the charming velvety pillow to rest upon, and Virgo becomes serious and task oriented. Even though Virgo would do anything for their partner, they are a slave to duty and dedicated to their daily tasks.

Virgos do not always communicate their concerns, and Libras are not good at reading between the lines, which creates misunderstandings in this relationship. Libras are remarkable at getting what they want, and they tend to mold their partner into a version of themselves and merge them into their own lifestyle. Because Virgo is mutable, they will usually bend for their Libra's wishes. However, Libra needs to remember that Virgo is an individual with different wants and needs of their own. If Libra does not catch on to this soon enough, Virgo may lose themselves in the relationship and resent Libra for it. Virgo may not seem like they have the willpower to go, but if they feel it is the right thing to do, they certainly will. Virgo is much stronger than they lead on and will not settle for less than what they need in a partnership. However, it takes two to tango, and Virgo must put the effort in to tell their Libra what they need and work on getting comfortable with using a direct approach, even though it is not their preferred method.

The truth is that Libra needs Virgo's soothing presence to help calm their indecisive mind, and Virgo needs Libra's romantic lightness to brighten up their sky. Libra will teach Virgo what life is like with balance, which is something they so desperately need. They will have to find a secret formula together, and it is there, just waiting to be discovered. Virgo is the splendid forest, and if you can see past the trees, Libra is the glittering sunset in the distance that paints the heavens above with pink and orange hues. Libra's light dances through Virgo's foliage, and their breeze rustles their branches. Together, they make an entire picture and create a work of art. Their canvas has some cracks, and storms brew in the distance, but collectively they are a masterpiece nonetheless.

☼ ☼ ☼

VIRGO & SCORPIO

♍ ◈ ♏

Aspect: Sextile
Elements: Earth and water
Modalities: Mutable and fixed

Virgos are naturally attracted to things that are mysterious because they are filled with so much clarity. Scorpios are naturally attracted to things that are pure to protect their intricate nature. When they combine their passionate affinity for one another, they create an evenness to their energy that magically enables them to create their own sanctuary. Virgo's mutable and Scorpio's fixed modalities are wonderful complements to the virgin's earth and the scorpion's water elements. Furthermore, Virgo has a stationary element with a variable modality, while Scorpio has a moving element with a static modality. This intriguing blend is distinctive to this match and creates a balance of power and understanding. There is nothing to stop the inevitable science of the natural attraction between Virgo's placidity and Scorpio's obscurity.

Virgo is mental, and Scorpio is emotional, so the angel and the scorpion have much to teach each other. Scorpio will initially take Virgo's innocence as naivety, and Virgo will see Scorpio's distrusting nature and want to show them the light. Scorpio will initially fight the love that Virgo gives, but when they realize Virgo's intentions are unalloyed, they will willingly give in. Virgo must understand that Scorpio takes time to let their guard down, and what Scorpio needs to understand is that Virgo is incredibly particular when it comes to the one that they want, so if they choose them, it is genuine. Virgo grasps things in a more complete way when they are tangibly measurable, but Scorpio will be able to teach Virgo about the things that are wonderfully unquantifiable. Scorpio will impart Virgo with gifts of content love, and Virgo may even feel things with Scorpio they did not know existed. Virgo is always consumed with the day-to-day, but Scorpio will show Virgo the big picture. However, the most important thing Scorpio will have to teach Virgo about is sex.

Virgo may think they have sex all figured out before they meet their Scorpio, but making love with a Scorpio is like stepping into another astral realm. To a Virgo, sex is simply a physical act, but Scorpio will show this sun sign that there is also the emotional and spiritual side to oneness that brings wholeness and completion. Scorpio must have patience while teaching Virgo this secret. Virgos are perfectionists and will blame themselves for not being able to disconnect from their physical bodies, but once Virgo is guided down the path of sexual holiness, the two will have an undying bodily connection together. Just the sight of their scorpion will make Virgo lose their train of thought now that they know how to make love with their body *and* soul.

Virgo is wildly imaginative thanks to their ruling planet, Mercury, and these two will be mental playmates. Their sextile vibration gifts them with an undying unity of friendship, and this match will have no problem talking about anything and everything under the sun. When it comes to being emotionally controlled, Virgo will beat Scorpio in that department every time. Virgo's purity of thought and simplicity of action will be something Scorpio will do good to learn from. When they argue, Scorpio will go into a cold silence, which will make Virgo irritated because they want to understand everything. One thing Virgo must realize is that their scorpion's depth is something that no one will ever reach other than Scorpio themselves. The best thing to do is just be there for them, and Scorpio will come around.

Virgo is known to make guarantees with pure intentions, and most of the time they keep their commitments, but other times they do not follow through. However, in a Scorpio's world, vows outweigh practicality, which brings us back to the fact that Virgo is mental and Scorpio is emotional. Because of this specific variance, Virgo will need to think before they make a promise because Scorpio will hold Virgo true to their commitments. Most of the time, these two will have no problem resolving issues because Virgo is one hell of a communicator and will be able to talk Scorpio off any ledge. However, too many broken promises and too many ledge talks will send Scorpio in search of sturdier ground. Contrastingly, Scorpio's outbursts of anger will scare Virgo out of their skin. If there are too many eruptions that Virgo feels like they must fix, they will leave to find a place to calm their nerves. The trick with these two is a lot of balance and understanding of one another's differences to make room for compassion.

Virgo will never see their Scorpio as ruthless, cold, or dangerous. Instead, they'll see them as warm, generous, and caring. Scorpio will never see their Virgo as picky, fastidious, and nervous, but rather they'll see them as peaceful, devoted, and healing. Virgo must slow their mind and feel with their heart, and Scorpio must slow their passions and think with their head. If they both do not reach the destination of where they intended to get, they will still take away beautiful lessons from one another that they will never forget. The similarities and differences of their merging energy is truly a magnificent dynamism.

☼ ☼ ☼

VIRGO & SAGITTARIUS

♍ 💎 ♐

Aspect: Square
Elements: Earth and fire
Modalities: Mutable and mutable

Virgos treasure their solitude. However, when the virgin meets the centaur, they seem to willingly give up pieces of their single life that they never anticipated. Virgo is first attracted to their bright aura and chatty wit. Sagittarius always has a thing or two to say, but being that Virgo is also a mutable sign, they will always have a comeback or two. They will most likely meet through mutual friends, and Sagittarius, of course, will make hilarious remarks, and Virgo will have something clever to retort. The difference between their banter is that Sagittarius does not think before speaking, and Virgo most certainly does. Surprisingly Sagittarius loves that Virgo always has a slick reply, and Virgo knows that even though Sagittarius blurts everything out, it is usually backed by good intentions. One thing they certainly have in common is that every action they take is motivated by decency and kindness.

Let us not forget though that these two are squarely aspected to one another, and that makes their relationship more challenging than most. Sagittarius is known for being hilarious and loves to play jokes on people. There is nothing more satisfying to a Sagittarius than successfully pulling off a good prank or getting a crowd of people to laugh. On the other hand, Virgo is more of a serious creature at heart and does not necessarily appreciate hilarity and jokes at the expense of dignity. Virgos have a great sense of humor, but they believe that there is a time and a place for everything, whereas Sagittarius does not have the perceptiveness to pick up when that time may be. Virgo is characteristically a neat freak in one way or another, while the centaur is not exactly the epitome of tidiness. Sagittarius's mind has bigger fish to fry than taking a toothbrush to tile thanks to their free spirit. If this pair plans to cohabitate, hiring someone to clean would be worth it because it is better than squabbling about whose turn it is to scrub the toilet.

Sagittarius is a yang fire sign, and Virgo is a yin earth sign, so they will need to find a way to balance their inherent dissimilar energies. Sagittarius will see that Virgo loves them for all their attributes and flaws, and Virgo will sooth them in a way that helps them forget their painful past. There is just something about looking into Virgo's clear eyes that puts a sense of safety and security into Sagittarius's soul, and this is something that the archer has needed for a long time. You may look at these two and wonder how they work, but as different as they are, there is something about them that is uncannily similar due to their matching modality. This shared modality makes them both so honest, which is not so easy to come by. Sagittarius is a difficult creature to capture, and Virgo is looking for a love that is unattainable. Somewhere these two somehow meet in the middle of their differences and find each other—both mentally and physically.

In the bedroom, Sagittarius is as fiery as ever, while Virgo takes more of a cool, grounded, and practical approach. Here they can both teach one another things about oneness that the other never knew. Virgo loves to simplify their life as much as possible, but they also need to learn how to lighten up. In the bedroom, Virgo will enjoy Sagittarius's sense of adventure, and Sagittarius will enjoy Virgo's uncomplicated approach. When they are finished and cuddling with one another, Virgo will kiss Sagittarius so sweetly on the forehead that it may melt the centaur's heart into a puddle, causing a tear of pure joy to run down their cheek. Sagittarius needs this type of solidity and sweetness to make them feel safe enough to stick around.

Virgo will find themselves feeling enough comfort in their union to tell Sagittarius things they never thought they would tell anyone because Sagittarius's open mind never judges them. Sagittarius never analyzes things as sternly as the virgin does, and this reminds them not to be so hard on themselves. They are both intelligent in different ways, and they both have a lifetime of learning from one another to look forward to. The archer loves that their angel can be firm yet sweet all at the same time because they need that balance. Virgo can teach Sagittarius how to soften their tongue, and Sagittarius can teach Virgo to look at the world through their rose-colored glasses. Sagittarius is not always the easiest creature to figure out, but Virgo can see right through their naive nature to the beautiful person that they truly are. The way they challenge each other is what keeps their sharp, mutable minds coming back for more.

☼ ☼ ☼

VIRGO & CAPRICORN

♍ ⬥ ♑

Aspect: Trine
Elements: Earth and earth
Modalities: Mutable and cardinal

When Virgo and Capricorn first meet, they will feel a karmic tug. Things happen fast with this pair, but it does not feel overwhelming to them because it is as though they have known each other all their lives. Their auras blend and lock, and they will understand one another instantly. It is difficult to get these two apart because they communicate so beautifully and truly enjoy being around one another. Separating them is like trying to untangle a knotted necklace. Thanks to their trine aspect, the energy that their union creates is effortless.

Virgos are anything but desperate to be in a relationship. In fact, the idea of changing their entire lifestyle to fit someone else's sounds petrifying because they have a notion that marriage is not all that it is cracked up to be. They are not necessarily afraid of commitment, but they are afraid of losing their freedom. However, the sea goat is brilliant at building a solid foundation, which will allow Virgo to get rid of their fear and anxiety. Furthermore, if Capricorn can make them feel free in a commitment, they can form a bond stronger than any.

Capricorn's steadiness and patience create a space where their relationship can flourish. This earthly connection between them is filled with copious amounts of love that will eventually lead to permanency. They will find a lot of peace and beauty in their sex life because they are eloquently in tune and magnetically drawn to one another in ways only earth signs can really understand.

They will only grow closer and stronger the longer they stay together, making their unity unshakable. They do not make their perfection a show, but rather it is one of quiet appreciation. It is as though they have known each other for eons even though they have maybe only been together for a short time. They will start syncing with one another simultaneously, and this will be applicable for their sex life as well. They are both cool characters, but with sex they can warm one another, creating a deep passion that trembles like an earthquake.

Capricorn loves making plans, and Virgo will enjoy helping them come to fruition, which makes them a formidable team. They will each have their own successful ventures to contribute to their empire, making them one hell of a power couple. They will admire and respect each other in the way that they become their own individual sources of strength. Their relationship may seem perfect, but just like with any love story, one should expect days with cloudy skies.

These two earthly beings have their spats, and they're usually because Virgo is nagging about something, and Capricorns truly do not enjoy being nagged. Sure, no one likes it but especially not Capricorn. Virgo is also always on the go and has a hard time relaxing. They are constantly busy cleaning, reading, exercising, cleaning, working, and then cleaning some more. Capricorn, on the other hand, is always working. They will both enjoy the productivity of the other, but it will be hard to cut out the time needed to spend quality time together. They may get irritated with the "work first, love later" attitude, and they may even break things off because of this, but it is difficult for them to stay away from each other long. With Virgo's excellent communication skills plus Capricorn's natural ability to lead, finding a resolution for their issues should be a cinch.

If these two ever do separate, it will usually be for career, power, ambition, or money. What they may not realize at the time of parting is that they are making a huge mistake. They are both stubborn, so they may never admit to their fault, but they will always feel it—no matter how much time passes. That is why it is smart for them to not only look at the present but far into the future as well. Understanding that their quiet oneness is better suited for each other than the exhausting, loud, and tiresome single life is an imperative to them staying together. They must always cherish the familiarity, stability, and intimacy between them and hold dear the way they subliminally understand each other. That is how they will know they have hit the real jackpot in life; they have something that money cannot buy.

☼ ☼ ☼

VIRGO & AQUARIUS

♍ ◊ ♒

Aspect: Quincunx
Elements: Earth and air
Modalities: Mutable and fixed

Virgos are undoubtedly the singletons of the zodiac, but Aquarius is a very close second. Virgos are perfectly content waiting for the perfect person that may never show, while Aquarius enjoys doing whatever they see fit without needing companionship until the end of their days. With that in mind, you can imagine that it would have to truly be in the stars for these two to end up in a relationship, but when they do, there will be something uniquely binding that keeps them together. An outsider may not figure it out, but that is because only these two could possibly understand it.

Virgos fall in love with water bearers because they can spot potential no one else can, and Virgo thinks it would be wonderful to chase rainbows with Aquarius. Aquarius falls in love with the virgin because they did not laugh at their ridiculous dreams. The reason being is that Virgo can see that Aquarius's rainbows are painted in practical colors. Even though Aquarius is full of eccentricity, they are surprisingly traditional when it comes to picking their life partner, possibly because they know there is only enough room for one variable in the house. Virgo is wonderful at being the constant and delights in keeping things straight, and that is how these two can nicely blend. Astrologically speaking, they quite literally have nothing in common. Their quincunx aspect will be what attracts and simultaneously repels them, and this dichotomy between them is what makes their love story one of a kind.

It will take Virgo some time to get used to Aquarius's many odd and unusual friends who show up without warning. There will be times when Aquarius takes advantage of Virgo's kindness, but the water bearer needs to remember that the virgin does not breathe to be with them. Virgo may feel neglected when Aquarius is off chasing those rainbows, and Aquarius would be smart to take Virgo with them on their adventures. That being said, Virgo would be wise to let Aquarius chase their dreams alone occasionally, especially in the beginning of their relationship. Like all air signs, they need space and time to breathe, and if they are allowed this space, they will realize that it is more fun to have Virgo come along for the ride. Two heads are better than one, especially when it's a sharp, intelligent Virgo mind paired with the futuristic Aquarian viewpoint. Virgo can be quite critical, but Aquarius is considerably serious about getting things right themselves. They are both dreamers at heart, regardless of how acute their minds are. However, their dreams are not wispy but rather crafted from solid intellect.

There is a kind of secret surprise to their sexual compatibility. In fact, their sex life is a lot better than anyone would ever think and even better than they would have even imagined. Virgo will love Aquarius's quirkiness and willingness to think outside the box when it comes to sexual escapades, which gives their sex life variety. Aquarius keeps Virgo's intellectual mind stimulated with their zany humor, bringing a lot of fun and laughter to their lovemaking. Virgo has surprises up their sleeve as well. At first Aquarius will assume their angel is a model of innocence and purity, but behind closed doors, they are in for a sweet surprise. Passion and attraction will not be lacking in their relationship because to Aquarius, Virgo represents the eighth house of the mysteries of sex on the karmic wheel. Therefore, Virgo may arouse more desire in Aquarius than other partners have accomplished in the past, which will delight Virgo and make them feel wanted.

Secretly Virgos are most pleased when they feel wanted and needed by their partner. Aquarians like to tease, but it would be a mistake for them to tease Virgo to the point of frustration. After long deliberation, virgins can decide to cut out their partner with ice-cold surgical precision. Humor is what will get them through tough spats. Virgo is a mutable sign and quite clever, and Aquarius has an eccentric sense of humor themselves. They enjoy their intellectual banter, and their jokes and laughter are what they love most about each other. Aquarius always searches for a friend first and a mate second, and very rarely is it ever the other way around. Virgo makes an excellent friend and becomes the backbone to their relationship, allowing Aquarius to be the free and fun character they are meant to be. On the other hand, Virgo is looking for their one true love. If they can be these things for each other, they will make it through almost anything. Even when the world may seem upside down, their love has roots grown in true adoration and friendship that will always give them a sense of home in one another. When they stop chasing those rainbows and stop believing in their dreams is when trouble will strike and storms will begin to form. They must remind each other to keep visualizing their colorful ambitions that keep those magic arches in their sky.

☼ ☼ ☼

VIRGO & PISCES

♍ ❤ ♓

Aspect: Opposing
Elements: Earth and water
Modalities: Mutable and mutable

No matter how sweet and innocent Pisces may seem, there is always a clever strategy hidden behind their ocean eyes. At first Virgo will only see the fragility that they feel compelled to protect, but they will soon find that what lies on Pisces's surface is not what lives deep inside their heart. Pisces encompasses a wide range of energy because they are the last sun sign in the karmic wheel, meaning they have absorbed a little bit of every sun sign along the way. Pisces may be naive, but they also inherit an innate wisdom from all the lessons in their previous lives. Pisces's empathetic nature makes them a beautiful listener, which is something Virgo's mutable modality craves in a partner. There is very little that is orderly about the Pisces mentality, and this differs from Virgo's methodical mind. However, Pisces's charm has many different colors that depend on whom they are around due to their ability to blend with anyone, which is something Virgo can learn from.

There will be immense love between them, but like with all couples, there will be days that are trying. One of the biggest topics of dispute between them will be money. In Pisces's mind money has no matter, whereas a typical Virgo will find that outlook irresponsible. Pisces is overly trusting and generous to the point that they continually lend their money out or even give it freely to friends and family. Pisces will find Virgo's critical comments about this matter nagging and as though they are trying to take their financial freedom away. It's quite the opposite; Virgo is just looking out for their fish's best interests. However, if Pisces continues to feel as though they are failing their partner, they will find a way to escape the pain. This can mean becoming distant by drowning themselves deep in their dreams and emotions. Money can bring stress to relationships, so they must find a balancing act when it comes to finances. One place they can always resolve a quarrel is with physical oneness.

Their attraction to one another is strong due to their opposite natures. Earth and water signs naturally blend sexually in sheer delight because of the earth's ability to absorb water. Their physical oneness may come a lot faster than they both anticipated due to the extreme attraction they have for one another. The passion they share is deep, and there is something so pure and vulnerable about their sex that they both wholly enjoy. They are both delicate and sweet underneath the sheets, and their love for one another is almost like a poem—too perfect for most to even understand. Their sacrificial natures are both so unselfish that they easily can give each other whatever they desire.

The fact that Virgo can be vulnerable around Pisces is soothing to their soul, and Pisces will never take advantage of this gift. In return, Virgo makes Pisces feel incredibly safe, which is something they desperately long for in love. Together, they share a mutable modality, meaning they will be wonderful communicators. However, one thing Pisces will not stand for is if Virgo builds a wall around their heart that becomes impenetrable. If Virgo is sparing with love, money, personality, attention, or really anything, for that matter, this will cause Pisces to swim the other way. The fish craves a love that is all-encompassing, and if Virgo cannot—or will not—give that to them, this union will not end the way it should. All Virgo needs to know is to never criticize Pisces, to give freely, and to act natural around them. Go with Pisces's flow, and they will never be disappointed. As for Pisces, they must understand that Virgo loves order because it helps their anxious mind. This is not the Pisces's brand of business, but they must try for their angel.

Pisces has their own flavor of alchemic elixir that Virgo will be happy to consume. However, Virgo also has their own brand of magic, which is that they are immune to distortion. This specific trait of Virgo is something that Pisces desperately needs. They require a partner who will gently point them in the right direction. Pisces is a sun sign of duality, which can be an incredible blessing or a mixed bag of tricks. Pisces refuses to let their dreams disappear while simultaneously succumbing to their fears. Their absorption of energy works in the same way; it is a blessing to know things before they take place, but it can also be exhausting to feel everything around them. Virgo is immune to falsifications and will assist their fish by being their own personal fear breaker and energy saver. Together, they can make their own enchanted potion that will have them both covered in stardust. Because of their kindness to one another and the fact that they give each other what the other one is missing, they make one complete component in a way that only opposing sun signs can.

☼ ☼ ☼

Chapter 7

Libra

Libra's love archetype is the diplomatic lover. They are an intellectual, assertive, vibrant, and romantic companion who holds love in a significant way to create harmony and balance. Libra's lesson in love is to impart that love is splendor and absorb that love is synchronization.

Element	Air
Modality	Cardinal
Polarity	Yang, positive, and masculine
Mantra	"I balance."
Hue	Pink
Deity	Hera, goddess of marriage
Glyph	♎
Flowers	Roses and hydrangeas
Tree	Poplar
Jewel	Opal
Crystals	Rose quartz and rhodonite
Fragrance	Rose
Body Parts	The kidneys and equilibrium
Animals	Lizards and small reptiles
Food & Herbs	Wheat, berries, apples, pears, grapes, artichokes, asparagus, dried beans, mint, goldenrod, parsley, borage, and cereals, such as oatmeal and barley

Libra's Ruling Planet: Venus

Venus rules love, marriage, and attraction. It also reveals your capacity for affection, beauty, and harmony in your partnership. Venus represents the colors, sounds, music, and varieties of love. Venus is there to provide couples with smooth sailing through stormy seas and brings beauty and blessings to partnerships. Combined with Libra's air element, Venus gives its children true physical beauty. Libras are naturally charming and social while enjoying luxurious, airy, and sweet surroundings. They are blessed with the cardinal masculinity of Libra while adorned with Venus's feminine and romantic touch. Because this sign possesses a perfect balance of masculine and feminine energy, they are considered to be one of the most admired sun signs of all.

Libra Mythology

Libra is one of the oldest known constellations due to its relation to the Greek goddess of justice Astraea. Astraea went to the heavens and became the constellation of Virgo. In the stars Virgo carries the scales of justice, which is the constellation of Libra. The fall equinox takes place on the day that the sun enters Libra, which is when the days and nights are of equal length and the sun and moon are in perfect balance. This is why the scales are commonly depicted holding a sun on one side and a moon on the other.

Libra's Positive Qualities and Negative Forms

Libra's positive qualities are justice, intelligence, charm, gentleness, and emotional balance. Expressed in their negative forms, they become lazy, prone to procrastination, indecisive, argumentative, pleasure-seeking, and temperamental.

How a Libra Loves

Libras are the diplomats of love, handling romance in a valuable way to create harmony and balance in their relationships. As Libras move through partnerships, they become incredibly wise. They can beautifully see every side to every love story so well. Therefore, Libras have the reputation of being indecisive, which they do not mean to be, but when you are able to see both sides so clearly and without emotion, you want to walk in two directions at once, which frequently leaves them in the same spot. Libras rarely act like they know something when they do not. They will ask, discuss, deliberate, and then act fairly, which makes this sign so incredibly trustworthy. Libra is the sign of the scales; one side is for fairness and the other is for morality. Libras always weigh their decisions for a long time, so if you happen to be chosen by one to be their partner, you should feel quite flattered.

Libras treat their lovers as they want to be treated, and while their ambiguity may make them seem detached, they are anything but. Libras wholeheartedly know that love is what makes the world go around, which is why they are in a constant state of searching for companionship. They are fabulous at adapting and engaging themselves to other's energies and make a superlative effort to fit in, which is why they are incredibly likable. Their even temper and charm are what allures romantic partners to them, and their unbothered attitude is what keeps those love interests hooked. If, for any reason, a Libra in love feels as though their companion is unfair, it will throw their scales out of balance, and they will justly leave them high and dry while they blow a kiss goodbye. Libras often dream of finding their soul mate and wish for a perfect fairy-tale ending, which is why many become disappointed in relationships. For this reasoning, Libras often get the title of serial daters, always searching for an unrealistic and idealistic happily ever after.

Something wonderful and unique about Libra is that they are the only sun sign to be a masculine sign ruled by a feminine planet. This is all too appropriate considering that they are the most balanced and fair sign of the zodiac. Libra is also the only sign that is not represented by an actual living creature; they are represented as the scales. This gives Libra a beautiful balance of energy that is not possessed by any other sign and the reason they are so cherished, charming, and loved. Their allure is potent to most, but Libra is usually unaware of their effect because that is just their natural character.

Libra loves to be in love, and if they are not in love, they will consistently search for the paradise that it brings. They are the archetypal romantics of the zodiac, and their search for partnership drives their every move. Because of their Venusian gifts, they will work hard to make their relationship last by making it extraordinary. When Libra finally finds the one they want to partner with, there will be little that gets in their way of using cupid's bow to tranquilize the one their heart desires. Even though their love can be hasty once they make the choice to commit, their sentiments are always in the right place. The joy that they feel when they are in love is worth any pain that may come down the road, which makes this poetic sun sign incredibly companionable in love.

How to Spot a Libra

Libras are arguably the most beautiful sign in the zodiac. Because they are the only masculine sign ruled by a feminine planet, they are marvelously attractive, balanced, and pleasant. There is no "typical" Libra. However, many of them have dimples on their sugary faces, which are surely one of Venus's gifts that adds to their enchanting charm. The real giveaway is their voice, which is usually as clear as a bell and sweet as cherry pie. Their laugh is bright and unforgettable. They rarely yell and would much rather speak diplomatically. They are interested in a dialogue, not a monologue. Their expressions are neutral and delightful. Their smile is silky, and their eyes sparkle with stardust. Even though they seem soft, there is something as strong as steel about them. It is a strength you know is there but does not need to be spoken of.

Throughout their life, Libras seek what is reasonable yet beautiful. They have a graceful intelligence to them that attracts many. When you come to them, they are gentle, and when you need someone on your side, they are strong. These Venusian beings are fantastic to get advice from when times are tough because they are naturally gifted at seeing every side of the situation. They are genuinely a delight to be around, and part of their charisma is coming across as guileless while they run the show from behind their pink velvet curtain. They are experts at persuasion, and there is not a sun sign that can hold a candle to Libra when it comes to getting the things they want out of life. Their attractiveness and benevolence create a lovely cloak for their regime. The motives for their actions are always laced with an engagement to partner because they exist for love.

The Libra indecisiveness is true indeed, though many of them will deny being as such. Their rebuttal itself is an example of their indecision. No matter how you slice it, trying to get a Libra to decide is never an easy task. The more important the decision is, the longer it will take them to decide. At times they will even purposefully take a different side to start a debate for the pure pleasure of it. They truly seek harmony, but it may not seem like it because of their constant deliberations. However, their intentions are honorable, and their purpose is to mediate to bring peace and balance to their scales. They know that sometimes gaining reconciliation requires a war, but if you want a Libra to make up their mind, never ever push them. They will be gone faster than you can blink. Instead, gently persuade them but always let them take their time.

As Libra's scales dip up and down throughout their life, they will have times of relaxation and times of excessive effort. An object in motion stays in motion, and this law rings true for Libra. They are constantly trying to find balance between the excess that they commonly come across, which is a challenge that never seems to end. Libras are made of the mental air element, and their brilliant minds need frequent rest. What many may not know is that they also have a profound vibrancy to their emotions that most do not have privy to. There is a metaphysical beauty to their sentiments that wonderfully irons out wrinkles of tension.

Libras are gracious and charming individuals that are honest and harmonious. They enjoy surrounding themselves with beautiful music, art, food, wine, and company. The finer things in life are what they aim for. Even if they are down on their luck, they somehow always can make the best of their situation. Their love of peace and tranquility drives their every move. Venus bestows each Libra with its clandestine gifts of amorousness and intoxicating charm. Venus imparts an unassuming aura of pastel pink and scents them sweetly of roses. Experiencing their charisma is like drinking an intoxicating love potion that leaves you in a state of bliss, elation, and incandescent happiness. The best part is that you do not even know you are under their spell due to their low-pressure nature. When the phrase cloud nine was coined, surely they were referring to being in love with a Libra.

How to Lose a Libra

Libras are looking for a classy and poised partner who smells sweetly and looks at them with stars in their eyes. They enjoy partnerships for the mutual benefits and romance runs through their sugary blood. They want to show off their lover, so appearing effortless and charming will be sure to please them. They are very into the way things appear (all who are ruled by Venus come with an artful eye for beauty), so do not, I repeat, do not show up to a date with a Libra looking like you just rolled out of bed. To Libra, perception is reality, so spend time on your appearance while seeming natural because Libra sure will be. They do not want something superficial but rather something unsurprisingly lovely. They appreciate when things are unforced and easy, so having a cool and calm energy will be enticing.

Libras are very indecisive, which can be irritating, but that is just how it is with them. Having patience in this department will be absolutely necessary with this sun sign. Giving them ultimatums will never help you get what you want from them. In fact, forcing them into a decision will only make them leave. Take your sweet time and allow them to think it is their idea. Pairing this with a lot of compromise is the way around their indecision. Libras will charm your heart into submission, but they do not want someone who is clingy. They love to be wanted but not necessarily needed. It is easier said than done, but do not completely fall for their charisma. However, you do not want to act like you do not care about them at all either. You will have to find a balance to keep them interested, which is tricky but necessary. This is not a game that they are playing, but simply a balance that they need in their partnership between independence and interdependence. It is hard to know where the line is with Libra because they will not tell you—they do not even know themselves. It needs to feel right and natural, not forced and full of work. Self-control will be required when falling in love with this air sign. Do not forget to keep living your life as you did before while making time for them.

Libras are not impressed with anything too extreme. They are looking for someone who is classy, smart, balanced, and secure. Do not sell yourself to them; let your confidence do all the talking. Libra's senses are touchy and extremely heightened thanks to their ruling planet of Venus, especially their sense of sound. If your voice is shrill or the music is turned up too high, they will be gone in a flash. They require serene surroundings filled with beauty along with a peaceful and relaxed environment. They enjoy a fun debate, but they detest heated arguments. They are in a constant state of achieving harmony in love by balancing their scales, so if you are constantly picking fights, they will have no problem leaving for more peaceful pastures. Libras love the finer things in life, so if you are too practical with your dollars, it will rub them the wrong way. The way that Libras show love is by spoiling and with romantic gestures, so if you do not show appreciation for these things, they will look for someone that does. To keep a Libra is quite a balancing act, but it is a total breeze once you find the right amount of weight to even out their scales.

How to Bed a Libra

Libras encompass all the enchanting beauty of the Venus de Milo. They appeal wonderfully to the senses by being soft and sensual. They taste like apples and smell like roses. But do not let their romantic gentleness fool you into believing they are feeble. Behind the pink smoke, they are strong as steel. Libras are equally as stoic in their poised statue as they are soft, which also translates to how they make love. Their sexuality is filled with gentleness and strength that increases and contracts in a balanced way, which makes one wild with delight.

Libra's poised mind is excellent at summing someone up in moments. They do not fall in love easily or foolishly as they may lead you to believe. They will share their thoughts with you in such a way that would never leave you offended. Sexually they will boost up your ego and your head in a way that you will think you are the best on earth. They want a lover who knows their way around the bedroom and have no desire to teach their sexual partner from scratch. Finding someone sexually worthy of a Libra is a true task.

Keep the crude and crass comments out of the bedroom because Libras like to keep things classy. They appreciate strength that does not need to be spoken of. As they say, insecurities are loud. They also like to be the one in charge, and you better not mind it. Handling them with finesse and balance is critical to getting a Libra to surrender because they are a hard one to lock down. However, once you do, you will be flying in the clouds. When they do surrender, the sex is so harmonious, you will hear bells ringing.

There is a duality in their sexuality that gives their companions a taste of salty and sweet, light and dark, kind and cruel, and masculine and feminine. Their character is defined in dyad, which is why they are a hard sun sign to sexually pinpoint. Libras are constantly being pulled in two directions at once, which is why it is important for their partner to bring variety to their love-making. Libra's mind is always open to new possibilities and colorful sexual escapades. The dichotomy of this sun sign makes them easy to love but hard to keep happy, easy to adore but difficult to be with. Libras always wonder if they are missing out on something bigger while being fully committed to someone, but if you are able to consistently spark their interests and enthuse them, their minds will have an easier time staying put.

Their sexual standards are high, especially when they want you forever. Sex to a Libra is something that is not just physically pleasurable but mentally enjoyable as well. The romance of a relationship is so thrilling to this lovely sun sign. They will entangle you in their web of cotton candy love, and you will anticipate the act of sex with them up to the very last second. They will take control of your body and have you flying high in the sky on cloud nine. All of this will be done with poise, charm, and Libran beauty. You will be engulfed with their sweet pink seduction and go to a place that only lovers know.

☼ ☼ ☼

LIBRA & LIBRA

♎ 💎 ♎

Aspect: Conjunct
Elements: Air and air
Modalities: Cardinal and cardinal

Two Libras together only doubles the charm. They will love to spend a lot of time talking about all the logical and romantic topics that run through their minds. The air element is known for its clever nature, and what is important to Libras is the excitement of a mutually stimulating intellectual debate that they find mentally energizing. Unlike most couples, if they are unable to agree, they are completely comfortable agreeing to disagree. It is when other sun signs rush them into decisions that their scales dip out of balance, causing more mental, emotional, and physical damage than anyone would ever guess.

Two Libras have more in common than debating, indecisiveness, and their good looks. They also have a love of their home and an eye for beauty. They will take pride in appearing attractive together, and when they find mutual passions that encourage loveliness, they will help each other flourish in those areas. They both require a lot of rest too. Libras have exhausting spurts of energy and social periods where they spend a lot of time with friends, and they then need a big break to recharge. This is why resting is productive for Libra. If they are unable to do so, they become downright crabby. Their reenergizing periods may not always match up together, so they need to keep this in mind and be respectful of one another's individual space. These two cannot expect compatibility unless their metabolisms are counterbalanced. That way, they can give each other a helping hand by boosting one another's spirits. When they are both portraying their positive aspects to one another, it is very harmonious indeed. They will enjoy long evening walks, relish reading in bed together, and love to compliment one another. They will enjoy shared interests and hobbies so that they are able to intellectually talk about their tandem experiences afterward. Being that they are the sign of beauty, they will also enjoy inspired topics about things such as art and music.

Sexually they both create mental variety for one another. It is rare that boredom will strike between them in bed because they are such an imaginative sign. Their creativeness will always keep things sweet and fresh. The only thing that will come between their physical union is business at work, being bogged down with stress, or raising a family. The wonderful thing about them, though, is that no matter how long they do not connect, they will reconnect beautifully, as though their relationship was brand new. Small things, such as the way they smell or looking at a love note they wrote for each other, will trigger their spark for one another. Nearly every double-Libra couple will dedicate a song to their relationship. It will be an anthem for their love, and whenever they hear it, they will think of their wedding or the first time they met because they are both sweetly sentimental in this way.

Libra is known in astrology as the peacemaker, and one of the most beautiful things about two Libras is that they possess the wonderful ability to bring peace into one another's mind. Venus always gives its children brightness and beauty, and together, their dreams have wings. When two cardinal signs join forces, the heavens seem to open up for the impossible to happen. Their love can make hopes come true, and they become the epitome of splendor, fairness, and hard work to make their story an enchanted one. They gently fill one another's hearts with truth and justice, and together, they help beautifully balance each other's scales, creating an energy filled with peace, love, and prosperity.

☼ ☼ ☼

LIBRA & SCORPIO

♎ 💎 ♏

Aspect: Semisextile
Elements: Air and water
Modalities: Cardinal and fixed

Scorpios are intimidating, but Libras are not easily intimidated. Libras are charming, but Scorpios are not easily charmed. Scorpios are deeply sensitive behind their façade of self-sufficiency and confidence. Libras are as strong as steel underneath their charming voice, beautiful features, and sparkling dimpled smile. Scorpio is a water sign ruled by the fiery planet of Mars, but Scorpio's modern ruler, Pluto, keeps all that smoldering passion below the surface. Meanwhile, Libra is the only masculine sun sign ruled by a feminine planet. So, you see, these two will learn that there is much more to one another than meets the eye, which works out perfectly seeing they both love a good challenge.

Libras are naturally intelligent, beautiful, logical, and can make a fair decision about everything—except when it comes to falling in love with a Scorpio. The challenge that Libra presents Scorpio is one of unattainability because Libra has a hard time deciding if they are in or out. In relationships, Librans love ease, and Scorpio presents difficulty with their emotional depth and mystery, which presents a challenge for Libra to understand them no matter how many years have passed. Libra will never cease to amaze Scorpio with their true to form logic, and their starry eyes and Venusian features will be a distraction for Scorpio when Libra's indecisiveness is hurtful.

Scorpio is aware of Libra's beguiling effect on them and may sometimes suspect that they are not completely leveling with them by hiding their true thoughts and feelings. This is a dual problem because Libra will be troubled by Scorpio's subtle and secretive manner. Libra is naturally curious, but most of the time, it will not be worth it for Libra to argue with anything Scorpio feels strongly about, especially when it comes to commitment. Scorpio takes a black-and-white approach to love, and they are either all in or all out. Libra lives in gray area, which is something that Scorpio cannot fathom. However, where Scorpio can find solace is to know that Libra can be undeniably convincing of the fact that they are relaxed and simple, but behind their cheerful face and clouds of pink smokes, they will not truly be happy unless they form an important bond of partnership.

Libra rules the seventh house of marriage and partnerships, which is why there is an intrinsic importance in this area of life. Libra does not just want to be a partner, though; they need a challenge and mental stimulation as well. It is important that their scales are balanced with a peaceful companionship and an equal partner. Scorpio is the ruler of the eighth astrological house, which rules other people's money and shared resources. On the karmic wheel, Libra falls in Scorpio's second house of money and material possessions, which gives these matters more importance with this couple than with most. The income of either—or both—will be the subject of much emphasis in their relationship. If there is a lack of financial stability between these two, there could be some serious issues.

Libra will be the one in the relationship who creates the social atmosphere, and their fondness for fun, people, and entertaining can be wonderful for Scorpio. On the contrary, taking Scorpio's focus away from work and priorities can be a bad distraction. Mingling frequently also creates financial stress that concerns Scorpio much more than Libra, but the scorpion will conceal their stress to please their Libran. Scorpio is not as naturally balanced as Libra is, and they usually need their time alone to do their best work. If they start their love story later in life, this will usually be no issue because Scorpio will know their boundaries by then.

These two are not as emotionally passionate as they are mentally. Sexually they can anticipate each other's wishes, but they are not always aware of how to satisfy them. Scorpio's intensity may make Libra a little nervous at first, but if Libra is able to relax and unwind, they will be able to enjoy Scorpio's sexually fervent nature. Depending on the day—and which way Libra's scales are tipping—Scorpio may need to lighten up a bit to be able to blend with Libra. Libra will teach Scorpio how to comply by showing them that there is a certain time and place for everything when it comes to sex. When they harmonize, Scorpio can satisfy every sensual and erotic longing—every secret need of affection and fierce devotion—that Libra has ever dreamed about romantically.

After they can figure out their finances, communication, social life, and sexual harmony, they will most likely marry or move on. With patience and adjustment, they will see that they both fall in love for keeps; they just have different ways of getting there. It is a blessing when this pair falls in love because Libra can provide an idealistic outlet for Scorpio's controlled and driving ambition, and Scorpio's deeper wisdom will check Libra's airy indecisions, gently molding them into a sensible approach to make their daydreams into reality. Their love has an excellent chance to expand outside themselves into a tremendous energy.

☼ ☼ ☼

LIBRA & SAGITTARIUS

♎ ❤ ♐

Aspect: Sextile
Elements: Air and fire
Modalities: Cardinal and mutable

Libra respects a partner who is honest and optimistic because they themselves encompass these qualities. They love parties, art, music, learning, and mental challenges, including a good debate. Sagittarius respects a partner who is outgoing and mentally stimulating because they are on the search for their equal. They love freedom, animals, spontaneity, and having people to talk about their dreams with. Libra and Sagittarius share many of one another's qualities, and their sextile aspect brings a strong friendship vibe to their love. Sagittarius will first notice Libra's classically good looks, and Libra will first notice Sagittarius's bright energy. When they start conversing, they will realize they both break each other's mold.

These two are truly wonderful together, but if they meet when they are not ready to commit, this love may be hard to hold on to. Libra is the sign of partnerships, and Sagittarius is the sign of travel, adventure, and continued learning. Libra has urges from their ruling planet, Venus, that pull them toward relationships and marriage, while Sagittarius has urges from their ruling planet, Jupiter, that pull them toward wanderlust and curiosity, not necessarily rings and vows. Libra has two options: let their archer go and hope they will come back or stay with them and hope they eventually see that permanent partnership is an adventure in itself. To suffocate or force Sagittarius into a union will never work.

It is not that they are against marriage, they just need time to bask in their freedom. Libras rarely move quickly into permanency as well due to their deliberating nature, which is why this pair will usually date for a long time before they marry—if ever. The timing in this love story is everything.

Libras are supremely smooth and superior to most because they are born leaders, but their charm allows them to lead gently and intelligently. The more Sagittarius gets to know Libra, the more they will see what an incredible teammate they would make for their endeavors. Sagittarius is much happier with someone by their side, and together they are a witty, smart, and fun couple. It is an excellent idea for the Libra who loves an archer to go along with them on their journeys rather than to try to force them into a societal mold. Libra's indecisiveness is something that will irritate Sagittarius, and it will be something that Libra will have to improve upon. Sagittarius will help Libra understand that they do not need to go through life trying to weigh out every single decision that is ever presented to them. Sometimes they just need to go where the wind takes them because spontaneity in life is what makes it beautiful. The way that Sagittarius communicates is blunt, which will occasionally hurt Libra, and this is something they will need to work on. Sagittarius is way more impulsive than Libra is, but over time Libra will calm their centaur down enough to realize that deliberation can save them from making mistakes.

There is something about Libra's air element that is soothing and cooling to Sagittarius's fiery and wild nature. Maybe it is their dimpled smile or languid nature, but whatever it is, it works wonders on the centaur. They will enjoy stimulating each other's minds just as much as each other's bodies. Sagittarius is eager to get Libra in bed as often as possible because Libra sparks so much sexual curiosity. Sagittarius is quick to sense every unspoken mental, emotional, or sensual desire in Libra, almost before they even know it themselves. With both of these sun signs so attractive and exuding such a love of life, they rarely get bored with one another. People can fall out of love as quickly as they fell into it when they have only their sexual chemistry, but with these two, part of the attraction has to do with the lovemaking between their minds as well. Their sex is cheerful, free, and fun, and they connect through conversation just as much, if not more, than sex. They feel like they can even see the world a little clearer after oneness with each other.

They will always have plenty to talk about because Libra sees the childlike wonder behind Sagittarius's big personality and would like to spend their whole life being Sagittarius's personal love guru. The archer is so curious about everything, and Libra truly enjoys that about them. Libra has an incredible way of talking themselves into believing anything, and Sagittarius will be attracted by their fine mind and touched by the optimism they share. It is that same optimism that can turn the tough times of their love story into positive ones through the steadiness of faith that they have in each other. Within every cloud, Libra looks for the same silver linings as Sagittarius does. Together, they live in a world of imagination where troubles are never real and negativity is not invited. Their sharp minds can figure out the tricky turns throughout life and solve any problems by painting rainbows over the dark skies. They will turn their backs to ugliness, and that is what makes these two amazingly capable of a great and lasting love.

☼ ☼ ☼

LIBRA & CAPRICORN

Aspect: Square
Elements: Air and earth
Modalities: Cardinal and cardinal

As challenging as this relationship will be, there are positive aspects to it that both sun signs will greatly benefit from. Libras enjoy a powerful and independent partner, and Capricorn checks both of those boxes. Capricorn is thoughtful, logical, reasonable, and always wants to hear all sides of any argument, which is something Libra will love about the sea goat. Both sun signs are born under the cardinal modality, which means they are both natural-born leaders. Capricorn enjoys guiding themselves and everyone else around with the attitude that they always know what is best. They are brilliance combined with a cool and strong common sense. Libra's way of guiding is strong yet soft, like whiskey in a teacup. They will have to make compromises between their cardinality so that they both have the opportunity to be the one in charge.

With Libra's fairness and Capricorn's sagacity you would think these two would see eye-to-eye on everything, but unfortunately, the reason that this relationship has its challenges is because they prefer to be in control. Sometimes when Capricorn gets into a relationship their significant other becomes their career. Capricorn will never guide their partner to failure, but Libra does not take well to having themselves be anyone's "project." Libra is an air sign, so Capricorn must learn that, like all air signs, they need freedom and movement. If you do not let this sun sign come up for air, their relationship will become like a stale and stagnant room that has had the windows closed for a long time. If Capricorn continues to try to contain and control Libra in any form, there will be several battles headed their way.

One weakness Libra has is their desire and need to always win an argument. Libra is so intellectually stimulated by being right that they may even change their mind on where they stand on something just so they are correct. That is not how Capricorn operates one bit. Once the goat digs their heels in about a decision, nothing will change it. Thanks to Libra's ruling planet, Venus, their nature is naturally optimistic and pleasurable, whereas Capricorn's ruling planet, Saturn, makes them pessimistic and practical. When they initially meet one another, they may not be attracted, but Libra will be able to coax Capricorn from behind their walls with their charming, dimpled smile.

When it comes to sex, Libra may think that Capricorn is too reserved for their taste, but Libra is wrong. When Capricorn makes love, it is nothing short of powerful, slow, and sensual. Libras tend to be verbal in bed and will always let Capricorn know how amazing they are. Capricorn will be able to teach this feathery sun sign how to make love like an earth sign by taking them out of the sky and bringing them to the ground. Libra will go willingly, but in return, Libra will teach Capricorn how to be lite and affectionate without holding anything back. Capricorn must learn from Libra how to be more verbally expressive. If they can make these tweaks, all will be well behind closed doors.

These two have so much to benefit and absorb from one another. Libra must learn to have patience with Capricorn and the hard walls around their soft heart, and the sea goat must let this air sign be free from their naturally restrictive view on how a relationship should be. Capricorn has secret wants and desires that take a very perceptive person to understand. Libra usually looks at things for exactly what they are instead of believing that there is a hidden meaning or conspiracy. Therefore, Libra will have to look a little harder if they want to love this sun sign the way they need to be loved. Capricorn needs Libra's rainbows and lightness because they are good for their soul. Libra needs Capricorn's steadfast dependability because it assists in grounding them. Some relationships grow rapidly, but this one will grow slow and steadily like a tree. Trees take years and seasons to grow to their full potential, but once a tree grows solid roots, it will be then be able to flower. If they can learn and love from one another, they will beat the odds of what astrology says about this square match.

☼ ☼ ☼

LIBRA & AQUARIUS

Aspect: Trine
Elements: Air and air
Modalities: Cardinal and fixed

Aquarius is all over the place when it comes to relationships. Even though these two sun signs are a match made straight out of heaven, there is nothing that can control the water bearer's truly Uranian energy. Aquarius just has a knack of always changing their mind about where they should be in their relationship. One day they will want to marry Libra, the next they will want to just live together until they are financially stable and they both finish goals they have, and the next day Aquarius will wonder what it would like to be single again. Regardless of the water bearer's sometimes confusing mind changes, Libra can assist in leveling everything out to make sense again for their partner's zany and ever-changing plans. Libra is also quite indecisive, which allows them to make space for the water bearer's variable views. Aquarius loves Libra's fair mind and beautifully dimpled smile that heals their aloof heart, and Libra knows that no one on earth would ever be able to love them for all their faults the way that Aquarius does. There is rarely a dull moment around these two.

Aquarius values friendship in a relationship more than anything. To a water bearer, the definition of love and the definition of friendship are usually the exact same. They are both very clever and enjoy playing practical jokes on one another, which can bring a childlike joy to their oneness. While friendship is Aquarius's number one, the important things to Libra will be having a peaceful and harmonious environment and committed partnership. Considering the fact that Aquarius is so unconventional, keeping the peace will be something that they must work to achieve for their Libra. Because of their brilliant mind, Libra often needs to rest more than any other sun sign. If Aquarius can take the time to join them, they will need to remember to lower their high vibrations, bring their voice down, talk about positive things, and stay as calm as they possibly can. When Libra is relaxed, they will want to connect both mentally and physically. The physicality is what separates Libra from any of Aquarius's friends and is an important piece of this relationship's puzzle.

Because of their matching air element, they are brilliantly compatible sexually. They will both love giving and receiving and have the power to heal one another when they blend. There is a lightness and beauty to their physicality that is poetic and fresh, as though they had known each other in a past life. They will learn each other's bodies as though they are their own and will remember it is as though it is the back of their own hand. There is something so familiar yet so new about the way they feel when they are one. They are friends first and lovers second, but their bond for one another has loads of complexity and significance. There is nothing aggressive or forceful about how these two make love because they magically vibe on the same wavelength without needing to say a word, which brings a special closeness and exclusivity to their union.

On their gray days, Libra will blame Aquarius of being stubborn, and Aquarius will allege Libra of being bossy. They are both correct in their accusations as Aquarius is fixed and Libra is cardinal, but instead of seeing these traits as a negative, they should view them as assets that allow them to strengthen their relationship. After they let one another know how they feel, Libra can appreciate the water bearer's stubbornness as tenacity while Aquarius shifts their gaze to see Libra's bossiness as responsibility. They both enjoy polishing their minds with one another's intelligence, which is how they will be able to see one another clearly. When they start to really think about it, Aquarius really does admire Libra's impartial approach and the way that they are graceful under pressure, and Libra appreciates how their Aquarius rarely wastes time or energy on trivial topics, which creates fewer arguments and makes space for a cordial dynamism that Libra needs to balance their scales. Their mutual cooperation will be necessary for their harmony.

There will be days when the Uranian unpredictability of Aquarius throws Libra's scales out of balance. However, it is also during those spontaneous surprises that Libra is most inclined to feel their deepest affection toward their water bearer. All the unique and unexpected experiences they have with their alien makes Libra remember that they are so fortunate to have such a witty and exceptional partner to spend their days with. This reminds them how lucky they are to not be alone or tied to someone who is boring. There is nothing dull about Aquarius, and odds are that even the way they meet will be an unexpected story. That is the thing with Aquarians that brings zeal to their love and lives. You never know what to expect, making every day different than the one before.

☼ ☼ ☼

LIBRA & PISCES

♎ ❀ ♓

Aspect: Quincunx
Elements: Air and water
Modalities: Cardinal and mutable

Together, these two create their own world made of pink mist and contentment. Libras are airy, dreamy, charming, and mysterious while being familiar all at the same time. Pisces are overwhelmingly sympathetic and even dreamier than Libra is, if you can imagine. These two are romantic and poetic together while both wise with different types of sagacity. Libra's wisdom is their intellect, and Pisces's is their emotions. Together, their alchemy is a bubbly potion of air and water that is pure magic. In Hellenistic astrology, Venus is in its domicile in the sign of Libra but exalted in the sun sign of Pisces. Even though this pair may come from two totally different worlds, one world they share is that of Venusian romance and love.

They can make each other very happy, but just like every love story, it is not a complete walk in the park. If the fish has any unpleasant habitual patterns, which most Pisces do, Libra will expect them to be corrected. However, Libra will have to stop being so judgmental and understand that Pisces is not in the relationship to serve them. They want and require a partner that is their equal, not their boss. It is hard for Libra to not be disparaging because it is in their nature to weigh every bit of information that is received. Libra is symbolized by the scales for this reason, and instead of feeling things out, they look at issues with their detached intellect. This is not how Pisces operates, and instead, they rely completely on their emotions and intuition to make their decisions. This can cause Pisces to see Libra as being hard-hearted and aloof, while Libra sees Pisces as illogical. This difference also motivates their decisions inversely. Neither one of them is very quick when making big choices, which can delay them from moving forward in their own relationship. However, once they can get their differences straightened out, they will see that they really do want the same things, which is for their love to be peaceful and harmonious. Libra is usually the peace, and Pisces is usually the harmony.

Neither one of them cares for conflict of any type, and they can avoid it by creating a romantic bond through their oneness. Their sex is rich, passionate, dreamy, and full of quality. They both connect at a different wavelength, but when combined, it is a sweet melody. Pisces uses their intuition to sense Libra's deepest desires, and they are happy to make them come true. Their quincunx vibration makes them powerfully attracted to one another, and together, they create a dreamy aura of amorousness. Their sex will be something out of a pastel-colored dream, but for them to stay together, they will need to make their dreams into a beautiful reality.

In most cases, these two are very happy together, and over time, they start to vibrate simultaneously on one wavelength. Pisces starts having faith in Libra, and Libra starts to support Pisces, which creates a strong base for any times of disagreement. Pisces will begin to see that Libra really is not coldhearted but that they are wonderfully fair, and Libra will start to see that Pisces's emotions are a necessary part of their logic, which makes them the beautifully empathetic person that they love. Together, they will come full circle back to their world of pink mist and contentment.

Pisces respects and admires Libra's strengths and knows that it is something that they could most certainly learn from them. Libra is fascinated and enchanted by Pisces's ability to know things without logic and reason and understands that tapping into their own intuitiveness is something they can certainly learn from them. These creatures are from two totally different worlds, but once they are caught in one another's nets, they will enjoy each other's beauty and appreciation for true romance. There will be days where they will wonder how this will ever work, and they will have to find a place of peace they can both cohabitate in. A fish may love a bird, but where would they live? If a bird and fish are to fall in love, they must live harmoniously where water and air mingle—in a haven of quiet pools and gentle zephyrs.

☼ ☼ ☼

Chapter 8

Scorpio

Scorpio's love archetype is the alchemic lover. They transform and create love through a seemingly magical process. Scorpio is a complex, secretive, introspective, and tactical lover. Scorpio's lesson in love is to impart that love is desire and absorb that love is relinquishing.

Element	Water
Modality	Fixed
Polarity	Yin, negative, and feminine
Mantra	"I desire."
Hue	Burgundy
Deities	Hades and Persephone, god and goddess of the underworld
Glyph	♏
Flowers	Chrysanthemum and amaryllis
Tree	Blackthorn
Jewel	Topaz
Crystals	Malachite and black obsidian
Fragrance	Anise
Body Parts	The nose, genitals, colon, blood, and urethra
Animals	Scorpions, eagles, snakes, beetles and other insects
Food & Herbs	Onions, leeks, shallots, aloe, witch hazel, catmint, capers, sarsaparilla, sanicle, olive leaf, sassafras, mustard, bitter-tasting food, such as cranberries and pomegranates, and vegetables with high iron content, such as beets and broccoli

Scorpio's Ruling Planets: Mars and Pluto

Scorpio is one of the few signs that have two ruling planets. Mars is its traditional ruling planet, but when Pluto was discovered, the powerful dwarf orb was assigned to Scorpio, making Pluto this sun sign's modern ruler.

Mars in love rules energy, physical stamina, and motivation. Mars reveals how we act out our sexual impulses, passions, challenges, and masculine sexual expression. Mars represents your physical energy and how you act and react in situations. Mars gives this sign its fiery passion. Unlike the other water signs, Scorpio is the only one that has an element of fire from Mars, which makes it arguably the most powerful sign in the zodiac.

Pluto in love rules transformation, your ability to reinvent yourself, change, and subconscious drives and forces. Pluto reveals rejuvenation, beginnings, and endings. Pluto shows you where you need to change your life, and the parts of your relationship that need to be torn down and then rebuilt. It is there for your ultimate good, or at least it tries to be, if you will not resist the change. Pluto is the planet of life and death—of the new you and the old you. It repairs and resurrects, causing you to reinvent yourself and your relationship throughout your life. Regarding Scorpio, Pluto represents sex, death, birth, and rebirth, and Scorpio's water element gives the sign deep complexity. Being a fixed sign gives it stability.

Scorpio Mythology

Scorpius was responsible for the death of the great hunter Orion. According to myth, the scorpion stung Orion in response to him bragging that he could defeat any creature. However, Scorpius stung Orion while Orion simultaneously stabbed Scorpius, causing their tandem demise. To further avoid conflict, Scorpius was placed on the opposite side of the sky from Orion, which is where you can find them in the heavens to this day.

Scorpio's Positive Qualities and Negative Forms

Scorpio's positive qualities are loyalty, willpower, magnetism, gentleness, insight, and amazing self-control. Expressed in their negative forms, they become ruthless, extreme, revengeful, cruel, suspicious, and have self-hatred.

How a Scorpio Loves

Being born while the sun was in Scorpio enriches a person with an inconceivable amount of emotional passion. It's not a loud in-your-face type of passion but one that smolders; it is a passion that is calm yet intensely felt, like the embers of a fire. The emotions experienced by this individual are so potent that they are barely able to be contained. When Scorpio is in love, they are known to create a lovely, calm façade for their feelings to keep them neatly confined. This only enhances their mysterious quality. One can feel that there is something powerful about Scorpio's aura but cannot quite pinpoint exactly what it is. However, there are a rare few who are privy to Scorpio's hidden desires.

Because of Scorpio's mysterious nature, they come off as unapproachable, which is exactly what they aim for. They know fully well that familiarity breeds contempt, so they conceal and control their energy because it makes them feel safe. However, when Scorpio does find someone that they are able to bare their soul to, their love for them becomes all-consuming and even obsessive. The loyalty they have for their loved one is unswerving and the one that they revere is worth any sacrifice. It is in this love that they attempt frantically to unite their feelings to the physical and spiritual vibrations of eternity.

The mastery of understanding Scorpio's love is to understand their desires. Scorpio's soul is blessed with the sense of knowing things others are not able to conceive. They sense things that cannot even be defined. Their feelings are black and white, making them either care deeply about matters or not at all. They are not quick to trust out of pure self-preservation, and because of their fixed modality, they are not easily swayed. Scorpio energy is dark yet safe, and it is in the shadowy, invisible, and mysterious place of their psyche that true connections are formed. Unseen yet indestructible ties are created for the ones their soul loves. It shows us that we do not have to be physically together to be linked. Scorpio's emotional ties are built in a place you cannot view with your eyes but must feel with your spirit.

The Scorpio lesson in love is to impart that love is desire and absorb that love is relinquishing. In traditional marriage vows, one says, "Until death do us part." But for Scorpio, until death do us part does not a promise make. They look for a love that is all-consuming beyond this world and dimension of understanding. They necessitate a connection that lasts through the limitlessness of the universe, through the trillions of stars, and in the vastness of time. They desire a love that travels through infinite lifetimes, through endless galaxies, and in every form of existence. That is what type of dedicated love, depth of emotion, and raw passion a Scorpio in love is capable of manifesting.

How to Spot a Scorpio

The surefire way to figure out if someone is a Scorpio is their eyes. Their look is piercing with strong intensity, and their eyes are always somehow dark, even if they are the lightest shade of blue. Their x-ray-vision gaze is penetrable and steady, and if you are stared down by a Scorpio, it may make you feel extremely uncomfortable, which is usually their intention. Most Scorpios have razor-sharp features (notably the nose, which they rule) and prominent brows that beautifully frame their mesmeric eyes. Scorpios have a powerful aura that says a lot without having to speak a word. Most Scorpios will have dark hair with a reddish tint thanks to their traditional ruling planet, Mars. Scorpios are poised, cool, and completely unbothered. Their bodies rarely have any nervous twitches, and they are able to stay still with all the composure in the world. Because of this, it is rare to find a tense or detached Scorpio. They prefer to hide their obsessive emotions where they are safely concealed. Scorpio's calm, collected nature is a façade to suppress their true feelings, which are locked away for a select few. Their many masks hide the passion that boils inside of them.

Scorpio knows what they are and what they are not, making them confident and sure. Quips will be laughed or stared off if anyone throws one their way. When Scorpio smiles it is genuine. Scorpio may not smile often, but when they do, you know their grin is coming from their heart. If you compliment them, they will take your praise with a smirk. There are some Scorpios with a friendly and outgoing nature, but their eyes give away the seriousness in their soul. The biggest mistake you could ever make is mistaking a Scorpio's kindness for weakness. Be on your guard with every Scorpio you meet because no matter how nice they are perceived to be, they are never naive or spineless. If you betray them in any way, they will happily cut you and any drama out with one swift slice, and depending on the severity of the situation, they will use their stinger to teach you a lesson as well. The twenty-sixth president of the United States, Scorpio Theodore Roosevelt, put it perfectly with "Speak softly and carry a big stick." This is a motto many Scorpios live by.

Scorpios live by their convictions and are black and white. They are not the "maybe" type of people. If you are looking for a straight answer, they will have no problem giving you one. Sensitive souls who need their egos stroked should not go to a Scorpio for advice. A Scorpio tells you what you need to hear, not what you want to hear. It is beneath them to dish out a compliment just to make someone like them, so if you get one, it holds weight. You either love, respect, and admire the Scorpio you know, or you loathe them. There really is not a lot of gray matter on the subject. Take them or leave them; that is all they ask.

This sign is represented as a snake, a scorpion, an eagle, and a phoenix. With Pluto as their modern ruler, they are constantly being broken down, rebuilt, and reinvented. There is no one who can rise from the ashes the way a Scorpio can. They are considered the darkest sign in the zodiac because they are ruled by Pluto, which is the planet of death. It is their constant life struggle to crawl out of the darkness and into the light and to evolve into one's highest sense of self. If you look at the Scorpio glyph, you will see that there is an arrow pointing upward, representing this struggle. Scorpios must remember to always find the light in the deep emotions that tend to drown them. However, they are also the most powerful sign in the zodiac because they are a fixed water sign, which gives them strength to harness and control their formidable element. Scorpios can use this force for both good or evil. The choice is theirs.

Scorpios are fiercely loyal and protective of their loved ones. If you are kind to a Scorpio, it will never be forgotten and richly rewarded. There is something hypnotic and transcending that transfixes people to Scorpios. It is as if they cast a spell. If they want something, Scorpios will resourcefully make it become reality. Yes, Scorpios are intense, but once you have one on your side, you will have gained a gentle soul, an amazing lover, a loyal friend, and a very strong ally for life. See that dark, mysterious character with the intense gaze who seems to know your secrets? Do you feel a shudder down your spine? You must be spotting Scorpio because they have certainly already spotted you.

How to Lose a Scorpio

Scorpios are secretive, and there are things that will remain secret about them forever, so it is smart to not pry or assume. If a Scorpio does not want to tell you something, it is to help you, not to hurt you. Do not snoop or dictate what they should or should not do, or you could be met with your Scorpio leaving you. They are a fixed sign, which means once they have decided, it will be very hard for you to change their mind. They stand strong in their convictions, so just trust that their intentions are in the right place. Scorpios do not want someone who is clingy, but even more so, they do not want someone who makes things impossible either.

Scorpios have zero time for games. Their emotions are intense like a volcano—suppressed until brought on by a disturbance. They want their partner to be sexy, but only for them. Their possessive nature will not appreciate a morally loose partner. They require complete loyalty from the one they love; you are either all the way in or all the way out. There cannot be an in-between. Scorpios are uncompromising when passionate about something, and they respect and admire a partner who stands their ground on their beliefs, even if they do not match up with their own. Do not be wishy-washy about who you are. Scorpios will see through your façade. Scorpios are human lie detectors, and once trust is broken with them, they will cut ties and never been heard from again.

Scorpios have no desire to be the butt of any joke. Underneath all their mystery is a sensitive spirit, so if you embarrass them, you will feel their sting. They need a partner who does not talk about their relationship to anyone other than maybe a licensed therapist. They like to keep their private life under wraps because it is sacred to them. The same also goes for their sex life. They do not care for a partner who kisses and tells. Scorpios rule sex, so if you are uncomfortable with your sexuality, that will be difficult for them to navigate around. Sex is a spiritual act to Scorpios, and it is imperative for them to connect to their partners physically and completely. If you are willing to learn, they would be happy to teach you.

Scorpios do not need to be pushed to commit. When a Scorpio wants you, you will know. They make their intentions crystal clear, so if they are only halfway in with you, there is a reason. They may not privy you to this information, so do not expect an explanation. While being involved with a Scorpio is intense, there is really nothing else like it. There is nothing watered down about the way they love, and it may even feel like control at first. But if you submit to their Plutonian potency, you will see that it is not control but rather a love so deep that even the gods envy. If you are unable to relinquish yourself to a Scorpio in fear of losing yourself, you may be missing out on the greatest love of your life. Release your inhibitions, and let their crimson waters take your heart away.

How to Bed a Scorpio

A Scorpio's energy is so intense that you can feel your skin start to move at the mere sight of them. Their piercing eyes stare directly into your soul. The gaze makes you feel naked, and you do not mind at all. The closer they get to you, the more nervous you become, and when they touch your skin, you become paralyzed by their magnetic desire. If you want a Scorpio, you must give yourself completely to them—body and soul. Sex with this sun sign is beautiful and fulfilling, and it can even bring the strongest of souls to tears and leave their body trembling with delight. After you've united with a Scorpio, you will be ready for more. Many become hooked on sex with a Scorpio because there is something addicting about their powerful, desirable, intense, and mysterious energy while they somehow keep a cool and composed poise. Scorpios are a master of uncovering what is not known to others and can sum you up in one quick glare. Few, if any, will ever leave the way they came when they truly fall for a Scorpio. Scorpios come with many karmic lessons in life and the bedroom that they must teach.

Sex with a Scorpio is like very strong coffee; it is an acquired taste that once you learn to like, you cannot seem to live without. One of Scorpio's biggest fears in love is feeling like they have no control, which is why they have a strong need to figure everything and everyone out. Scorpios understand that knowledge is power, and they will always be in control of how much they give of themselves, especially in bed. Scorpios rule sex, birth, and death, which they intrinsically know are all intertwined. Throughout their life, sex becomes something intensely yet intimately explored. This exploration becomes part of their evolvement of blending their emotionality and physicality into one. Because of this, Scorpio souls are traditionally never short of being sexual. However, what is commonly misunderstood is their promiscuity. Scorpio emotionality is not capable of easily detaching feelings from physical oneness. This makes it very difficult for them to share themselves intimately with someone they do not care for. Sex to a Scorpio is a religious act, which makes them a peculiar mix of amorousness and purity.

Scorpios are black and white, quick and to the point, and all or nothing, so you cannot have sex halfheartedly with them. They will capture you with the mere thought of being able to have them one more time. They dream to find a partner that is their equal and desire a partner that can match their passion. If they gift you with letting you see their real self, which is hidden under all the mystery that surrounds their elusive aura, you will find a very loyal and sensitive soul. Scorpios prefer dominating in the bedroom, but they also need a strong partner who can take the reins. There is a sense of security that a Scorpio needs from their partner in bed so that they know they can handle a personality and sexual nature of their caliber. A Scorpio's sex drive is high, and they need a partner to explore the realm and dimensions of sexuality with them. This sun sign is not for the faint of heart but the strong of soul. Do not be shy, and dive in; Scorpio's waters are just right.

☼ ☼ ☼

SCORPIO & SCORPIO

♏ ◈ ♏

Aspect: Conjunct
Elements: Water and water
Modalities: Fixed and fixed

A Scorpio partnership is a tricky potion made of sugar, spice, and mostly everything nice. This pairing will naturally challenge each other daily due to their mystifying blend of personality. They are both aware of each other's power and love how understood they finally feel with their equal. When things are good, they are good, but when things are bad, it is war. And thus is the story with every conjunct relationship in the zodiac. They will figure things out on their own as time goes on and come to see the best and worst of themselves mirrored back through their partnership.

To truly understand a Scorpio, you must be partnered or have had to grow up with one. Scorpios have layers upon layers of complexity to their souls, which they keep tucked away and out of sight and mind. Their memories are like filing cabinets, and they have the most incredible recollection second to Taurus. This knowledge is used for anything and everything that they wish to apply to throughout their day, including disagreements. Knowledge is this sun sign's deadliest weapon, and when they are in an enlightened state of being, they will use it for construction rather than destruction. Scorpios have lofty goals, and together, this duo can become quite the power couple when they choose to support one another.

A Scorpio pair can accomplish many marvels because of the immense force of blending their resources together. When one or both are not busy working toward an achievement, they can become depressed and even physically ill. Keeping each other motivated requires consistent, collaborative effort. If they can cope with keeping their arguing under control, their achievements as a team will be impressive. Scorpio rules the eighth house on the karmic wheel, which governs shared resources, intimacy, sex, and bonding. Therefore, the core of their partnership will revolve around these values. In addition, Scorpio rules childbirth, death, and the transition into another life. Because of this, it will not be uncommon for them to find pleasure and intimacy talking about these deep topics with one another. They may have different ideas of what death and religion are, but they do not feel that the topic is morbid. For Scorpio, sex is a spiritual and holy experience, and there is something undeniably haunting about the way these two create oneness with each other. They have a way of connecting their hearts, souls, and minds while making love because of their sensitive and deep nature. Sex is a way for them to fill those voids and create a bond that will make them inseparable.

A lesson that two Scorpios will learn in their relationship is that when they do disagree, negative actions and words inevitably return to the sender. When they seek to score against their partner, they are simply hurting themselves in the long run. This is a lesson that will take time for this couple to learn and inevitably be what separates them or what makes them completely unbreakable. Because they can understand each other so well, there will be more compassion and forgiveness than coldheartedness and revenge. Their negative traits are magnified by one another, but so are their positive ones, such as courage, dependability, protectiveness, and passion. Forgiveness is key with these two lovers, and they must learn to absolve one another to surpass the test of time.

Scorpios seem like they want to be feared, but their end goal is to be respected. This is something both will need to give the other. Throughout their partnership, they may not always be in the same place at the same time, but they will always hold space for one another. Scorpio naturally breaks down, and then rebuilds themselves over and over throughout their lifetime. They know that to truly love someone, you will watch old versions of them die and then support them during their rebirth. During these transitions, they may not always be in sync, but they can assist and support each other in one's transformation. This is how they grow to become intertwined, and together, they can build the tallest towers to which they are able to soar to the highest heights. If they use their power together, rather than against each other, there is next to nothing that this pair is unable to manifest.

☼ ☼ ☼

SCORPIO & SAGITTARIUS

♏ 💎 ♐

Aspect: Semisextile
Elements: Water and fire
Modalities: Fixed and mutable

Sagittarius will see Scorpio as a challenge, but what Scorpio does not know is that centaurs eat challenges for breakfast. The harder something is to achieve, the brighter the Sagittarius's flames will grow. The archer always has their eye on the target and aims their arrows that drip in optimism and luck toward the prize, which, in this case, is Scorpio. Scorpio is fixed, and Sagittarius is mutable. Scorpio is ruled by secretive Pluto, and Sagittarius is ruled by sanguine Jupiter. Scorpio is a water sign, and Sagittarius is a fire sign. Nevertheless, no matter their differences, nothing discourages either one of them from getting what they want, and if anything, their variations only make them more fascinated by one another.

These two share a common interest of discovering the truth behind life's most burning questions. With Sagittarius, it is called "inquisitiveness," and with Scorpio, it is called "control." The archer's curious nature is forever asking straightforward inquiries and demanding logical answers, never resting until they have been convinced. Scorpio goes about discovering the truth in a more subtle way. It is rather amusing to observe the two of them attempting to find out everything about one another. Sagittarius will be determined to rip off all of Scorpio's layers to truly understand their enigma, but Scorpio will not make it easy for them.

There is no denying that Scorpio has lessons of freedom, optimism, and self-honesty to learn from Sagittarius, which at times they will actively dislike. Yet, the situation will be somewhat softened by the Sagittarian's tolerance for Scorpio's faults and failings because they, somehow, are understanding of why they live life so intensely and with such great poignancy. Sagittarius likes to avoid such heavy emotional burdens and will always be happy to cheer Scorpio up when times get tough.

Just as in life, there is much to be learned sexually with each other. The way they look at sex is different, but that does not make them incompatible. Scorpio looks at sex as a sacred and silent act and wants an unspoken, shared ecstasy. Sagittarius will need to realize that sex is not always a time to say what is on their mind. They are both passionate in their own way and can even overpower one another with their shared intensity. Sex to a Sagittarius is a playtime and a way for them to release outwardly, while sex to a Scorpio is a way to connect spiritually and obtain closeness inwardly. The trick for Sagittarius is to know that there is more than what lies on the surface, while Scorpio will be required to let loose and free themselves during oneness.

Sagittarius never sneaks up on Scorpio from behind because there is nothing sneaky about a centaur. Their candor is a blessing from Jupiter and is due to the fact that they were born honest enough to kill you right to your face. They like to make their point loud and clear but never from a place of premeditated revenge. If they can connect through sincere communication, the Sagittarius will be happier with their scorpion, and they will become brighter and more cheerful as a couple. Sagittarius has a way of being able to bring anyone out of their shell and live life larger, and Scorpio is no exception to this rule.

There is also a positive and happy side to Scorpio's emotions, which is their passion. Sagittarius will not see that until later, but they will learn it was certainly worth the wait. For when a Scorpio is truly in love, they are loyal and fiercely protective of their partner. They will realize that behind Scorpio's mask is a warm and loving companion who is capable of intense devotion and who will still be there, whereas the ones before were like a revolving door. Sagittarius has never felt security like this with another person. However, if Sagittarius is not ready to settle down, then they should not be with this sun sign. Sagittarius could try to push their luck, but if they gamble with Scorpio's heart, they could lose it all. When Scorpio parts, they part for keeps.

Sagittarians want to wander on the wind and be free to answer the call of wild adventure. Yet, they have a genuine compassion for Scorpio's different outlook. They are both deeply sympathetic toward one another, which is what makes this couple so beautiful. This fire and water combination can be superbly combined to create a thick, warm vapor. If they find their perfect elemental blend, they will go on a lot of adventures and learn from each other along the journey. If Sagittarius cares enough to handle Scorpio's heart tenderly and watch their sharp tongue, they would be wise. If Scorpio can treasure Sagittarius's open mind and honest love without suffocating them with suspicion and accusations, they would be wise. Scorpio should not try to break the archer's golden optimism and blue-skied spirit because Sagittarius's starry eyes are what Scorpio deeply needs. Scorpio should go along with their visions and be the wise council so that together they can achieve wonders along their adventure through life and love.

☼ ☼ ☼

SCORPIO & CAPRICORN

♏ 💠 ♑

Aspect: Sextile
Elements: Water and earth
Modalities: Fixed and cardinal

When they first meet, Scorpio will admire Capricorn's quiet steadfastness. The sea goat rarely dominates any conversation, preferring to be more of the strong and silent type. Capricorn's reserved nature comes off to Scorpio as a challenge, and one thing Scorpio is fantastic at is seducing without needing to say a word. One of Scorpio's smoldering stares followed by a devilish smirk and Capricorn will be hooked. Scorpio seems so mysterious and intriguing; Capricorn must know more. Scorpio will then quickly act like the goat does not even exist, and after Scorpio has tortured them long enough, they will simultaneously give in and fall down the rabbit hole.

One thing that these two sun signs frequently have in common is that they are masters at concealing their emotions. However, once you get to know them, they both have beautiful imaginations and sensitive, deep souls. If they can get past each other's walls, they will connect in a private subterranean level, which is where they operate most comfortably. Capricorns require their partners to just know that they love them without large displays of romance. Scorpios are strongly intuitive and do not require an exaggerated type of idealism from their partners. They know that when their Capricorn shows love to them in a more practical way, it carries meaning and is coming from a place of sincerity, rather than something they are doing out of pure habit or spectacle. There is a strong, unspoken understanding between them that they are there for each other without having to put on a show, which is how they both like it.

One thing that Scorpio endears about Capricorn is that they are family oriented. Capricorn has their few close friends, but their family trumps all. Scorpio will have to get used to spending a lot of time with Capricorn's crew because that is where the sea goat will want to be. There may be times when Capricorn will depend on their family a little too much. Scorpio will need to step in and handle that in a way only a Scorpio really could: analytically, sensitively, and intrinsically. Scorpio is circumspect about everything, especially about their romantic relationship, and they will not appreciate their sea goat divulging their private life to anyone, even family. Scorpio is also possessive, and once things get serious between them, they will expect to be Capricorn's number one, requiring the health of their bond to come first and foremost. Capricorn will need time to understand that once they have a life partner, they must come before anyone, even their family. It will take them time, so Scorpio needs to be understanding and patient for this to naturally happen.

Capricorns love to be at home with the one they adore, and a close second is being at work. Capricorns are made to work, and if someone's career needs to take a back seat in this partnership, it could be Scorpio's. Scorpio will never sit at home without purpose, and they will find a way to succeed while supporting their Capricorn climber because Scorpio never lets anything hold them back. Capricorn will admire that the naturally resourceful Scorpio can make the best out of any situation given to them. Capricorn does not have to coddle and baby this sun sign. Scorpio is one of the most powerful signs in the zodiac, which makes them perfectly paired for the steely sea goat.

Sexually they will enrich each other's life in a way they never thought imaginable. These two are both masters of self-control and discipline. At first,

Capricorn will put high walls around themselves, but Scorpio's intrinsically solvable nature will find a way through their maze and into their heart. Once Scorpio breeches Capricorn's hard exterior, they will truly be able to fulfill them beyond what they could have imagined. Scorpio's loyalty will make Capricorn feel safe, and Capricorn's unwavering strength will allow Scorpio to intimately release. When they combine with one another, there is a strong sextile bond that only earth and water can create. As time goes on, Capricorn will make Scorpio feel safe and comfortable in a cozy way. Scorpio will feel like they're next to a fire in the dead of winter. If things ever do get a little dull, a change of scenery will do wonders for these two.

When you look at this beautiful pair, it is as though they have a secret that they are keeping from everyone else. It's something special only they understand. This secret is concealed in the intricacies of all their deep love for one another. It is not a sappy, over-the-top, innocent kind of love. It is much richer than that. It is a love that is tied together by life, by death, by memories, by karma, by family, and by their children. This love encompasses and encircles them, creating a bond and a private connection only they will get to experience with each other and only they can comprehend. Their unshakable union is met with sextile gifts of friendship and gives them their indestructible staying power. There really is not anything more priceless than that.

☼ ☼ ☼

SCORPIO & AQUARIUS

♏ ◈ ♒

Aspect: Square
Elements: Water and air
Modalities: Fixed and fixed

It will not take long for Aquarius to decipher Scorpio's smile. Scorpio always has a purpose to their stare and a precision in their reasons. They hold a secret in their aura that Aquarius wants to know. The water bearer's heart feels a soft pull every time Scorpio grins at them. Aquarius knows there is more to it than just the smile because they can see it in their eyes. Pump the brakes, Aquarius, and turn on your intelligent mind before floating away too far into the future. You need to realize there is more than what meets the eye with this soul. This is only the tip of the Scorpio iceberg that is being experienced because what you see is not what you get with a Scorpio. Ever. Water bearers have their own tricks up their sleeves, and if Scorpio suddenly starts to play hide-and-seek on them, Aquarius can become quite hazy themselves. Just when Scorpio thinks they have Aquarius in the palm of their hand, this sun sign will magically perform a vanishing act. When an Aquarius evaporates into thin air, not even the detective work of a sleuth Scorpio will find them. Aquarius will be somewhere high above the Milky Way, beyond all rainbows, floating to Uranus. They are certainly not going to stick around on earth to play Scorpio's cunning games.

Because of their similar fixed natures, neither one will want to be pushed into anything. They do not need to lead, but they certainly do not want to follow. They both significantly belong to themselves, which, at times, will make it hard for them to compromise with one another. A relationship between these sun signs is never going to be anything less than a learning experience that is both enlightening and fascinating. It will not be harmonious every day, but the lessons that they must teach each other will help both of them stretch and grow. They will need to learn to apologize and understand that any sort of change for either of them is hard. Both show regret through actions, so there will be a lot of reading between the lines, which may feel like game playing. However, if they can adjust to one another's varied vibrations, their harmony can be powerful and incredibly significant.

Scorpio is wise enough to understand that they have things to discover from Aquarius—although, they would never admit it in a million years. Aquarius has a much more casual approach to their problems and can easily forgive and forget. However, a Scorpio rarely forgets and is not the best at forgiving, especially when they experience Aquarius's shocking temper. Scorpio can stuff their emotions down a lot better than Aquarius is able. However, neither way is better than the other. If Scorpio can learn to be more upfront about their feelings and Aquarius can learn to cool their reactions, their disagreements will begin to lessen. Scorpio and Aquarius are aspected in a square, which means they will challenge and sharpen one another. Any friction they have can create tremendous growth and a mutual respect, which is better than being stuck in their fixed ways.

This combo can tend to be in a constant competition when it comes to sex, or if they choose, sex can be a truly healing experience for them depending where they are on their journey. Aquarius can experience Scorpio's energy in a way that makes them uneasy in the bedroom because they constantly feel as though they must measure up to Scorpio's intensity. Scorpio will feel as though part of Aquarius is actively and enthusiastically engaged in their feelings, while another part of them remains detached. Aquarius needs to learn to turn off their brain and just go with what emotions come naturally to them. Scorpio does not want a percentage of the water bearer's heart; they want them wholly. The problem with that desire is that Aquarius belongs to no one and everyone concurrently. Their soul is in a constant state of flux. They will have to meet each other in a parallel dimension and find one another in a world of compromise that they create together.

Scorpio may never grasp Aquarius the way they desire. However, they admire their independence and strong will. Together, they are beautifully determined so that even in their glaring differences, they will persist to discover how to adjust and respect one another. The universe will consistently pull them to each other until the karmic lessons are learned and understood. Sometimes they make it through, and other times, they do not. But either way, they will look back and know that there was love there. The trick of this union is when they learn to gladly give each other a wonderful interdependence and create space for one another so that they can do the things they love both apart and together. Their magic lies in the modern way of how they combine their divergences to where they are complete individuals while simultaneously being a couple. It is their strong wills and confidence that will keep them together because where there is enough will, the heart's wisdom can always find a way.

☼ ☼ ☼

SCORPIO & PISCES

♏ ◈ ♓

Aspect: Trine
Elements: Water and water
Modalities: Fixed and mutable

When these two star-crossed lovers meet, they will really believe they are soul mates, and they truly could be. Throughout a Pisces's life, they will meet and have all kinds of love interests but will rarely be sure if they are their soul mate. However, when Pisces sees the strong and mystical creature that is Scorpio, their heart will feel a zing they have never quite felt before. When their eyes meet, they will both smile because they know that it is the beginning of the end of everything that they used to know. The way they start falling in love is not because of any one mentionable thing—it rather organically unfolds. Little do they know that this relationship will change them both forever because they will not come out of this relationship the same as they came in.

Together, they will create a beautiful depth that is rarely dull. Pisces is magnetized by Scorpio's powerful aura, and Scorpio loves Pisces's dreamy vibe. They have a way of handling and understanding each other like no one else can. There is something so strange and elusive about Pisces that Scorpio wants to unravel, and every time Scorpio looks into the fish's watery eyes, they fall deeper under their enchantment. How is a human so tender, yet so haunting? Scorpio has fallen under the Neptunian spell that has tethered them karmically together for ages. This magic gives them the ability to talk to each other without having to say a word and connect no matter the distance or time. As with most water sign couples, this telepathic communication comes naturally, and it is a bonding gift from the stars.

There is so much compatibility between this match—it is incredible. They will give one another so much meaning and understanding in life. Their bond is something strong. It's a type of imperfect perfection. They will go through happiness and sadness like every couple, but they will always be able to feel one another's hearts on a level deeper than most. This intense connection is a blessing because they can understand one another yet a curse because when they are both in the deep end of sadness, it is hard for them to pull each other out of it. When water signs combine their energy and element, they must always create a checks and balances to ensure they will not go too far down for them to be unable to find the surface. If they fail to do this, the relationship can cause them to drown in a false sense of reality. Without knowing which way is up or down, they feel like they do not need anyone else and become consumed with one another. They must remember to come up for air and find independence in their union to keep it healthy.

The scorpion and the fish have much to learn from one another. Pisces will need to stop fabricating the truth, regardless of the fact that they never do it with malintent, because Scorpio detests secrets being held from them. Pisces also lives in a land of dreams, where they do not always feel as though they need permission to carry them out. It can cause a lot of problems between them if Pisces is consistently living in their dreamland alone. Being a mutable sign, Pisces is quite wonderful with words, so when Scorpio is about to get upset, Pisces will find something clever to say that eases the tension. Pisces is not one for confrontation and would rather avoid arguments altogether. However, this passive approach will not work for Scorpio because they want to get to the root of the issue and resolve it as soon as possible. If this difference causes them any discord, sex is where they can heal their disharmony.

One reason they profoundly connect with each other through intimacy more than they do in reality is because sex with this pair is pure ecstasy. They have had nothing like it before and will never have anything like it again because they reach a depth where not only their bodies connect but their souls become one as well. Their oneness is magical, passionate, intense, and transcending for both. When they are apart, they usually start to have problems, but when they are one, they can wash their troubles away with just one kiss. There is a silent force in the way they physically connect that makes even the angels look down in envy. The willingness of Pisces mixed with the surrender of Scorpio brings them to a precipice of unmatched height. Their modern ruling planets of Neptune and Pluto combine in a cool blue swirl of shimmer that creates a universal connection between them that not even death can disconnect.

Their love for one another can be both painful yet equally beautiful, making their story either epic or tragic. These two have the choice to sink, or they can decide to float into the best versions of themselves for one another and reach a level of fulfillment and serenity that most will never even fathom. If they are lucky enough to find one another, it means that they have been given a chance at a love that most can only hope for. This love will find them in an eternity of lifetimes until they can get it right, so why not get it right in this one?

☼ ☼ ☼

Chapter 9

Sagittarius

Sagittarius's love archetype is the explorative lover. They are an inspirational, assertive, energetic, and zealous partner who explores exotic realms both physically and philosophically. Sagittarius's lesson in love is to impart that love is sincerity and absorb that love is devotion.

Element	Fire
Modality	Mutable
Polarity	Yang, positive, and masculine
Mantra	"I see."
Hue	Purple
Deity	Zeus, king of the gods and ruler of the sky
Glyph	♐
Flowers	Carnations and dianthus
Tree	Birch
Jewel	Citrine
Crystals	Lapis lazuli and tourmaline
Fragrance	Bergamot
Body Parts	The hips, thighs, liver, veins, femur bones, and sacral region
Animals	Horses, deer, and hunted animals
Food & Herbs	Grapefruit, sage, currants, sultanas, celery, leeks, cinnamon, wild yam, lemon balm, blue verbena, costmary, bilberry, and bulb vegetables, such as garlic and onion

Sagittarius's Ruling Planet: Jupiter

Jupiter in love rules good fortune, benefits, expansive ideas, and social adaptation. Jupiter reveals individual ethics, philosophies, and personal growth. Jupiter represents the promise of good things to come and is the good luck charm in your partnership. It will be there to give you encouragement when times are tough to remind you that you are never abandoned.

Jupiter regarding Sagittarius makes this sign one of the luckiest. According to ancient legends, the gods feel a special affection for the Sagittarian children of the zodiac, watchfully protecting them from those who would harm them. This is the basis for the so-called Jupiter luck. It also gives centaurs a desire to discover a deeper meaning in life, as well as a desire to travel.

Sagittarius Mythology

Most of the centaurs were regarded in myth as bestial because they were, after all, half horse. However, the ancient Greeks had a great deal of respect for the horse and were reluctant to make the centaurs entirely bad. An example of this was the centaur Chiron, who was renowned for his gentleness. He was an excellent astrologer, archer, musician, and physician and tutored the likes of Achilles, Jason, and Hercules. Chiron was accidentally shot and wounded by Hercules with an arrow that had been dipped in the poison of the Lernaean Hydra. This inflicted great suffering for Chiron, and even though he was an incredible physician, he could not cure himself, giving him the renowned title of the "wounded healer." Chiron was immortal, so he lived in agony from his wound and was unable to find release in death. In an effort to end his pain, Chiron offered himself as a substitute for Prometheus. The gods had punished Prometheus for giving fire to humans by chaining him to a rock. Each day an eagle would devour his liver, and each night it would grow back, making his pain and punishment repeat indefinitely. At the request of Hercules, Jupiter agreed to release Prometheus if a suitable substitute could be found. Chiron gave up his immortality and went to Tartarus in place of Prometheus to be done with his suffering. In recognition of Chiron's goodness, Jupiter placed him among the stars.

Sagittarius's Positive Qualities and Negative Forms

Sagittarius's positive qualities are optimism, candor, cheerfulness, logic, honesty, bravery, and enthusiasm. Expressed in their negative forms, they become reckless, emotionally confused, careless, rude, fickle, and have a lack of tact.

How a Sagittarius Loves

There is not a drop of malice in the way a Sagittarius loves. Their adoration is experienced as expansive both physically and philosophically, opening doors to worlds that can only be explored by being loved by this fire sign. There is a dichotomy about the way they show affection because they crave closeness and distance simultaneously, making them hard to pin down. Part of them wants eternal freedom, and the other half wants someone to join them on their many adventures. They do not hide their hearts and wear them right on their sleeve for everyone to see. However, their contradiction can cause confusion to the people that they attract. They never hide their intentions, and they can even come off harsh. Even though they can be cutting at times, there is something refreshing about their candor, which does not leave one reading between the lines. With a Sagittarius, you will have to use a bit of both your head and heart to interpret them. If there are hopes to change the centaur, throw those plans to the wind because there is only one way to love them, and that is for exactly the way they are.

Archers are energetic, likable, and have an excitable spirit that inspires people to want to be on their team. Thanks to their mutable modality, they are quick talkers with all the right things to say. Joking around is one of their many hobbies but so is astrology, philosophy, and religion. Anything that gets their minds working and gives them something new to explore attracts them like a moth to the flame. Giving a Sagittarius space to roam is crucial to making them happy in their relationships. They want a companion but not always a commitment, so giving them the time and space they need allows them to figure out that companionship is a commitment. Nevertheless, it will have to be their discovery to make. Walking besides a Sagittarius, rather than behind or in front of them, is well worth the patience.

If—and when—love overcomes their reservations to calling one person theirs forever, they go in all the way and do not look back. Sagittarian spirits do not regret or doubt decisions they make and prefer to make the best of everything by pushing forward to the next possibility with their one and only by their side. Life in love with a Sagittarius is a quest into the future filled with visions of what they want to move toward as a pair. As long as the one they love continues to grip their heart and imagination, the sky is the limit, filled with endless possibilities. Sagittarius is fabulous at filling the journey with rich experiences that bring their life true meaning.

An archer's energy can be scattered and enthusiastic, taking them to wherever they point and shoot their optimistic arrows. The way they love is not easily contained and bubbles out of them like a bottle of shaken champagne. They live life to the fullest and need someone to keep them safe so they can stay wild. They love hard, and they move quickly with hearts full of eternal enthusiasm. If something does not work out, they brush themselves off and continue on their cheerful way, always keeping their eyes on the horizon. These firecrackers are hard to resist and hard to capture, but if you do get a Sagittarius to remain at your side, it will be a wild ride.

How to Spot a Sagittarius

See that person at the center of the crowd with this big voice that is making everyone laugh? That is a Sagittarius. These people will walk right up to you and greet you with some sort of shocking honest statement that will either charm you or make you cringe. They shamelessly wear their bright grin and are often cheery in attitude. The archer is typically free of cruelty, and their shockingly direct communication never intentionally comes with malintent. They are clever yet, at times, hilariously tactless.

Their physical characteristics are easy to remember. Their features are usually open and inviting. They usually have large foreheads, and their movements will be quick. They walk proudly, with their heads held high until they trip over something, laughing at themselves when they do it. They are known to be a bit clumsy. Their eyes are bright, sparkly, and laughing. They usually are tall and have athletic builds. Sagittarius rules the hips and thighs, which are usually a noticeable area of their body, either muscular or substantial in size. Their voices are bold and loud, commanding attention of whoever is in attendance. Sagittarians are also known for having a hard time sitting still and are always up and doing something.

They have many loves in life, such as travel, animals, and learning, to name a few. They are eternally students, believing that you should most certainly learn one or more new things each day. This is why most of them have some sort of higher education, which gives them loads of cleverness and drive. They love animals for they are centaurs themselves: half human and half horse. If you want to find one for yourself, you have a good chance seeing them out on a run with their dogs or volunteering at a local shelter.

Whatever is on the Sagittarius's heart or mind is usually coming out of their mouths. They are frank and honest from day one. Archers will gain a lot of loyal friends that find them endearing because of their guilelessness, and in return, centaurs are warm and generous to the ones that they love. There are few people that can be mad at this character long. If you are blue, they will always do what they can to cheer you up. For as chirpy as they are, they also have a rebellious streak in them. They are born without an ounce of fear and are brave souls who will take a chance at just about anything. They are not big on authority or arrogant people. However, if they are challenged, they are not ones who will take a back seat. They are gamblers by nature, knowing that the greater the risk, the greater the reward. If anyone dubs them as dishonest, you will see their tempers flare because truthfulness is next to godliness to them. They are a fire sign, after all.

Archers will usually speak before thinking, shooting arrows of truth from their mouths. They are not interested in sugarcoating what they have to say. Overall, Sagittarius characters are happy clowns. They are lucky, bold souls who are generous idealists. They are hilariously unreserved, and when they aim straight, they always hit their target. Their arrows are dripping in clever wit and genius intelligence that will get them through life with Jupiter's luck in a fun and inspiring way. Their fire is always ready to surge into the open at any chance they can get.

How to Lose a Sagittarius

Keeping an archer for yourself is never an easy feat, but with enough freedom and fun, it can be done. Sagittarians are born with wanderlust and need a partner to take adventures with them; they need a soul that is as liberated as their own. If you are not down for an escapade here and there, you could be sans Sagittarius. Centaurs prefer to take the road less traveled because they have a zest for the life less led. They require a stimulating partner, so spicing things up is a must with this sun sign. There is not a moment to waste when you are in love with this fiery soul. They are sporadic, so if you need to have control of every situation, you will see Sagittarius leaving as fast as they came. There is no way to keep them contained, and it is better to let them roam free while giving them a home base.

Sagittarius loves to clown around, so if you are overly sensitive and take offense to bold remarks easily, they will take off in a flash. This sun sign is constantly sharing their thoughts and cracking jokes, which could be about you. However, if they are not giving you a hard time, they probably do not like you that much. Sagittarius is a mutable fire sign, which means they are fast and furious. If you prefer a slow pace, you may get left in the dust. Because of their mutable modality, they always have someone to talk to and somewhere to go and prefer to stay busy. They require a partner to keep up with them and support their endeavors. Sagittarius is a wild, free, and usually quite educated spirit, so if you are dull and do not have much to say or an opinion of your own, they will probably talk right over you. You do not need to be as voluble as they are, but you cannot be a doormat either.

Archers prefer to spend their money on experiences rather than material items. If you are in any way materialistic or shallow in your way of thinking, they will be turned off. If you are worried about what other people think about you, Sagittarius will find you narrow. Sagittarius values ideals and philosophy over labels and societal norms. They are not looking for a relationship that people dub as "normal" but one that is more customizable and modern. They need a partner who is effortless, not someone who is self-absorbed. They also require an independent partner, so if you need to constantly ask for money and approval from your friends or family, it will be distasteful to them. They prefer a companion who makes their own way in life and has the ability to be free of restrictions or expectations. Sagittarius appreciates being financially and mentally liberated from constraints that could potentially weigh their relationship down. Keep things light, fun, and spirited, and their heart will be yours to hold.

How to Bed a Sagittarius

A Sagittarius has no problem getting hot and heavy quick. They will laugh when you look surprised as they start stripping you down to nothing. Sex is playtime for a Sagittarius, and you will soon find that they are wild and a ton of fun. In the morning, as you start to open your eyes to the sun, you will realize they are gone; they collected their clothes and left without a trace of them in sight. All they left was the scent of bergamot in your sheets and the memory of them in your head. You would think such a wild child would have not a care in the world, but you are oh so very wrong. The archer cares a lot about their future, which they view through their rose-colored glasses. This sun sign is intelligently hopeful and craves a partner that can take care of their heart. If you can keep a Sagittarius safe, they will keep you wild.

As much as the centaur wants a safe place for their heart, they will equally need independence. They are innately hilarious, boisterous, and zealous but under all that hoopla is a soft, vulnerable, clever, and very capable soul. Sagittarius has no interest in putting restraints on their lover, and they expect the same in return. A Sagittarius in bed is not shy about pleasuring themselves in front of you, and they are blessed with amazing stamina that just keeps going and going. You may want to get a few workouts in before hitting the sack with a Sagittarius. Whatever you cannot finish, they are more than happy to take care of themselves. They are not big on emotions in the bedroom because they would rather keep things hot and fun.

Sagittarius knows that life is way too short to be taken too seriously, which is why they love to turn anything into a joke. There is something refreshing and exhilarating about their sexuality that keeps things uncomplicated and stress free. They do tend to overthink their feelings and what to do with them, which is the only thing that can become complicated with this sun sign. Though most of the time, the sex will be natural, fun, and wild. Sagittarius loves a good adventure and will be in search of some excitement and new things to try in the bedroom. Traveling really sparks their lust, so a change of scenery is always a good idea with a Sagittarius. They are bold, brave, and willing to try just about anything experimentally with their open-minded approach.

Sagittarius does not require grand gestures but does necessitate an honest kind of love. They enjoy being chased and longed for, so if you just had the night of your life with this fiery sun sign and they fled your bed, call them up and propose another spontaneous date. Do not be like the rest of the stagnant, serious partners they have had before you. When you can show a Sagittarius that they are secure with you, they may just stick around a little longer next time. If you are lucky, maybe even for breakfast.

☀ ☀ ☀

SAGITTARIUS & SAGITTARIUS

Aspect: Conjunct
Elements: Fire and fire
Modalities: Mutable and mutable

It is quite astounding when these two find each other because the timing will have to be just right for this to truly work. You see, these two are both so fiery, both incredibly independent, and both always on a journey with no destination necessarily in sight. If they happen to cross paths and decide to start traveling down the same rode together, it is really something quite rare and spectacular.

Sagittarius is a mutable sign, meaning they are experts when it comes to language, communication, jokes, and word games. When they first meet, they will notice one another's fiery energy from across the room and be drawn to each other thanks to their mirrored natures. Sagittarians are not shy, so without much time, one centaur will end up going up to the other with a big grin on their face and saying something to them like this: "Have you ever tried to eat a clock?" Now, if this was any other sun sign, you would get an expression of shock or confusion, but this is another Sagittarius we are dealing with. There is little that shocks them, so they will play along and say, "I can't say I have." And the first Sagittarius will reply, "It's very time consuming." There will be a second of silence, and then they will both break out in laughter. That's how their relationship is—full of hilarity, ridiculous banter, and quick-witted one-liners.

It is not all fun and games, though, because they are both very intense beings. One second they will be fighting, and the next they will be making up. Not many can move at their pace, but they enjoy keeping up with each other. Just as funny as they can be, their honesty can be a bit brutal at times as well. When emotions are high, they are not the best at fixing things verbally, so it is usually best to just take some time apart to let things cool down before coming back together. They also tend to exaggerate the truth on occasion, which to them is not necessarily lying; they just like to make things seem more interesting than they really are. They need to remember to keep the truth at the core of everything they do, no matter how boring actuality can be. Relationships are built on trust, so building a solid foundation in this area is crucial for their love to last.

Centaurs do not do anything halfway, and sex is no exception to this rule. There will be little that needs work in the lovemaking department. When it comes to sex with these fire signs, there will be a lot of talking, touching, laughing, warmth, and fun. There is so much in common with them that they will vibrate with ease on the same wavelength. There is much affection and expressive love that brings a sense of safety and security that all archers secretly long for. No matter how independent they are, they are a sign that is most definitely known for wearing their heart on their sleeve. Two Sagittarians will be able to have a vulnerability and an unbarred romance that most people could only dream about. They can achieve a fiery love that does not hold back even an ounce. These are things that they should most certainly cherish about one another.

Money will be something that comes and goes with these two, and it is most definitely not at the forefront of importance in their relationship. They will make it, spend it, and then make some more. They would rather experience life than sit at home and check their bank account while eating leftovers. To them, money is to be earned in exchange for experiences in life. If these two could be independently wealthy and travel the world together, experiencing new cultures, trying different cuisine, and hearing the philosophies of others, that would be the perfect life. However, most are not independently wealthy, so they will work to gain those experiences one paycheck at a time and then enjoy them together. Their travels will be some of the best days of their love story and will enrich and strengthen their bond. Making travel a priority with this pair is a must. The Sagittarian philosophy is that you cannot take your money with you when you die, so you might as well spend it on a good time.

Throughout the years, these two will only become closer to one another because they have so much luck to get them through the hard times, enough fire to get them through the cold, and enough laughter to keep it all together. They will love telling their children and grandchildren about the many adventures and travels they had together and the people they met along the way. They will have a full life of color, adventure, learning, movement, seeking, chasing, traveling, fighting, making up, and experiencing time in the way only two Sagittarians really can: all the way.

☼ ☼ ☼

SAGITTARIUS & CAPRICORN

Aspect: Semisextile
Elements: Fire and earth
Modalities: Mutable and cardinal

When Sagittarius meets Capricorn, they will feel like all the other partners in their life were children compared to this sun sign. Maybe it is because Capricorn is not aggressive but old fashioned. Or perhaps it is the fact that they do not try too hard to sweep Sagittarius off their feet but rather approach love in a manner that is proper. Capricorn's romance toward Sagittarius is tinged with timidity, but Sagittarius loves their sea goat's shy grin and knows there is more to them hidden under that steely exterior. There is something about Capricorn's quiet and mature eyes that feels safe to the centaur. It is their emotional maturity that the archer needs to absorb most, and they are fully aware of this. In return, Sagittarius's optimism and bright energy will rub off on Capricorn's practical nature in a way they also need.

In the beginning of their love story, they will both need to soften their approach with each other in very different ways. Sagittarius's mouth is what will get them in trouble with Capricorn, and Capricorn's negativity is what will get them in trouble with Sagittarius. When the centaur is angry, they will tell Capricorn that they are selfish, cold, heartless, insensitive, and harsh. Capricorn will probably just walk right out the door because Sagittarius's words are biting and powerful even to this steadfast sun sign. The archer must use a softer dialect with a similar connotation to get their point across. Sagittarius should instead tell Capricorn they are being too practical, economical, and careful. Capricorn will be a lot more receptive to those words than the previous and will be more open to softening themselves with constructive criticism.

Capricorn is afraid to show too much emotion, which is why they can come off cold, but they admire the way Sagittarius can be so open and freely converse about their own feelings. If the archer is patient with them, Capricorn will love them a little more each day and gradually let them past the high walls that guard their soft heart. Loving Capricorn's family is a huge piece of the pie because they put their family over everything, including their partner until they are officially family too. Sagittarius does not have the tug to be with their family the way that Capricorn does, so there will need to be compromise and adjustment here. One way that Sagittarius can get them alone is by telling Capricorn that they are craving one-on-one time to be intimate. That is always a sure way to get the sea goat's attention.

Sexually there is a genuine curiosity that they will have with one another. Sagittarius is fast and fiery, while Capricorn prefers to take their time and enjoy every moment. They are so different, yet something about their sexual oneness makes sense. They will study each other as though they are seeing each other for the very first time. Capricorn will approach Sagittarius sexually with caution, but Sagittarius will have no problem jumping in headfirst. There will need to be adjustments, but once they are able to make them, their sex life can be quite unifying. They must both have patience with one another, but after time, the familiarity they create will bring them warm affection. Once there is trust from Capricorn, things can get brassy in bed.

Capricorn does not require the same types of freedoms that Sagittarius does and can even find them selfish and disorderly. Sagittarius views Capricorn's obsession with work exhausting and as an enslaved way of living. What they both must realize is that the way they choose to lead their lives is their own, and if this is to work, they must somehow meet one another in the middle. Time is something that will be good for them because the more of it that passes, the stronger they will become. They have so much to learn from each other, and they will only gain respect and understanding through accepting one another's differences. Capricorn will curb the archer's impulsive nature and channel their energy into something with more direction and fruition. Once Sagittarius has the key to unlock the gate to Capricorn's heart, they will help the sea goat become emotionally free to live life more liberally. There will be days that are trying for them, but if they are able to absorb one another's strengths, they can create a formidable team.

Capricorns have a desperate need to climb to the top, but Sagittarius does not share this desire. However, Sagittarius does like to have a goal to reach and something to look forward to so that things stay interesting. Sagittarius's fiery spirit craves adventure, so if things start to feel mundane, they should book a trip that is somewhere far away from Capricorn's career and crew and Sagittarius's side hustles so that they can mentally and physically focus on one another. It should be a journey to a mystical place where they can both take a deep breath simultaneously and fall in love all over again.

☼ ☼ ☼

SAGITTARIUS & AQUARIUS

Aspect: Sextile
Elements: Fire and air
Modalities: Mutable and fixed

Water bearers are whimsical and out of this world. This sun sign does not belong to anyone, yet they are loved by everyone. This makes them incredibly popular, which is how they acquire their many acquaintances. Aquarians like to change their mind quite frequently because they soon forget their passion for one thing and move all their energy to their next futuristic mission. This can also happen in their relationships when they are not fully committed and especially when a relationship is brand new. Archers are not short of friends either. They are flirtatious charmers and will talk to just about anyone that has the time to listen. Sagittarians usually start out just wanting a friendship and somehow find themselves in a relationship they do not necessarily want. This tends to make several of their relationships short lived because many of their love stories are operated with their heart before their head.

On the day that the water bearer and the archer meet, they will most likely be hanging out with their friends or at a social gathering. At first, Aquarius will want nothing to do with this loud and boisterous character, but when Sagittarius sees Aquarius, they will want everything to do with them. Sagittarius has met many different types of personalities, so when they see their Aquarius, they will know that they are different than most. They can tell that Aquarius is intelligent and will switch gears to show that they are not all noise but that they also have a philosophical and spiritual side to them as well. Sagittarius has so many wonderful stories about all the places they have traveled and the interesting people they have met. This is when Aquarius's interest will spark; they start to realize that the two of them really are not so different after all. Sagittarius is the one who will have to pursue Aquarius because odds are the water bearer will forget all about their meeting. Aquarius will make them work for it, but centaurs are always up for a challenge.

Their friendship will develop after some adventures they take together, and their love will only continue to grow as the days pass. This is a couple that takes a trip every other month, exploring new tastes and sights, meeting new people, and divulging in new experiences. These two share an unbreakable friendship thanks to their sextile aspect, and they will also discover their sexual union is giving and coy. When they connect physically, Aquarius's air element will feed Sagittarius's fire element, creating a bright blue flame. They will enjoy sharing each other's bodies and will find oneness freeing. Their escapades will keep their love life fresh and new because they are always looking to the horizon. Together, they can go places—both mentally and physically—they never imagined. The conversations they share will be about religion, reality, science fiction, utopians, politics, and various other topics that will keep them fascinated with one another for eternity.

What is beautiful about this match is that they give each other so much freedom to be themselves while remaining together. They are both optimistic about life and love and share an attitude that things will just work out the way they are supposed to. The two things that get them in trouble are Sagittarius's harsh honesty and Aquarius's forgetfulness. They will tiff sporadically because Sagittarius frequently puts their foot in their mouth, and Aquarius can be very stubborn about forgiving them for it. Sagittarius innately runs hot, while Aquarius runs cool, so when Sagittarius gets loud and their temper flares, they usually will not get the reaction they are looking for from their water bearer. Aquarius has no patience for nonsense or games. However, Sagittarius's sense of humor will have them forgiving and forgetting much sooner than they planned. They are both good about letting things go and refocusing their sights on the positives, which is a blessing in their relationship.

Sagittarius needs Aquarius to persist, to grow, and to become their full self, while Aquarius needs Sagittarius to keep their cool persona warm and wild. It is Aquarius's quirkiness that made the freedom-loving archer want to settle in one place, and it was Sagittarius's spontaneity that keeps Aquarius on their toes and made them fall in love. They will always be friends first and lovers second, which is the glue of their union. One morning, when Aquarius wakes up in a foreign country on a pristine beach with the sound of the waves rolling on the sand, they will look at their wild child and think, "How is this person real? Did I dream them up?" The answer is that Sagittarius is a mixture of both dream and reality, but so is Aquarius, and that is what makes this relationship tangibly surreal.

☼ ☼ ☼

SAGITTARIUS & PISCES

Aspect: Square
Elements: Fire and water
Modalities: Mutable and mutable

These two genuinely enjoy the truth, but they enjoy it served in diverse ways. Pisces likes their truth sugarcoated, while Sagittarius prefers their truth served straight up. The fish is beautifully sensitive and appreciates being managed delicately and thoughtfully, whereas the centaur sees passive communication as a waste of time. In fact, it is usually the archer's mouth that will end things for them before they even get started. The centaur's crass sense of humor will not get them far with the fish's delicate nature, or not at least until they really get to know one another. Therefore, there is something inexplicably strange about when these two decide to partner—something odd and yet spectacular.

Even though this pair is square in aspect, there is something that they just understand about one another that no one from the outside would ever really get. Sagittarius is a free spirit, and Pisces loves that about them because they themselves enjoy going where the water takes them. The archer and the fish both share the love of spontaneity in life, never having the same day twice, which is connected to their shared enjoyment of travel and philosophy. Yet, there is something about one another that makes them nervous. They will not be able to put their finger on it at first, but there will be things that need adjustment over time. However, the heart will win over the head because these signs both allow love to bring them wherever their dreams take them.

They are so different yet similar thanks to their matching mutable modalities. Once Sagittarius has Pisces's attention, they will soon learn what a wonderful listener they are, which is perfect for Sagittarius because they have a lot to say. Listening is truly a gift that not many possess, but Pisces is naturally empathetic, making it easy for them to absorb what others say. The archer's heart so desperately needs to be heard, and they can tell by looking in their Pisces's watery eyes that they really care about their point of view. There is nothing more satisfying for Sagittarius than to be understood. Pisces can chat quite a bit, too, because they also operate under the mutable modality. They will have wonderful conversations together of how the world could be a different place, and this is where they will connect the most. Their transmission will be an endless stream of energy that unites them.

Their communication may be solid, but when it comes to physical intimacy, they have much to learn from one another. Sagittarius will discover that Pisces craves more gentleness and tenderness, which they will find alluring. A centaur's desires are much fierier and more forward than Pisces's will ever be, which they will not mind from time to time. However, Sagittarius should not be afraid to be deep with sentiment and emotions. When there is compromise here, they will attain what they both desire, and it will be nothing short of amazing. Pisces finds the spirituality of Sagittarius exciting, and the way that they can connect through this medium can even bring them to tears. They can turn one another's dreams into reality without even leaving the bedroom by escaping into their sexuality. They will have their best memories from their travels, and all the various places that they will make love together will bring them both immense joy and excitement.

Pisces's depth of emotion can be difficult for Sagittarius to grasp, and at times, it can even feel dampening and depressing. Sagittarius is a genuinely optimistic person, but Pisces often takes a dip into the melancholy pools of their mind where Sagittarius cannot reach them. Pisces is like a psychic antenna, soaking up the energy around them, and Sagittarius is the total opposite. Negative vibes ricochet off a Sagittarius like a bullet on concrete. There will be many times when Sagittarius cannot sympathize with Pisces's gloomy moods, but for this match to work, they really need to try. These sun signs are both represented by dual-bodied constellations. Pisces is characterized as the two fish, and Sagittarius is depicted as half human and half horse. Pisces simultaneously swims toward fantasy and reality, and Sagittarius congruently desires independence and togetherness. Differences are what gives a relationship its sparkle, but they can also be what dulls it. They will have to decide whether they will take the time to shine up the dull spots, which takes consistent energy and effort.

If the archer and the fish ever feel each other slipping away, a trip and some time alone will be very healing for them. Getting away from it all will allow space for a wonderful opportunity to get to know each other all over again. New sights will spark up that beautiful gift of gab they both possess, and Pisces will love to intently listen to Sagittarius talk about their amazing days together. It is here that they create a space for one another that is full of compassion, adventure, worldly minded thinking, and love. If love is the center—and if there is enough independence and compromise to dissipate the differences—these two can make it on all the journeys they ever imagined and beyond. For it is with love, empathy, and compromise that this unlikely match can turn into a true love story.

☼ ☼ ☼

Chapter 10

Capricorn

Capricorn's love archetype is the ruler of love. They are a guarded, introspective, and tactical lover who exercises love through structure and responsibility. Capricorn's lesson in love is to impart that love is understanding and absorb that love is altruistic.

Element	Earth
Modality	Cardinal
Polarity	Yin, negative, and feminine
Mantra	"I use."
Hue	Black
Deity	Cronus, god of agriculture
Glyph	♑
Flowers	Pansies, aster, and hollies
Tree	Pine
Jewel	Garnet
Crystals	Onyx and galena
Fragrance	Musk
Body Parts	The teeth, bones, kneecaps, and skin
Animals	Goats and other cloven-footed animals
Food & Herbs	Meat, potatoes, barley, beets, spinach, malt, coffee, medlar, onions, quince, chicory, burdock, mullein, hemp, comfrey, knapweed, hemlock, henbane, and starchy food, such as pasta

Capricorn's Ruling Planet: Saturn

Saturn in love rules careers, values, public relations, and growth. Saturn reveals one's loyalties, commitment to family, sense of responsibility, and stability. Saturn represents familial bonds in partnerships. It also shows the importance of career and climbing the ladder professionally. Saturn regarding Capricorn gives them their calculated and controlled personality. Capricorns tend to have an older soul even when they are young.

Capricorn Mythology

The constellation Capricornus is depicted as a sea goat with the top of its body resembling a goat and the bottom half a fish's tail. This comes from the legend of when the serpentine giant Typhon attacked the Olympic gods on the Nile. The deities transformed into various creatures to disguise themselves from the deadly monster while Zeus stayed back to fight the monster. During the battle, the giant serpent stole Zeus's power, leaving him helpless. Pan, the god of the wilderness, who had taken the form of a fish-tailed goat, went to assist Zeus to defeat Typhon by regaining Zeus's lost strength. As recompense, Zeus placed his morphed figure into the heavens as the constellation known as Capricorn.

Capricorn's Positive Qualities and Negative Forms

Capricorn's positive qualities are determination, stability, wisdom, dependability, sureness, and tranquility. Expressed in their negative forms, they become selfish, narrow, ruthlessly ambitious, rigid, arrogant, depressed, and lonely.

How a Capricorn Loves

The way that Capricorn loves is filled with substance because they are built with structure and responsibility. Under their several layers of cool control is a warm and tender heart that longs for companionship. No matter their longing, they will never make it easy to get past their high walls, but they always make it worth the effort. Capricorns are anxious about choosing the wrong partners, but they will exude supreme confidence once they do find the one. Capricorns are loyal and loving companions who use practicality in nearly every single decision they make. There is something distant about the sea goat, but once they can trust you, they will be as supportive as steel.

A Capricorn's heart is sacred, and winning it will be like solving the solution to a difficult riddle. Because of their protective nature, they can be experienced as cold and uncaring. However, just because they are slow to move into romance does not mean that they are not capable of an earth-shattering kind of love. Over days, weeks, and even years, they gently unfold themselves layer by layer, making their partner prove that they really want to be there. Capricorns are people of depth, so they naturally deter superficial and shallow-minded people and gladly leave them chilled to the bone. Capricorn's aspirations in life and love are way too high to take someone along who only sees what is in front of them. Instead, they want sincerity and grit to ensure their partner has staying power.

Capricorns are quite sensitive to criticism because they aim for sky-high accomplishment. There is nothing out of a Capricorn's reach if they really want it. There is a dire need to deliver and generate throughout their life and in their relationships. They are devoted, honest, driven, and dependable to the person that they love, letting nothing stand in their way. Their responsibility and acumen make for a sturdy life partner that will be there when the going gets rough. When they feel secure in their relationship, you will see their dry and hilarious sense of humor shine through. Capriciousness is a hidden component of their personality.

Sea goats are notorious loners because they fear being dependent or weak, but if they are treated with patience and care, they can melt. There are many Capricorns that have great loves whom they let pass by because of their fear and caution, which can cause them to end up settling for a safe choice or no one at all. However, as our world continues to modernize and allow more space for uninhibited, altruistic love, this stereotype will fade. Being with this sun sign takes a confident person who is independent in their own light. Capricorns date with the intention of marrying up, so they will not settle for a partner that is not beneficiary to their life as a whole. They expect a lot because they are a lot, and they impose the same high standards on themselves as they do the ones they give their hearts to.

Capricorn's powerful personality and innate caution often creates a buildup between them and the person they are falling for. The emotion that lives within them is ready to be released, and when it does, it is overwhelming. They love in an old-fashioned way that takes its time because they know that slow and steady always wins the race in love. They never put the carriage in front of the horse and continually put their duty before pleasure because it provides the security and structure that their devotion thrives in. Their love lives tend to be quite complicated for such an uncomplicated sun sign, but their steadfast determination always has them trying to be the best partner that they can be, and it never allows them to give up on believing in a love that can last eternally.

How to Spot a Capricorn

Out of all twelve zodiac signs, Capricorns are the hardest to spot. This is because there really is not a "typical Capricorn." They are easily able to merge themselves into a group of people undetected to watch, listen, and learn. One thing they all do have in common is that they are tough and carry a heavy and methodical energy that is laced with wisdom. Their knack for strategy is impeccable, and their method is to take their time to get to the top. Their self-presentation is polished, and sea goats love to wear black because to Capricorn, black is always the new black. There is a timeless security of the monochromatic that the sea goat greatly enjoys. Metal accessories are a must for Capricorn because they love it all: iron, silver, copper, brass, and gold. They also can make gemstones glitter more than any other sun sign because of their cardinal modality and earth element. They love wealth, and they love to wear it even more; the tangibility of jewelry gets them excited.

Capricorns rule the teeth, skin, and bones, which blesses them with beautifully structured faces, high cheekbones, magnificent smiles, silky skin, and a sturdy build. It is as though they grow roots wherever they stand. Capricorns rarely wear heavy makeup because they prefer a more natural look. There is something dark about their eyes, no matter what color they are. Their actions are calm, steady, and deliberate, making them look cool to the touch. Capricorns are also blessed with aging in reverse—a gift from Saturn. To everyone's envy, the older they get, the younger they tend to look. Children of winter never grow old.

The sea goat is not a wild partier, but they are at the party, mixing themselves with people who share the same goals and ideals. They are a firm believer that you are the people you surround yourself with, so they intend to surround themselves with the best. If a Capricorn chooses you as a friend, take it as a huge compliment. They love success, they respect authority, and they honor tradition. This does not mean that they are not adaptable; it is quite the contrary. Sea goats may not be chasing after wild dreams, but they are able to adapt and push to achieve whatever they want to obtain. Capricorns are champions; they like to win, and they usually win. Going toe-to-toe with one will leave you in second almost every time. This is their cardinal energy and earthy ambition doing its work. No matter how gentle this sign may act, they are made of cold, unyielding steel. They easily push past barriers, and if they want something bad enough, they will climb the mountain to get it without deviating.

These old souls will surprise you with how sweet they really are once you completely get to know them. They are not ones who will outwardly push their way to the front because they know that is not necessary. Their disciplined nature is something to be admired and learned from. The sea goat is not made of magic fairy dust but rather of jet-black onyx that provides them and their loved ones with protection, vigor, steadfastness, and stamina. If you see someone with a clean, fresh, and aristocratic look who effortlessly glides into the room completely unbothered, you are spotting a child of Saturn. A Capricorn, that is.

How to Lose a Capricorn

Capricorns are all about a plan. They have one for everything, and they expect their partner to do the same. This cardinal earth sign is looking for someone who knows what they want and has a will of steel to get it. Capricorns are busy and have a demanding schedule to stick to. They will pencil you in, but you will have to earn it first because they have business to address. They are constantly climbing the ladder at work, which takes time, and they need a partner who is supportive of their workaholic habits and can help them relax after a long, grueling day. They are enthusiastic about what they do and do not want to be nagged about anything. On the other side, if a Capricorn feels like they are always competing with their partner, they will get exhausted. They want someone to take it slow and steady with, not someone who wants to race them to the top.

Capricorns are rocks, and they enjoy being leaned on. They want you to come to them for advice, and they enjoy feeling needed, which gives them purpose. They rarely ask for help or advice themselves, and they must be able trust their companions completely before showing any sort of their own weaknesses. A Capricorn has walls high around their heart, making it nearly impossible for just anyone to get in. They require a partner who is up for the challenge of climbing past their façade to reach their soft core. Capricorn values quality over quantity, and the people in their life mean everything to them. If their partner tries to avoid spending time with their friends and family, it will be a deal breaker. Try to take their crew away, and you will have one mad sea goat on your hands. Family is always first with a Capricorn, and they need someone by their side who appreciates and understands that.

Capricorns long for a partner to read between the lines to understand that there is more to them than what the eye meets. If a Capricorn cannot trust you, it will be a deal breaker. Capricorns are all about practicality and plans, not fluff and faux, so if you try to woo them with ungenuine gestures and poems, it will make their skin crawl. Just be patient, and let things happen naturally. They crave someone who is secure and understands that love is more about actions than words. Quality time and acts of service are what they appreciate. It takes a long time to get to their heart, but once you do, you will have gained an incredible lover who has staying power. Durability is Capricorn's middle name.

How to Bed a Capricorn

Sex with a Capricorn may not be riveting the first night you two do the deed, but that is only because this sun sign takes time to really open up. The longer you get to know them, the better and better it will get. Capricorns are demanding in the bedroom, so get used to it or get out. If you choose to stick around, their challenges will bring you to a sexual state you never knew you could reach with someone. It is tough yet rewarding in every sense of the way. Their ruling planet, Saturn, is all about hard work and then reaping the rewards once the work is complete. Sexually the sea goat is no different. They enjoy being fulfilled repeatedly, so if you can help them achieve this, the rewards will be endless.

Capricorns are innately traditional and advantageous daters who enjoy being with someone who can complete their high-level empire. They will not let feelings get in the way of their road to success unless they really find someone to break their strong barriers down. They love security in all aspects, which includes sex, so they require a resilient partner to complement their own robust nature. Many Capricorns are attracted to more experienced or older partners who know the ropes. Their sexual nature is both simple and complex, sensual and cool, and uninhibited yet restricted. They prefer intimacy rather than a one-night stand because if they put energy into anything, they want there to be a reward for their efforts.

Capricorns are not outwardly transparent of their curiosity in a lover at first, so if you are interested in a Capricorn and they seem cold to you, look for subtle clues that they are attracted. The sea goat has patience for days, and things in their world take time and diligence, which is why they thoroughly enjoy any sort of delayed gratification. Capricorn's stamina and libido are hard to beat, and they can go for hours without tiring. They need a plan and sure footing before jumping into anything, especially love. Even though they may not seem like it, they really do want to be swept off their feet and put to bed. Capricorns are tough to please sexually, and if you are incompetent, you will have to see your way out. This sun sign is one to know exactly what they want and will always find a way to get it.

It may be a month before you get them to laugh, two months before the first kiss, and maybe even longer to make love with them, but it will all be worth it in the end. Capricorn is always climbing to new heights in their life personally and sexually. If you can keep up, you will reach the peak with them, and you will see that behind their high walls is a youthful, bright, and warm soul that can fulfill your every whim. Be patient.

☼ ☼ ☼

CAPRICORN & CAPRICORN

Aspect: Conjunct
Elements: Earth and earth
Modalities: Cardinal and cardinal

When two Capricorns meet for the first time, it may quite possibly be during the season of their birthdays, when snow is falling, when a fire is crackling, and when the scent of pine fills the air. There is romance and magic, even on the coldest nights, and Capricorns know exactly how to warm one another up. Capricorns are not necessarily known for their over-the-top romantic gestures, but when two sea goats fall in love, the whole game changes in so many ways.

They are both hard to get to know initially, so this relationship may need a few hot cocoas by the fire to get them to feel safe and open up. Capricorns prefer to keep their tender hearts behind high walls, where no one can damage them. Capricorns do not like to show any type of weakness because they are way too tough for that. They also believe that they do not need anyone because it seems ridiculous to imagine that anyone would need another person. However, Capricorn will learn that it is okay to rely on another from time to time because no one can do it all. No one is that strong every moment. Being vulnerable with another person is the closest thing to heaven on earth—no matter how scary it may be. After a while, someone is going to have to let their walls down, and when these two become vulnerable with each other, a relationship can really begin. To love and be loved fully, including one's flaws, is what life is all about. With patience and time, they can teach this valuable lesson to one another.

Two Capricorns in love are as stable as a couple can be in almost every aspect of life—finances, careers, emotions, and the relationship itself. Not only are they an earth sign, but they are also the last earth sign on the karmic wheel, which blesses them with an innate wisdom. There is so much they appreciate about each other, especially the matching qualities that they possess. Capricorns hold a special magic that they seem to age in reverse. They are so serious about building a life for themselves early on that they learn later on how to enjoy the fruits of their labor. If these two meet at a young age, they will be extremely independent of each other so that they are able to focus on their own careers and life paths. If they remain together all the way through their retirement, they will finally act like kids together and see that their later years will be some of the best of their lives. This is something to keep in mind for when the road gets rough at any point in the relationship. They must remember that their best years together are yet to come.

One thing two Capricorns will always get right is their intimacy. They both keep a tight lid on their expressions for one another at first, but that will not last very long. They both feel the passion all the way down to their solid, earthy cores. If they can release their inhibitions and feel free while they are one together, their sex can bring contentment and peace because they can wholly trust one another. There is a sweet, vulnerable sensuality and a gentleness that only they will share, which is such an amazing break from the usual coarse façade that they put out to everyone else. Their sex is bonding and makes them unbreakable. Once they break past each other's walls, they will start building their own fortress together to keep their relationship safe from anything that could ever tear it apart.

A Capricorn couple has the power to soften each other in a way that their friends and family never thought was possible. As the soft snow is falling and the moon makes the ground look like it is glittering, they will feel a tug on their hearts and a love that they never knew existed. It is nothing practical, nothing logical, and nothing that they can even put into words. Their love is abstract, which is not a feeling that a Capricorn is familiar with. Marriage is a natural step for Capricorns because a lasting love is what they strive for in life. Perpetuity and permanency are the pillars of their past, present, and future. The past was where they were able to break down each other's barriers, the present is where they build a beautiful life, and the future is where they will grow young together.

☼ ☼ ☼

CAPRICORN & AQUARIUS

Aspect: Semisextile
Elements: Earth and air
Modalities: Cardinal and fixed

Capricorn thinks Aquarius is quite peculiar when they first meet. However, it is this strangeness that is intriguing to the sea goat because they can watch the water bearer through their steady, quiet eyes. Capricorn admires and understands Aquarius's eccentricities. They can see the brilliance and potential that is hidden beneath their oddities. Capricorn likes keeping their cool, especially in a public setting, but Aquarius will want them to join in their loony song and dance. This will make Capricorn uncomfortable, but if they want to win over this alien, they are going to have to break out of their comfort zone in more ways than one. Aquarius makes Capricorn get nervous, and they never get nervous.

Aquarius is a fixed sign, which means they do not want to follow or lead; they just do their own thing without worrying about what anyone thinks. Capricorn is a cardinal sign, meaning they do like—and need—to lead, and opinions of them hold weight. The good thing is that out of all the fixed signs, Aquarius's air element is the most changeable, which gives this pair some room for adjustment. They would both be wise to take a page from each other's book. Though they are different, they do share the same planetary ruler of Saturn. Saturn regarding Capricorn gives them their calculated and controlled personality, while Saturn regarding Aquarius gives them their wisdom, knowledge, and social structures. The thing that Saturn gives them both is that they enjoy keeping their distance, getting close to a very select few. This shared attribute is where they will find their bond.

Capricorn's world is entirely invented and designed by their careful planning, while Aquarius lets their world naturally create itself. Capricorn wants a world where their calculations create space for the conventional to happen, and Aquarius wants a world where the unusual can happen. Through careful thought and deliberation, Capricorn can show Aquarius that you can have your cake and eat it too, which is a concept Aquarius will enjoy. The water bearer will return the favor in teaching Capricorn that when things are planned there is no room for surprise or serendipitous happenings and that if you veer off the path, there is magic that no one has yet to experience. This is how Aquarius has collected their group of zany friends and acquaintances over the years.

Aquarius has loads of friends who will come in all different shapes and sizes, genders, ethnicities, backgrounds, and religions. There will be ex-lovers, circus performers, office workers, and more—you name it, Aquarius has it. Capricorn will wonder how one collects such a vast array of characters and will not be a fan of the ex-lovers that are friends due to jealousy. However, they are all an integral part of Aquarius's life, and Capricorn will have to get along with them for this to work. Capricorn prefers to have friends in high places and selects their company with precision, but they will not pry or nag which, will be great for such a free spirit.

It is Aquarius's eccentricities that Capricorn will adore and simultaneously find challenging. Capricorn has little patience for someone who tells them one thing and does another, which is what Aquarius is famous for. If Aquarius wants to keep their sea goat around, they need to start keeping the promises and commitments they make, which will be something they must work hard on. Aquarius can be self-absorbed at times—not on purpose but simply because they are in their own head, thinking about how to make the world a better place. They occasionally need a tug from a strong partner to come back down to earth, and Capricorn has the strength to do that. If they make it through the tough times, Capricorn will be rewarded with a partner who gives them interesting days, fascinating nights, unexpected trips, and enough excitement to last a lifetime.

Capricorn believes that if they are going to do something, they are going to do it right, and that includes their physical relationship. Sex with these two is changing and unpredictable every time, but then again, it is rare when an Aquarian ever does something the same twice. The water bearer will make Capricorn interested, and sex with them will be out of this world and dreamy. If they can accept each other's differences, they will be able to achieve sexual harmony. There may be minor adjustments because of Aquarius's aloofness, but they will adapt quickly to make their lover pleased.

Love begins in the minds of those born in the air element. To those born in the earth element, love begins with security. Aquarius is a little short on reliability and security, but with enough tolerance and patience from Capricorn, they can learn. Capricorns are fabulous at spotting possibility that no one else can see, so even though Aquarius lives behind their eccentricities, the goat knows that they are just scratching the surface of their vast potential. Aquarius can teach Capricorn things if they are able to open their mind, unlock their heart, and discard the word *impossible* from their lexicon because with Aquarius, you can believe as many as six impossible things before breakfast.

☼ ☼ ☼

CAPRICORN & PISCES

♑ 💎 ♓

Aspect: Sextile
Elements: Earth and water
Modalities: Cardinal and mutable

Capricorns are made up of class and quality, while Pisces are made up of dreams and romance. Capricorn is attracted to Pisces's wonderful ideas, and the fish will ask the sea goat the night they meet to fly away with them to somewhere only lovers go. Their eyes will sparkle with delight as Capricorn starts planning the rest of their life together. Pump the brakes. One thing to know is that these two signs are cut from completely different cloth. When Capricorn talks about dreams, they have a strategy set in place on how to get there, whereas when Pisces speaks about dreams, they are simply spewing them from their heart without a plan in place. This is one of the many areas of life where they will be able to help each other. Pisces will have the dreams, and Capricorn will figure out a way to make them happen.

Pisces will be able to feel Capricorn's emotions, and the fish will love them in a way that the sea goat has only read about in fairy tales. At first, Capricorn will fight the urge to be scooped up by Pisces's Neptunian net, but it is only a matter of time before they let go and allow the fish's waters to sweep them away to their magical abyss. They will then ride the waves of whatever comes, which will be a nice break from climbing their mountains. Capricorn can tend to be quite stubborn, but Pisces is flexible and sensitive. Capricorn is always wanting more in life, but Pisces will show them how to find joy in the present. Capricorn sets harsh rules and expectations that cannot be met, but Pisces will show them how the rules are made to be broken. If Capricorn can ease their directness and open their heart to feel their partner's sentiments and if Pisces can try to be a bit less passive and feel secure in their strength, they can make it through nearly anything together.

Pisces should keep in mind that Capricorn is patient but will not have any tolerance for indolence. Capricorns have every intention of climbing to the top and will bring whomever they love right along with them. Pisces do not really climb but rather swim, so Capricorn will need to learn how to be patient with their lack of matching ambitions to get to the top. Pisces has other plans, which do not include reaching certain statuses. Instead, they crave abstract and spiritually meaningful experiences. Pisces will teach Capricorn how to swim with them through the magical waters of life and impart that life is not all about climbing vertically. There are a lot of places to go other than up, which is a foreign idea to a sea goat. Capricorn will be the rock in their relationship, which is something that the fish desperately needs in their life. But if Capricorn really wants to connect with Pisces, they will have to learn to compromise and let go of control.

There is not a fish who would prefer to swim in a tank over a large body of water, so Capricorn will need to sympathize that their creative partner's mind will need room to venture off—even if that is not something they personally require. Even though Pisces is a free spirit, there is something deep down in their heart that is looking for a place to call home. Capricorn will be the rock Pisces needs, and Pisces will be the gentle love Capricorn has been looking for. The greatest gift Capricorn will give to Pisces is comfort and dependability, and the greatest gift Pisces gives to Capricorn is their compassion and imagination.

Pisces loves variety and surprises and will look to their partner for their source of entertainment and excitement, especially in the bedroom, which is something that they will both enjoy. At first, Capricorn will be a little shy with their dreamy fish, but Pisces will penetrate their earthy exterior with their magical water qualities in no time. Capricorn is very direct when they express themselves sexually, but Pisces adds a mystical and dreamlike element to their lovemaking that gives it dimension. Pisces will teach Capricorn that sex can bring them to worlds other than the one they tangibly live in. This blending of sextile energy will bring one another different facets of life and create a true depth of friendship between them.

Earth is a very solid and structured element, while water is much more variable and freer because it flows where the earth takes it. However, over time, water changes earth, making it greener and more fertile, carving rivers into valleys, and creating cliffs next to the sea. It happens gradually, taking months and even years to see changes. Nevertheless, once the changes are made, they are permanent, making water the strongest element known. Pisces will gently change Capricorn ever so slightly and for the better without them even realizing it. Pisces will soften them and bring new perspective to their life, and Capricorn will ease into becoming a gentler version of themselves.

☼ ☼ ☼

Chapter 11

Aquarius

Aquarius's love archetype is the love maverick. They are an intelligent, cool, active, principled, and eccentric lover and independent-minded future maker. Aquarius's lesson in love is to impart that love is patience and absorb that love is solidarity.

Element	Air
Modality	Fixed
Polarity	Yang, positive, and masculine
Mantra	"I know."
Hue	Electric blue
Deity	Prometheus, god of humanity
Glyph	≈
Flowers	Orchids, iris, and bird-of-paradise
Tree	Elder
Jewel	Aquamarine
Crystals	Fluorite and sodalite
Fragrance	Patchouli
Body Parts	The lower legs, ankles, varicose veins, and circulatory system
Animals	Hawks and other large birds
Food & Herbs	Kiwi, starfruit, citrus fruits, elderberry, peppers, chilies, rosemary, nettles, prickly ash, seasonings with sharp and unusual flavors, and food that preserves well, such as dried fruit

Aquarius's Ruling Planets: Uranus and Saturn

Aquarius is one of the few signs that have two ruling planets. Saturn is its traditional ruling planet, but when Uranus was discovered, the revolutionary orb was assigned to Aquarius, making Uranus this sun sign's modern ruler.

Saturn in love rules careers, values, public relations, and growth. Saturn reveals one's sense of responsibility, loyalties, commitment to family, and stability. Saturn represents familial bond in partnerships. It also shows the importance of career and climbing the ladder professionally. Saturn regarding Aquarius gives the water bearer their wisdom, knowledge, and social structures. They enjoy getting to know many while keeping a distance and getting close to a very select few.

Uranus in love is the planet of change and rules the ability to experiment, innovate, change, and find pleasures in the sudden and unexpected. Uranus reveals our reckless side, where we seek our thrills, and our eccentricities, representing the rock and roll of a person's chart. Uranus is what you look at when you want to know your partner's unplanned and uninvited ideas. It comes in and makes electrifying, sweeping alterations, but it is not unpleasant unless you resist the change. Uranus regarding Aquarius gives them sharp intellect and their emphasis on society and humanitarianism.

Aquarius Mythology

The constellation Aquarius is revered as Ganymede, who was a handsome Trojan prince. While tending his father's flocks on Mount Ida, Ganymede was spotted by Jupiter. The king of gods was enamored by his attractiveness and flew down to the mountain in the form of a large bird, whisking Ganymede away to Mount Olympus. Ganymede served as cupbearer to the gods and for his service was placed among the stars.

Aquarius's Positive Qualities and Negative Forms

The positive Aquarian qualities are individuality, tolerance, friendliness, inventiveness, originality, and visionary genius. Expressed in their negative forms, they become eccentric, neurotic, detached, absentminded, and will refuse to cooperate.

How an Aquarius Loves

Aquarius is a maverick in the way they love, never following societal norms or guidelines, for the rules of love were meant to be broken in the water bearer's book. The way their amorousness is experienced feels like a cool blue electric wave that flows through your body, leaving you stunned. They are not wildly enthusiastic due to their fixed modality, which causes them to be experienced in an intellectual and controlled way. Their complexity allows them to love in a way that is not easily grasped because it is entirely of another dimension. The essence of true love to a water bearer contains friendship, support, encouragement, respect, broadmindedness, independence, and individuality.

Aquarians value friendship in a partnership over anything. They wholeheartedly know that when friendship is the strongest element, it creates an unbreakable bond. When the newness of love fades, the base of friendship will still be there. When a true alliance is made, they will allow themselves to tumble into a romance that will be filled with mutual admiration and respect. Aquarians are too modern to want a partner to take care of them or someone they need to take care of. Instead, they want an equal who can find their own independence in their union. They need someone who can consistently meet them halfway because the thought of a traditional marriage sounds tedious.

Aquarians fly around in their own time machines of eccentricity, moving too quickly to dwell long on sentiments. They would prefer to tether their emotions to something that is free flowing, which allows them to become multifaceted in the way they love. Their cool and impersonal approach to love is not something for the simpleminded. Water bearers are broadminded, and they are always thinking about the group rather than the individual, which is why they require an autonomous partner. Aquarius is never boring, and they are full of surprises, constantly morphing into different versions of themselves. Their uniqueness and willpower is what makes them endearing.

Aquarius's good nature is intriguing. They do not place value on material items but rather on intellectual ideas and achievements that they will want their partner to obtain on their own or by their side. Although Aquarius is unusual, they never get lonely because they have more friends than they know what to do with. It is something really special if this sun sign decides they want to hold hands with you through life. They do not want a conventional kind of love, but they do want one filled with excitement, chemistry, and friendship. Their progressive outlook on love nearly never leaves room for a conservative type of life, so get ready to strap on some moon boots and travel to the fourth dimension. When you fall in love with an Aquarius, you are going to have a feeling you are not in Kansas anymore.

How to Spot an Aquarius

Aquarius is neither cynical nor immature, neither passionate nor nonchalant. Their eyes have a strange faraway look to them that is wise, mysterious, and vague. They are laced with a dreamy, wandering expression that is filled with electricity. When thinking of an Aquarius, imagine a prism: clear, hard, precise, and multi-faceted. If the light hits that prism just right, it creates a rainbow. Aquarians are filled with rainbows, but they need to be in the perfect place at the perfect time for you to see their colors. Aquarius is tranquil by nature, but they love to shock and surprise those around them. Like a bolt of lightning, they will come out of nowhere with their odd and fascinating zingers. Their movement is erratic and unpredictable, but the easiest way to spot them is their zany garb, which is never quite in place yet somehow always fashionable.

Aquarius is usually taller than average, and their features are finely chiseled, as though they were cut from a piece of marble. Thanks to their rulers, Saturn and Uranus, they are a curious mixture of cold practicality and eccentric instability that makes their energy cool yet conductive. Water bearers exude an androgynous energy and physically display a mixture of feminine characteristics, masculine characteristics, and everything in between. This fact, along with the original way they dress, makes them incredibly interesting to look at and hard to miss. They are funny, proud, original, and independent, but they can also be diplomatic, gentle, sympathetic, and timid. It really depends on the day you catch them and the setting they are in.

Aquarians have lots of friends and are rarely alone. They desperately seek the security of crowds and saturate themselves with friendship. Then, out of the blue, they will fall into a spell of solitude and want to be strictly left alone. Despite their fixation on friendship, Aquarians do not have many intimate relationships. They seek quantity, rather than quality, and rarely settle down into permanent partnerships due to their restrictive nature. There is too much to discover to become exclusively tied to one of anything. However, if you somehow touch the heart of a water bearer and they leave you, they may eventually come back wanting more.

Aquarians are naturally rebellious and instinctively feel that the old way of doing things is never the right way to do them. There is often nothing traditional about the water bearer, and to this end, Aquarians are always analyzing situations, friends, and strangers. It can be alarming when they start asking point-blank questions with zero tact. When they think they have you all figured out, they become bored and look for their next puzzle to solve. It is good to remember to always keep a little to yourself around an Aquarius. Do not ever give them all the pieces at once if you want to keep them around.

A strange sort of loneliness hangs over their essence because they are often so misunderstood. This is simply because most have not yet caught up with their futuristic ideals. Many are not able to sustain the Aquarian way of thinking, and Aquarius would never move backward to conform to those who do not understand. They are usually found on their own journey through the cosmos. Astrology teaches us that we will come close to catching up with them later, but once we do, they will have already moved on to the next galaxy. This explains why Aquarius is the sign of genius. There is a fine line between genius and insanity, but an Aquarius does not really mind which side of the line they are on. They are on their own path and unbothered by what the social norm is.

Aquarians do not seem to have the best memories, but they really do not need to memorize much seeing that they seem to pick up knowledge out of thin air. They like to leave their minds uncluttered so that they can grasp more and more. They cannot remember what they had for breakfast, yet their power of concentration is incredible. They can carry on a complicated discussion and still not miss an intonation of what is happening around them. Sometimes you could swear they were not listening to anything you said, but the next day they can repeat it back to you verbatim. They have an insane way of soaking up knowledge while they seem to be oblivious. This is how they can plunge into the unknown and absorb transcending mysteries without even trying.

The soul of the water bearer is constantly torn apart by Uranus, the unpredictable and radical planet of change, which lets them see the future with electric blue lucidity. Aquarius represents the collective's truest dreams and deepest values. Aquarius is often the hardest sun sign to grasp, and only those that are very close to them can break open their enigmas. However, it is only for an instant that you can see into their solitary heart, which was long ago permeated with Saturn's ageless wisdom. The only way in is if you decide to take an outrageous leap into the future with them. If you are ready to leave the past behind, spot the character who looks like they live in the future and hop in their time machine. Do not ever look back.

How to Lose an Aquarius

If you are looking for a scoop of vanilla, an Aquarius is not going to be your flavor. If you have the patience, though, you will find that life with an Aquarius is never boring. It will be like a rainbow sherbet—filled with multiple tastes, experiences, and colors. Aquarians are known to wear outlandish clothes and have far-out ideas, but if you try to change them, they will vanish into thin air. Aquarians are unusual, but they are not necessarily undignified. If you have trouble accepting their quirks, go ahead and see yourself out because they are not going to change. They require a partner who is quite open-minded. Aquarians are naturally individualistic and need a lot of time alone, which entails them to obtain a companion that has their own interests. Aquarians live in their own world and on their own timeline, and they are not worried about what everyone else is doing. If you need to keep up with the Joneses, you have got the wrong sun sign.

Aquarians have lots of friends, and if their friends do not like you, start packing your bags because their friendships never end. Some of these friends are old lovers, which means their current partner must have an open mind and a trusting heart. Possessiveness and jealousy are two things water bearers will not stand for. They are faithful to the one they give their heart to, but they are not going to ditch their friends because you ask them to. Aquarius values friendship in their relationship more than any other quality. They are interested in partnering for life to someone who is also their best friend. If you cannot wait to build a base of friendship before diving into a romance, they will not stick around. Aquarius's fixity never responds well when they are put under unnecessary pressure. Patience is a necessary virtue with loving an Aquarius.

Aquarians like to look at the big picture when it comes to the greater good. If you want to impress them, get into doing some community service for something you are enthusiastic about, and they will fall even deeper in love. They are attracted to people who do different and interesting things. Having a humanitarian and futuristic mind is imperative to keeping an Aquarius around. They need a companion who can see more than what is just in front of them. They want a partner with confidence and a pair of cojones, but they also need a nurturer.

There must be a mix of both these traits to keep your Aquarius by your side. Never crowd your Aquarius's energy, but instead, make space for them to be the brilliant individual they are. They may be buzzing around somewhere out in the galaxy, chasing the future and catching stars. There is even a good possibility that their detached nature will neglect to put companionship as a priority now and again, but if they love you and you are their friend, they will never lose you forever. When they are ready, they will take your hand and ask you to come with them on their spaceship to glide through the cosmos.

How to Bed an Aquarius

The water bearer belongs to everyone and no one all at the same time. No one could ever truly own this soul because they are an eccentric anomaly in every sense of the way. When in love, this sun sign is tried and true, but if you do something to break their trust, they will disconnect from you as though you do not even exist. If you are looking for an extremely passionate lover, an Aquarius may not be for you. They make love without ever giving you all of them, making their partners consistently come back for more.

Nothing is ever too heavy with an Aquarius, and they would prefer to keep things light and detached. Friendship is the number one factor when wanting to become a lover of this sun sign, and you may very well have to become best friends with them before you ever see what is under their acid-washed jeans. What has sex with this sun sign so intense is the buildup of desire that will have you going crazy while they make you wait to create a solid base of friendship. Then suddenly, out of nowhere, when the time strikes them right, they will let you in, and it will be explosive, unexpected, and electrifying. Aquarians do not have sex to just have sex; they are looking for a multidimensional experience with someone they care about.

Aquarius loves freedom—freedom to experiment, freedom to explore, and freedom to give. They can be hard to keep up with because predictability is not their style. They are a wild child at heart but can contain it under their statuesque façade. They obtain an aura that is bright electric blue and can translate to cool sex that feels as though a lightning bolt traveled through your body. How they have sex depends on the mood they are in that day, and odds are you will never know ahead of time because the element of surprise is part of their sexual attraction.

This intellectual is looking for more than physical connection, and they require an uncomplicated dexterity when it comes to sex. As an air sign, the connection of the mind is much more important to the water bearer than that of the body. There is a dominance in their sexual energy that is subtle and appealing. Because of their ascendency, they are not the best at attuning to their partner's needs, which requires their sexual playmate to match their strength in gaining what they want as well. However, their openness to trying new things will be exhilarating and a fun way to connect to this sun sign. Having the confidence to think outside the box sexually is key in connecting to Aquarius's fourth dimension.

If you are looking for one of these zany entities to have as your own, search for the character who looks like they live in the future. The element of surprise is laced in their extraterrestrial nature, and when you finally get them behind closed doors, you are in for an out-of-this-world experience. Aquarius is a beacon of self-confidence, and you will truly feel that energy when you are alone with them. What is sexier than a confident partner in bed? Not much.

☼ ☼ ☼

AQUARIUS & AQUARIUS

Aspect: Conjunct
Elements: Air and air
Modalities: Fixed and fixed

Aquarians are hard people to pin down. I guess when you are from another planet, it would be difficult for anyone to really understand you right off the bat. But when two Aquarians see each other for the first time, they will smirk a bit because they can recognize a universe traveler when they see one. They will most undeniably be friends first and lovers later, which is the code to crack any Aquarian's heart. Without a strong friendship in their relationship, an Aquarius would not survive.

Two water bearers will most typically meet through friends because life is all about who you know as an Aquarian. They both will have large circles of acquaintances of unusual backgrounds, and they will enjoy getting to know each other's peers. Their social groups are nothing to scoff at because these two are a popular pair who know many. Once they have built a friendship with one another and have discovered each other's acquaintances, habits, ups, downs, and quirks, they will start to "fall" in love. I use "fall" in quotations because Aquarians do not really fall anywhere. Instead, they put a great deal of thought into serious actions such as love. They will be more than just partners. They will be each other's travel companion, their shoulder to lean on, their saint, their sinner, their magic, their darkness, their dreams, their reality, and, of course, their best friend. You see, Aquarian lovers expect a lot out of their partners, and they will settle for nothing less than the best.

Not everything is always stellar between them, especially if they do not like each other's friends. In most relationships, there will be a time when leaving one's friends behind is part of being in that committed relationship, but that is usually not how an Aquarius operates. They often hold on to their network no matter what—even if the friendship is not necessarily healthy for their relationship. Aquarius is a fixed sign, which means that they do not lead, but they also do not follow and would rather stay precisely where they are. For lack of better words, they are stubborn. However, if these two can focus their energy into their naturally humanitarian ways, the inherent fixity in their personalities can help them achieve huge change in the world together.

Aquarius is a unique breed in the fact that they are indeed a fixed sign, which tends to avoid change, and yet, the typical Aquarius is dying for change in civilization. This may seem confusing, but Aquarians want change on a large scale for the better, specifically in humanitarian efforts. They are just unwilling to change the personal ideals they have. Once their mind is set on how a way something should be, it will often be ridiculously hard to make them see it in another way. If these two can join efforts in a cause, there will be no stopping them. This is where they shine as a couple and where they could even create a legacy with their combined efforts. The stars would have to align for this to happen, but it could most certainly occur. If there are any disagreements or hiatuses taken, sex will smooth those rough patches over.

When it comes to physical unity, they will both expect the extraordinary from each other because they know what one another is capable of. Once they can figure out each other's sexpectations, lovemaking will come naturally. They have immense consideration for one another, and their sex is so friendly because of it. The phrase "curiosity killed the cat" does not apply to a pair of Aquarians because their curiosity will rather open new doors to different worlds that they will enjoy exploring together in their physical oneness. It is in their experimentation that they will find an enlightened ecstasy together, which is something they hold sacred.

The most wonderful thing about a pair of Aquarians is their element of surprise. You never know what to expect when two extraterrestrials join forces, and they will constantly be surprising each other day after day. Their capacity for achieving celebrated philanthropical work is what sets them apart from the crowd, and their partnership is a look straight into the future. They may forget the details in life, but it is the big picture of love that really matters most to them. They do not sweat the small stuff, and they will elate together in the entirety of their alien-like beings.

☼ ☼ ☼

AQUARIUS & PISCES

〜〜 ⬡ ♓

Aspect: Semisextile
Elements: Air and water
Modalities: Fixed and mutable

Pisces are remarkable at recognizing things that other people are unable to, which includes noticing potential in people, especially the ones they love. Aquarians seem so strange and unapproachable to most, but a Pisces can see through their odd behavior because they have a few peculiarities themselves. These two sun signs' contrasts work out beautifully, creating an elixir of fourth-dimensional optimism. This adds to their attraction, and their energies spike one another's interests in a way that neither of them thought possible. Aquarius will do the most unexpected things for the shock factor, and Pisces will rarely have a dull moment with this extraterrestrial. Water bearers have a challenging time sticking around for the mundane, but little do they know, Pisces shares that same stance.

Pisces is not as exciting and eccentric as their Aquarian companion, but it is just as hard to shock a fish as it is to shock an Aquarian. Pisces understands people—all kinds of people—and is very tolerant and aware of all character traits. Pisces is innately charming and curious, which will be wonderful for Aquarius. The fish is also thoughtful, and they tend to be overly generous with the ones that they love. To Pisces, worldly things do not have the value that spiritual experiences give them. Aquarius understands that the most valuable things about their Pisces partner are their beautiful heart and the intangible blessings of their love, thoughts, and dreams. Aquarius can often be out in space, but they always know what is going on around them, which will help this pair keep one foot in reality and the other in the fourth dimension.

A water bearer's friends are a huge part of their life, which Pisces does not mind—unless they come before them. Aquarius puts their crew before many things in their life, and it may take some time before detaching from their friends becomes a priority for their relationship. Aquarius is a fixed sign, which means they are not big on change. Pisces will have to use their mutable charm to communicate their wishes and slowly work them into some new habits so they feel like Aquarius is not aloof in their relationship. Sex is a wonderful place to start.

These two are, surprisingly, very sexually compatible. There is a smooth, dreamy blend between them that is like reaching into an uncharted world. If Aquarius can understand that they will have to emotionally open up to let Pisces reach the deepest part of their inner being, they can make this union sexually stunning. They will not only connect bodily but will make love on a mental level as well. With their yin and yang energy united, sex will be something that happens often, and it will feel otherworldly for both, making their sex life quite an experiment. Aquarius lives for the miracles of life, and Pisces lives for a life of miracles, so if they learn how to combine their wishes, their blended lives can be quite enchanted. Before any of this happens, though, Pisces must prove to Aquarius that they are friends above all else. Friendship is tied into every relationship that Aquarius has and is crucial for them to feel close to their partner. On the other end, Aquarius must believe in Pisces's dreams for them to feel close to their Aquarius. Friendship and dreams are this pair's magical combination to their connection.

Now and then, Pisces will do something to trigger Aquarius's temper, and the water bearer will hurt the fish's sensitive feelings. Aquarius will usually not react when they cry because they would never react in such a way themselves and because they rarely believe they are wrong. It may take years of learning but Aquarius will understand that it is best to tread lightly when dealing with their partner's emotions. Concurrently, Pisces will learn that Aquarius's stubborn attitude does not mean they love them any less. Once they regulate these variances, they will prefer to lead a private life and protect their love behind closed doors. Pisces helps Aquarius when needed but on most days leaves their alien alone to travel to the future and back. Pisces does not mind because it feels wonderful to be loved by such a brilliant and futuristic character.

Their story may be crazy, but it is never boring because they both like to wake up not knowing what is coming next. A Pisces's greatest weakness is that they give too much of themselves, but Aquarius does not see it as a weakness and never takes advantage of the trait. Aquarius finds self-sacrifice to be a strength and the root of what friendship is about. Aquarius's greatest failing is their inflexibility of not wanting to conform to the norm and their constant need for change, but Pisces does not see these characteristics as flaws because they are what made them fall for their Aquarius in the first place. These two are a little zany together, but that is where their magic happens.

☼ ☼ ☼

Chapter 12

Pisces

Pisces's love archetype is the mystical lover. Pisces is an empathetic, enigmatic, meditative, and intended lover who believes in spiritual love that is beyond a worldly understanding. Pisces's lesson in love is to impart that love is empathy and absorb that love is complete.

Element	Water
Modality	Mutable
Polarity	Yin, negative, and feminine
Mantra	"I believe."
Hue	Seafoam green
Deity	Poseidon, god of the sea
Glyph	♓
Flowers	Lilac, water lily, and calla lily
Tree	Willow
Jewel	Amethyst
Crystals	Labradorite and spirit quartz
Fragrance	Ylang-ylang
Body Parts	The feet and toes
Animals	Fish, whales, and dolphins
Food & Herbs	Fish, lettuce, seaweed, ground ivy, redroot, and fruits and vegetables that grow on vines, such as cucumbers, pumpkins, melons, and other gourds

Pisces's Ruling Planets: Jupiter and Neptune

Pisces is one of the few signs that have two ruling planets. Jupiter is its traditional ruling planet, but when Neptune was discovered, the dreamy orb was assigned to Pisces, making Neptune this sun sign's modern ruler.

Jupiter in love rules good fortune, benefits, expansive ideas, and social adaptation. Jupiter reveals individual ethics, philosophies, and personal growth. Jupiter represents the promise of good things to come, and it is the good luck charm in your partnership. It will be there to give you something positive even when times are rough to remind you that you are never abandoned. Jupiter regarding Pisces gives the fish its wisdom, deep concepts, and philosophies on life.

Neptune in love rules illusions, imagination, visions, and misconceptions. Neptune reveals idealism and romantic fantasies where you can become deceived. Neptune is the planet of deception, and it can cause confusion and mix-ups. Sometimes it tells lies to fool you, bringing you false hope through dreams and illusions. Everyone needs Neptune for a little bit of magic, but this planet likes to sugarcoat the truth. Neptune creates a dreamlike comfort zone and shows us our dependencies. It is the place we like to escape to when the world feels cold and callous. Neptune regarding Pisces gives them their watery depth and makes them the dreamers and make-believers of the zodiac. Neptune is the planet that carries us over from one life to the next, which is why Pisces is the last sign in the karmic wheel.

Pisces Mythology

The deathly colossal serpentine Typhon unexpectedly appeared, startling all the gods into taking on different animalistic forms to veil themselves. Jupiter transformed himself into a ram, Mercury became an egret, Apollo took on the shape of a crow, Diana hid herself as a cat, and Pan disguised himself as a sea goat. Venus and her son Cupid were also there that day and took on the shape of a pair of fish. They tied themselves to one another so they would not lose each other in the water. Minerva, the goddess of the arts, later immortalized the event by placing the figures of the two tethered fish among the stars.

Pisces's Positive Qualities and Negative Forms

Pisces's positive qualities are humility, compassion, sensitivity, spiritual awareness, psychic comprehension, philosophic insight, and a healing potential. Expressed in their negative forms, they become timid, apprehensive, lazy, dishonest, have a weakness of will, and find pleasure in pain.

How a Pisces Loves

Love with a Pisces is experienced in a dreamy and most evolved way that is mystical beyond a worldly understanding. This sun sign is not afraid to love and will swim into their emotions without hesitation. Even if a great love is left or lost, they continue to hold love in an altruistic light, placing it high on a pedestal. Pisces are dreamers, especially when it comes to relationships, and they can believe their visions into reality. Dreams do not always do well in reality, so many of them will be shattered, but Pisces will never lose their self-respect and will always hold a beautiful hope of tomorrow.

Pisces will do the most they can in their relationships to make them harmonious until the pressure becomes too great for their delicate souls and they swim away and do not look back. They will find a new beacon of hope and a new star to wish upon so their dream of love will remain alive. Neptune bestows the fish with a foggy view of love that seems like a dream. When the dark sides of love present themselves, Pisces will try to turn it back, but if they cannot use their magic to make things right, they know they must have just fallen for the wrong one. Pisces was born to love and to be loved in return. They seek a nirvana in their relationships, and if it is not found, they will not settle for less.

Because they are the last sign on the karmic wheel, there is something that is old about their soul, and they have an innate knowledge and deep understanding of the way things are. They take this wisdom into their unions and apply it through their copious amounts of empathy. They have lived many lives and loved many souls. When they want to swim life's waters with one person, it is usually because their intuition tells them to. Like everyone else, they want to be loved, protected, and cared for, but for Pisces, it is a matter of their soul.

Pisces are devastatingly appealing to many because of their kindness and ability to listen with an open and gentle mind. They will stand by their partners through the toughest of times and with a loving heart. When they find faith in a relationship and their partner loses hope, they will not have room to stay. Pisces are not the most practical of people, but they are the most loving while supplying endless amounts of affection and attention to the one who holds their heart. Pisces is eternal, ethereal, fascinating, and vague. Their elusive nature makes them hard to comprehend, but their intricacies are where their beauty lies. Their enigmatic nature creates dualities of highs and lows where they are swimming in the shallow end one moment and in a raging deep sea the next.

The sign of Pisces is represented by two fish that swim in different directions but are tethered by a cord and always connected. One side of Pisces is pleasant, caring, and easy to digest, while the other side is emotionally unstable, depressing, and searching. When loving a Pisces, you will experience their dichotomy because their duality is connected by an impermeable cord of stars. Therefore, there will be times of immense joy and times that compassion is required. They need a partner who is brave enough to weather the storms and offer stability in many forms. This takes an evolvement like their own, but in return Pisces offers an alluring love that is full of intuition, thoughtfulness, and benevolence. There is a magic about Pisces that makes not only their own dreams come true but also the dreams of those they adore. This leaves their lovers feeling completely, perfectly, and incandescently happy.

How to Spot a Pisces

Pisces souls come in many colorful and shimmering types. Most are born with loads of charm and a relaxed good nature. An easy way to know if you are in the presence of a fish is by telling them something shocking. If they sweetly smile with an empathetic look on their face, you have yourself a Pisces. Their eyes are simply beautiful; they are liquid, heavy-lidded, and full of peculiar lights. Their features are often variable and always shifting. Pisces's aura is full of grace and extraordinarily captivating. They are naturally sardonic, but the cool waters of Neptune continually wash away any resentment.

Pisces rarely stays in one place for too long because they enjoy exploring spiritual settings, visiting art galleries, going to concerts, and being in various social settings. They are naturally creative and artistic, and therefore, they enjoy more leisurely and esoteric surroundings. Their heart is essentially free of greed, leaving more room for love and imagination. Pisces have a lack of intensity about the future, for they are happy to swim wherever the water takes them. There is an intuitive knowledge of yesterday and a gentle tolerance of today. To swim upstream is the challenge of Pisces, but doing so is the only way they ever find true peace and happiness. Taking the easy way is a trap for those born under this sun sign. It is a glittering lure that attracts them while it hides the dangerous hook: a wasted life.

Pisces were born with the desire to see the world in a positive light, always finding faith in humanity. They know that there is plenty of evil in the world, but they prefer to live in their own watery, gentle realm where everyone is beautiful and all actions are lovely. If reality becomes too terrible to face, they will try to escape whatever threatens their utopia. Their favorite place to go is their optimistic daydreams, which rarely come to fruition. They find themselves tenderly remembering yesterday and hazily hoping for tomorrow—all while forgetting about the present.

The opposite directions the fish swim in the Pisces symbol represent the continual decision given to Pisces to either swim to the top or to swim to the bottom, never quite reaching either. A fish's eyes are always looking to their sides, and they have difficulty seeing straight ahead. Because of the innate dichotomy this sun sign continually faces, Pisces often either retreat to the sublime heights of a dedicated professional life or to tonics, synthetic emotions, and erroneous enthusiasm.

Pisces are often born with a fabulous power of interpretation that lets them project a myriad of emotions. Even though most are shy, they often become some of the finest performers in the theater. Pisces's memory is legendary, and life itself is a huge stage. Their love of music and art and their deep wisdom and compassion come from the combined knowledge of every human experience. Pisces represents death and eternity because of their position on the karmic wheel, and they possess a composite of all that has gone before them. Therefore, their nature is a blend of all the other sun signs, which is quite a lot to cope with. Because of this, they have a strange power to stand outside of themselves and see the collective unconscious. Thanks to Neptune's great oceans, Pisces's internal nature is unfathomable to most. The altruistic fish is filled with an inexhaustible, tender love for every living creature, and this trait is truly saintlike when it is not turned inward in self-pity. Pisces have hearts big enough for the troubles of everyone they meet, and they can sympathetically absorb hundreds of stories and feelings.

Those who want this mystical being for themselves must use their imagination to grasp the heightened level of their mind and emotions. Pisces must live in cool, calm water and always be moving. Much like salmon, a large part of Pisces's life is the struggle to go against the current and swim upstream. Salmon are anadromous, a term that comes from the Greek word *anadromos*, meaning "running upward." In Pisces's case, they must find their strength and use their intuition to fulfill their destiny's calling by running upward, or they will live a life full of the depths of downstream regret. For this reason, it helps for them to have a partner who is able to assist in giving them the courage and encouragement to do what may seem impossible—a companion to assist in fulfilling their wildest dreams and to help them reach a place of cool contentment.

How to Lose a Pisces

Pisces has an immense emotional depth that makes them natural lovers of the arts. Music, photography, dance, opera, and other arts are mediums they use to connect to their soul. If you cannot appreciate artistic vision, this sun sign is not the one for you. Because of their imaginative vision, Pisces also has an entrepreneurial mind, which is why they need a supportive partner, not someone to tear them down with practicality and impossibilities. Pisces wants a partner to imagine and hope with. They want someone they can share aspirations with, wishing upon the same star. Pisces is almost always coming up with new ideas, and they require a compassionate partner to help them make their dreams become a reality rather than be shot down. Just hear them out because they are usually onto something.

Pisces is usually not one for confrontation, so if you find your fish making some passive-aggressive comments, start reading between the lines because this inert type of communication is what makes them comfortable. They prefer to not take things head-on but rather softly from the side. This requires their partner to have the intuition to check in with them and the compassion to adjust, even when they are not being forced to do so. One way to make anything up to Pisces is with thoughtful and romantic gestures. Pisces adores fantasy and sentiments, so if you are not swooning your Pisces, they may go find someone that will. Pisces has no problem finding lovers, so make sure you are doting on them in a way that they deserve.

The fish already has so many serious and heavy thoughts in their head, so they need a partner who can cheer them up. If you are always down in the dumps, they may have to swim to clearer waters. Pisces are like sponges because they tend to absorb the emotions and hardships of everyone around them. They need a lover who can help them unwind and refresh their aura. They get dumped on by other people all day, so do not add additional stress to their plate.

Instead, you must become a safe place for them to rest their head. They are incredibly sensitive by nature, and being such an empathetic soul is exhausting. Having compassion for this will get you far with them.

Pisces needs a strong shoulder to lean on, but they do not want someone who is too available either. They are looking for someone who is confident and able to give them their space when they need it. Because of their mutable modality, Pisces fluctuates and transforms many times throughout their life, and their partner must adapt and shape-shift with them through all life's waters if they want this love to work. Catching Pisces at the right time in life is everything. Never underestimate their strength and willpower, for if you mistake their kindness for weakness too frequently, they will wake up one morning and swim away without so much as a look over their shoulder. They know what they are, and they know what they deserve: pure magic.

How to Bed a Pisces

Get in line with everyone else in town; there are many who have a crippling soft spot for this mystical sun sign. Pisces has a way about them that attracts many, and their transcending charm and deep watery eyes seem to magically pull people into their soul. Pisces is never short of romance or sentiment, capturing many in their Neptunian net. There is something naive about them that makes you want to be strong for them, but that nativity covers up their tender, strong, and wise heart.

Pisces is 100 percent sensuality at its finest, which beautifully translates in the bedroom. They are an emotional water sign, and sex with them is experienced as penetrating depth. When you make love with Pisces, it will feel like you are able to breathe underwater in a comforting and deeply intimate way. They can show you what a true sense of affection really is and provide a wisdom in lovemaking you never thought attainable. If Pisces ever senses that you are dissatisfied with their lovemaking, they will use their empathetic abilities to sense what you need, which lets them know what you want without you having to say a word. They profoundly enjoy sexually pleasing their lovers by creating a healing and emotionally charged experience.

Be conscientious with your fish because they can swim both ways. They are elusive and an escapist when trouble and hardship present themselves. The ocean speaks to them, and if there is ever a point when it tells their soul that you can no longer connect to their heart or fulfill their deepest needs, they will swim away without a trace. Tangibly, fish are slippery, delicate, and hard to hold on to. To keep them, you must love them deeply and empathize with their emotions. Then they will stay by your side forever. These rules apply both in love and in your sexual relationship because Pisces connects sexual experiences to their soul and psyche, which makes it more than just a physical act—it is a spiritual one.

Pisces's placement on the karmic wheel makes them a sexually stunning combination of every sign before them. They will show their many sexual sides if you can hold their heart in your hand and appeal to their deeply spiritual nature. Do not mistake your Pisces's passiveness for submissiveness. No matter how wonderful things seem, there is constant work that needs to be put in to keep a Pisces sexually satisfied. It would do you good to remember that line of eager suitors waiting for you to get it wrong.

☼ ☼ ☼

PISCES & PISCES

♓ 🖤 ♓

Aspect: Conjunct
Elements: Water and water
Modalities: Mutable and mutable

Pisces has a view on love that not any of the other sun signs are able to possess. It is something that they understand in a more complete way because they have been through the karmic wheel and have felt all the other methods to love. They have a wisdom about love and a calm understanding that they want to find it. Therefore, when two fish meet each other and their deep watery eyes link, there will be a moment when they see themselves in each other. They will think: "Oh, there you are. Where have you been my whole life?" There is a magic and a dreaminess that connects these two souls through lifetimes of searching and swimming around the ocean to find the one their soul has yearned for. However, just like any conjunctly aspected sun sign pairing, there will be a few storms at bay.

256

Pisces are known to enjoy escaping reality and to be unrealistic, emotional, weak willed, and naive. They will tend to drown from time to time, and these two will have to work on bringing each other up for air when needed. If the two fish fall into a pattern of bad habits, it would be very hard to get them out. They should use the positive aspects of their sun sign, such as their humility, sensitivity, spiritual awareness, psychic comprehension, philosophic insight, and healing potential, to stay constructive. To one another, they are kind, compassionate, wise, intuitive, and come up with incredible ideas that the world needs. If they can support one another's dreams and push each other to the finish line of their goals, they will reach a state bordering on complete euphoria.

There will be nothing bossy in the way they handle their romance. They are so in tune with how the other is feeling that they can even complete one another's sentences. There is nothing brash or harsh in their mannerisms, just kindness and compassion toward each other that we could all learn from. They are both talkers once you get them going because of their mutable modality. They take pleasure in telling stories and will love to converse about anything and everything together: music, philosophy, the weather, what they had for breakfast, and what they dreamed about last night. They have so many beautiful, fluid ideas and thoughts in their head, and they need a canvas to paint them on, which is why and how they communicate so colorfully.

If a Pisces pair is swimming together at the right place and right time, things will tend to stay nice and smooth. There is nothing demanding or wild about their sex; it is easy, sweet, and fresh. They are deeply intimate with one another and can reach depths that most would never understand. The way they love is so ethereal and classic while somehow feeling new yet traditional. They are fluid and versatile, and no matter how long they stay together, they are constantly finding out new things about each other. Just like the ocean, depending on where you are, how the sun is hitting it, or what the weather is like, you can never really see it the same way twice.

These two will be there for each other constantly and yet in vastly diverse ways, depending on what the other needs. There will never be a dull moment between them, and they will constantly be feeling each other out to see what the other needs. It is almost as though they blend and become one person in many ways. If ever they start to feel astray from one another, all they have to do is look into each other's eyes and remember that very first day they saw their twin soul. It will help to remember how they intuitively knew that no matter what happened, this person was the beginning of the end, and all they need at the end of it all is each other's love. If they can keep that narrative alive, the rest will have a way of figuring itself out, and it always seems to with two Pisces in love.

☼ ☼ ☼

Conclusion

There really is not a right or wrong way to go about falling in and out of love—just your way. I have been observing and writing about astrological compatibility for decades, and there are still things to be learned. Each relationship is like a snowflake; there are no two that are just alike. In a similar fashion, your natal chart and your synastry is completely original as well. There has never been, or will ever be, a love story quite like yours. Every relationship has its highs and lows, its blessings, and areas of opportunity. My hope is that this book gives you a new set of eyes to see your partner through, as well as room to grow and understand your companion on a new level in hopes of prolonging and bettering your love or in finding love.

All love is capable of energizing wishes into reality, but love between two people whose personal auras have harmoniously blended creates the kind of vibration that is able to manifest marvelous magic. Billions of relationships exist on earth, and they are all on their own journey. There are those who are attempting to attain or who have attained a satisfying contentment and fulfillment together; those who are still struggling through heavy karmic work; and those rare ones called "soul mates," who finally find one another even if they may have fought against their fate for lifetimes and struggled in vain to escape their linked destiny.

No matter how your story unfolds, remembering to love one another every single day is a choice that is never too late to make. Whether you are searching for the one your heart aches for, meeting someone brand new, or celebrating your fiftieth anniversary, I encourage you to use the pages of this book as a reference and inspiration to know that there is always hope along the way. Even if your path in love leads you down a dead end, know that you will walk away with learned lessons that are invaluable to continuing your journey and unique narrative. Moving through the pain of breakups, hardships, and lessons are an integral part of your story. These experiences will help you appreciate when you find true love even more fervently down the road. Regardless of transitory voids, there is a relentless vibration that the universe gives you to transmit with the one your heart belongs to. I believe that not even death can separate this connection because you are linked by an unbreakable and invisible thread that ties you over the astral realms, universes, and heavens.

Now that you are armed with this ancient magic of understanding the stars, I invite you to go back through the chapters and read about you and your partner's rising signs, moon signs, Venus signs, and so on. As I send you on your way with this new knowledge you have obtained, I hope you make some space in your heart for one another's differences. I pray that the words strewn across these pages bless your connection with grace and peace down the road or strengthen the connection you already have. Never forget that you are worthy of a love that lasts through infinite lifetimes, through endless galaxies, and in every form of existence. I would wish you luck, but you do not need it because the universe already has an intricate and beautiful plan for you.

As above, so it is below.
That which has been, will return again.
As in heaven, so on earth.

Recommended Reading

This is a list compiled of books written by astrologers that I both respect and admire. You can study astrology your whole life and still have things to learn because the avenues of knowledge are endless. *Linda Goodman's Love Signs* was my first book and gateway into astrology, and it is still my favorite to this day. I felt as though she was speaking to me and teaching me directly from the pages of her writings. It is important on your journey through studying the stars that you find an astrologer that resonates with you in this way. I invite you to continue your journey through the stars with some of my favorite astrology books below to continue your learnings.

Aspects in Astrology: A Guide to Understanding Planetary Relationships in the Horoscope by Sue Tompkins

Astrology and the Authentic Self: Integrating Traditional and Modern Astrology to Uncover the Essence of the Birth Chart by Demetra George

Astrology for Beginners: Learn to Read Your Birth Chart by David Pond

Astrology for Life: The Ultimate Guide to Finding Wisdom in the Stars by Nina Kahn

Astrology for Yourself: How to Understand and Interpret Your Own Birth Chart by Douglas Bloch and Demetra George

The Astrology of You and Me by Gary Goldschneider

Astrology: Using the Wisdom of the Stars in Your Everyday Life by Carole Taylor

Birth Chart Interpretation Plain & Simple by Andrea Taylor

The Complete Guide to Astrology: Understanding Yourself, Your Signs, and Your Birth Chart by Louise Edington

Cosmic Power: Ignite Your Light: A Simple Guide to Sun Signs for the Modern Mystic by Vanessa Montgomery

Essential Astrology: Everything You Need to Know to Interpret Your Natal Chart by Amy Herring

Hellenistic Astrology: The Study of Fate and Fortune by Chris Brennan

Horoscope Symbols by Robert Hand

How to Get Along with Anyone (Yes, Even That Person) by the AstroTwins, Ophira and Tali Edut

The Inner Sky: How to Make Wiser Choices for a More Fulfilling Life by Steven Forrest

Linda Goodman's Love Signs: A New Approach to the Human Heart by Linda Goodman

A Little Bit of Astrology: An Introduction to the Zodiac by Colin Bedell

Magickal Astrology: Use the Power of the Planets to Create an Enchanted Life by Skye Alexander

Moon Signs: Unlock Your Inner Luminary Power by Narayana Montufar

The Only Astrology Book You'll Ever Need by Joanna Martine Woolfolk

Parkers' Astrology: The Definitive Guide to Using Astrology in Every Aspect of Your Life by Julia and Derek Parker

Parkers' Astrology: The Essential Guide to Using Astrology in Your Daily Life by Julia and Derek Parker

The Private Lives of the Sun Signs by Katharine Merlin

The Secret Language of Birthdays: Your Personology Profiles for Each Day of the Year by Gary Goldschneider

The Sex Files: Your Zodiac Guide to Love & Lust by Rowan Davis

Sextrology: The Astrology of Sex and the Sexes by Stella Starsky and Quinn Cox

Star Power: A Simple Guide to Astrology for the Modern Mystic by Vanessa Montgomery

Wander the Stars: A Journal for Finding Insight through Astrology by Nina Kahn

You Were Born for This: Astrology for Radical Self-Acceptance by Chani Nicholas

To Write to the Author

If you wish to contact the author or would like more information about this book, please write to the author in care of Llewellyn Worldwide Ltd. and we will forward your request. Both the author and the publisher appreciate hearing from you and learning of your enjoyment of this book and how it has helped you. Llewellyn Worldwide Ltd. cannot guarantee that every letter written to the author can be answered, but all will be forwarded. Please write to:

Desiree Roby Antila
℅ Llewellyn Worldwide
2143 Wooddale Drive
Woodbury, MN 55125-2989
Please enclose a self-addressed stamped envelope for reply,
or $1.00 to cover costs. If outside the U.S.A., enclose
an international postal reply coupon.

Many of Llewellyn's authors have websites with additional
information and resources. For more information,
please visit our website at http://www.llewellyn.com.

Notes